Sound: A Reader in Theatre Practice

Readers in Theatre Practices

Series editor: Simon Shepherd

Published:

Ross Brown: Sound: A Reader in Theatre Practice

Forthcoming:

Penny Francis: Puppetry: A Reader in Theatre Practice
Scott Palmer: Lighting: A Reader in Theatre Practice

Readers in Theatre Practices
Series standing order
ISBN 978–0–230–53717–0 hardcover
ISBN 978–0–230–53718–7 paperback
(outside North America only)

You can receive future titles in this series as they are published. To place a standing order please contact your bookseller or, in the case of difficulty, write to us at the address below with your name and address, the title of the series and the ISBN quoted above.

Customer Services Department, Macmillan Distribution Ltd
Houndmills, Basingstoke, Hampshire RG21 6XS, England

Sound
A Reader in
Theatre Practice

Ross Brown

palgrave
macmillan

First published 2010 by
PALGRAVE MACMILLAN

Palgrave Macmillan in the UK is an imprint of Macmillan Publishers Limited,
registered in England, company number 785998, of Houndmills, Basingstoke,
Hampshire RG21 6XS.

Palgrave Macmillan in the US is a division of St Martin's Press LLC,
175 Fifth Avenue, New York, NY 10010.

Palgrave Macmillan is the global academic imprint of the above companies
and has companies and representatives throughout the world.

Palgrave® and Macmillan® are registered trademarks in the United States,
the United Kingdom, Europe and other countries

ISBN-13: 978–0–230–55187–9 hardback
ISBN-13: 978–0–230–55188–6 paperback

This book is printed on paper suitable for recycling and made from fully
managed and sustained forest sources. Logging, pulping and manufacturing
processes are expected to conform to the environmental regulations of the
country of origin.

A catalogue record for this book is available from the British Library.

A catalog record for this book is available from the Library of Congress.

10   9   8   7   6   5   4   3   2   1
19 18 17 16 15 14 13 12 11 10

Printed and bound in Great Britain by
CPI Antony Rowe, Chippenham and Eastbourne

To Kate and Eliza

Contents

Acknowledgements

Thanks to Paul Arditti, John Bracewell, Steve Brown, Karen Burton, John Collins, Geoffrey Colman, Jonathan Deans, Igor Drevalev, John Levack Drever, Scott Gibbons, Kate Haines, Hans Peter Kuhn, Andrew Lavender, Sally Mackey, David Mayer, Susan Oman, Joanna Parker, Simon Shepherd, Rick Thomas, Andrew Wiskowski. Special thanks to my erstwhile collaborators Jonathan Holloway, Adrian Johnston and Mike Roberts, with whom I discovered most of what I know about sound and theatre, and to Alan Brown, who bought me my first reel-to-reel tape recorder when I was nine and from whom I inherit my audiophile genes.

The author and publishers wish to thank the following for permission to reproduce copyright material:

John Bracewell for an extract from pp. 206–7 from John Bracewell, *Sound Design in the Theatre*, Prentice Hall (1993);

Cambridge University Press and the author, for quotations taken from Philip Butterworth, *Magic on the Early English Stage* (Cambridge: Cambridge University Press, 2005), Chapter 5, pp. 98–100; 102–4, © Philip Butterworth 2005, published by Cambridge University Press, reproduced with permission;

Cambridge University Press and the author, for extracts from Bruce Johnson, 'Hamlet: voice, music, sound' in *Popular Music* (2005) 24(2), pp. 257–67, © Cambridge University Press, reproduced with permission;

Cambridge University Press and the author, for an abridged extract from David Mayer, 'The Music of Melodrama', pp. 49–64 in D. Bradby, L. James and B. Sharratt (eds), *Performance and Politics in Popular Drama* (1980), © Cambridge University Press 1980, reproduced with permission;

Cassell Illustrated, a Division of Octopus Publishing Group Ltd., for an extract from David Collison, *Stage Sound*, Cassell (1976);

Susannah Clapp for an extract from her article 'Noises On and Off' in *The Observer*, 26 December 2004;

Cressrelles Publishing Company Ltd. for extracts from *Noises Off: A Handbook of Sound Effects* by Frank Napier, published by Frederick Mueller, used by permission of Cressrelles Publishing Company Ltd.;

Harvard University Press for extracts from *Vitruvius: Volume I*, reprinted by permission of the publishers and the Trustees of the Loeb Classical Library from *Vitruvius: Volume I*, translated by Morris Hickey, Cambridge, MA: Harvard University Press, 1914. The Loeb Classical Library ® is a registered trademark of the President and Fellows of Harvard College;

Don Ihde and The British Society for Phenomenology for an abridged extract from D. Ihde, 'Parmenidean Meditations' in *The Journal of the British Society for Phenomenology* (1970) Vol. 1, No. 3, October, and D. Ihde, *Sense and Significance*, Duquesne University Press (1973);

Mic Pool for an extract from 'Manifesto on theatre sound' from The Aural Imagination, http://www.micpool.com;

Taylor and Francis Group, LLC for an extract from pp. 45–7 from *Sound in the Theatre*, Copyright © 1979 from *Sound in the Theatre* by H. Burris-Meyer, V. Mallory and L. S. Goodfriend. Reproduced by permission of Taylor and Francis Group, LLC, a division of Informa plc;

University of Chicago Press and the author, for extracts from Bruce R. Smith, *The Acoustic World of Early Modern England: Attending to the O-Factor*, University of Chicago Press (1999), © 1999 by The University of Chicago Press. All rights reserved;

Richard K. Thomas for 'The Sounds of Time';

Igor Drevalev for his address to the 2007 Prague Scenofest, for Reading 4.3 © Igor Drevalev, Reading 4.4 © Scott Gibbons, Reading 5.2 © Paul Arditti, Reading 5.3 © Hans Peter Kuhn, Reading 5.4 © John Collins, Reading 5.5 © Jonathan Deans, Reading 9.1 © Steve Brown, Reading 10.1 © John Levack Drever.

Every effort has been made to trace copyright holders, but if any have been inadvertently overlooked the publishers will be pleased to make the necessary arrangements at the first opportunity.

Series Editor's Preface

This series aims to gather together both key historical texts and contemporary ways of thinking about the material crafts and practices of theatre.

These crafts work with the physical materials of theatre – sound, objects, light, paint, fabric, and – yes – physical bodies. Out of these materials the theatre event is created.

In gathering the key texts of a craft it becomes very obvious that the craft is not simply a handling of materials, however skilful. It is also a way of thinking about both the materials and their processes of handling. Work with sound and objects, for example, involves – always, at some level – concepts of what sound is and does, what an object is and does ... what a body is ...

For many areas of theatre practice there are the sorts of 'how to do it' books that have been published for at least a century. These range widely in quality and interest but next to none of them is able to, or wants to, position the *doing* in relation to the *thinking about doing* or the thinking about the material being used.

This series of books aims to promote both thinking about doing and thinking about materials. Its authors are much more than mere editors, however. All are specialists in their field of practice and they are charged to reflect on their specialism and its history in order, often for the first time, to model concepts and provide the tools not just for doing but for thinking about theatre practice.

At the heart of each craft is a tense relationship. On the one hand there is the basic raw material that is worked – the wood, the light, the paint, the musculature. These have their own given identity – their weight, mechanical logics, smell, particle formation, feel. In short, the texture of the stuff. And on the other hand there is theatre, wanting its effects and illusions, its distortions and impossibilities. The raw material resists the theatre as much as yields to it, the theatre both develops the material and learns from it. The stuff and the magic. This relationship is perhaps what defines the very activity of theatre itself.

It is this relationship, the thing which defines the practice of theatre, which lies at the heart of each book in this series.

Simon Shepherd

Preface

PURPOSE

This book is about relationships between sound and theatre. It is about sound's interdependence and interaction with human performance and drama, and about places that are defined through the sonic performances that happen in them. It suggests different ways in which sound might be understood and create meaning. It collects together some key writings on sound design, but also some perspectives from beyond the immediate discipline.

The book is intended as a resource for teachers, students and researchers of theatre practices and theory, and anyone else interested in what it is to be a member of the audience – or to be audient – in the theatre. It can be selectively dipped into or read in sequence, as the reader chooses. I begin each chapter and section with a brief resume of what has been previously discussed to help the non-linear reader.

STRUCTURE

The book is divided into two Parts, framed by the essay *The Theatre of Sound*, which serves both as an introduction and a conclusion but which can also be read as a standalone essay. The main body of the book brings together reprints, extracts, newly commissioned articles and extended quotations within an editorial narrative, which intentionally offers both thesis and opinion. The narrative is contained in the introductory sections to each extract, and in some extended passages which weave quotations together in order to establish key themes. Thus, for example, the introduction to an extract from David Collison's text book on sound, deals with the impact of mediatized culture on theatre sound. The introduction to a chapter on phenomenological approaches to sound outlines some of the problems of considering sound as scenography.

Broadly speaking, Part I looks at designing sound in relation to dramaturgy: the construction of auditory sign-systems in relation to the theatre text within changing auditory culture. Part II then looks at the way theatre sound is perceived as a spatial and temporal phenomenon, and the ways in which perceptual encounters with auditory environments affect the perception of meaning.

The Introduction proposes that theatre sound design has increasing relevance in the context of changing everyday auditory culture.

Chapters 1 and 2 gather together material on Sound Design as a specialist theatre practice. Chapter 3 looks at the ways in which the dramaturgy of sound practice has evolved in relation to key moments in theatre history. Chapter 4 proposes some alternative ways of thinking about theatre sound, and Chapter 5 presents five perspectives on sound design from contrasting theatre sound designers: Frank Napier, Paul Arditti, Hans Peter Kuhn, John Collins and Jonathan Deans.

Part II looks at theatre as an aural place that organizes the way we hear. It is introduced by Chapter 6, which looks at sound design as a branch of scenography and identifies some problems in trying to approach sound as part of an object-orientated theatre. Chapters 7 and 8 look at the phenomenology of sound – or sound as an environment experienced from a position of corporeal subjectivity – in particular relation to concepts of 'live' auditory space. Through examining three historical instances (Neolithic burial chambers, ancient Greek theatres, Elizabethan 'wooden Os') it suggests how the design of the built theatre environments worked with the sound which was performed in them. Chapter 9 then suggests how theatre sound contributes to the creation of 'alternate worlds', through looking at conventions of dramatic space and time.

Chapter 10, which serves as a coda, readdressing the overall scope of the book, is an essay commissioned from the acoustic ecologist, composer and sonic artist John Levack Drever, which reprises the main themes of this volume from his perspective.

QUOTATIONS AND NOTES

Where possible, I have included original emphases, and have not introduced any of my own into quoted or reprinted sections. Where extracts and quotations include footnotes, I have taken an editorial decision as to whether they are included here, based on their usefulness as further reading to the readers of this volume, or where I think it would be ethically incorrect not to, but I have not systematically included every footnote or endnote from source material.

List of Readings

Introduction: The Theatre of Sound I

In this opening chapter, I shall propose that theatre has an important role to play in exploring and making sense of the sounds and auditory culture of everyday life. If you are reading this book from cover-to-cover, then it leads directly into Part I, on Dramaturgically Organized Noise. It would also make sense, though, if you skipped straight to The Theatre of Sound II at the end.

We begin with two positions from which to approach sound. First, immersivity and then from a critical perspective.

IMMERSIVITY

> We are normally so immersed in sound that we seldom stop to separate the individual components except through the discipline of theater. (Bell, K, 'The Art of Theater Sound', 1997)

I became familiar with the use of this term in relation to ambient sound during the 1990s, particularly through the writings of David Toop, but recently and with increasing frequency, I seem to be encountering the words *immersive, immersion* and *immersivity* used in relation to art and culture in general, and theatre in particular.

Writing in relation to sound, the semiotician Theo Van Leeuwen saw this paradigm-shift coming at the end of the last millennium: 'aural perspective … has been challenged … by new forms and technologies of listening which aim at immersion and participation rather than at concentrated listening and imaginary identification' (Van Leeuwen, 1999, p. 29). In other words, forms which 'aim' themselves more squarely at the subjective experience of sound. Immersion is often described as the opposite of visual perspective and is conveyed in aquatic tropes of oceans, bathing, drowning, swimming, floating and so on. This apparent liquefying of the sonic environment seems to be connected with the increasingly opaque omnipresence of noise in our daily lives. The air around us, it seems, is no longer a reliably transparent medium for sonic signals. It has become saturated with noise to such an extent that distinction between 'ground' and 'figure' has become uncertain.

> There is noise in the subject, there is noise in the object. There is noise in the observed, there is noise in the observer. In the transmitter and in the receiver, in the entire space of the channel. There is noise in being and in appearing. It crosses

1

the most prominent divisions of philosophy and makes a mockery of its criteria. It is in being and in knowing. It is in the real, and in the sign, already. (Serres, 1995, p. 61)

Noise has not only increased in level as a whole, but has proliferated in its component detail and diversity. 'Lo-fidelity' or low ratio of signal to noise[1] (the state in which the modern world increasingly finds itself) is often presented as a bad thing, but human culture has ways of adapting to environmental change just as it has ways of revising the premises of *good* and *bad*. The post-industrial world is a place of new and reconfigured relationships to noise and post-industrial creativity and creative entrepreneurism are making the most of them.

On the one hand, there is economic opportunity in noise abatement solutions and legislation; in sanctuary spaces and in-ear noise cancelling technologies. There is also a market for noise-based *thrill*: tremorous home subwoofer systems; real and virtually simulated motor sports; immersive and surrounding sound technologies, as well as for counter-cultural noise-music, noise-art and so on.[2] Those who can afford it can create a personalized dynamic, designer-relationship to noise. On the other hand, as the composer-prophet John Cage foresaw, there are artistic opportunities. There is new music to be found within the overcrowded soundscape, and an opportunity to reconsider music as something necessarily distinct from, and clean of, the 'anecdotal' noises of the everyday.[3] Music is no longer the object of a studiously quiet listening space. Neither is it any longer a prerequisite that it come in its own self-containing form, nor that it manifests discernable intent, sense or order in contrast to the chaos of the random.

Music can be a part of the subjective experience of noisy, environmental randomness; and that same everyday randomness can itself be taken as music. In musicology but also in everyday aesthetic experience, musical and the sonic environments are becoming blurred categories – hybrids or mash-ups. Music leaks into the non-musical everyday from headphones, open windows and shop doors and becomes part of the general ambience of place. And, conversely, environmental noise is becoming an increasingly assumed presence within music-à-porter, music composed and produced 'to go'. Sound effects and recorded samples of daily life are now commonplace in all kinds of music. And conversely, the soundscape at large, through the almost

---

[1] SNR, or signal-to-noise ratio is an audio engineering term adopted by acoustic ecologists. Signal means any wanted or useful communicative or orientational sound, noise means any sound that is unwanted or unhelpful.

[2] See Paul Hegarty, 2007; Douglas Kahn, 1999

[3] To quote Boulez: 'Any sound which has too evident an affinity with the noises of everyday life ... any sound of this kind, with its anecdotal connotations, becomes completely isolated from its context; it could never be integrated ... Any allusive element breaks up the dialectic of form and morphology and its unyielding incompatibility makes the relating of partial to global structures a problematic task' (Boulez, 1971. pp. 22–3)

inescapable presence or availability of music, seems to have become musicalized or musically framed.

Perhaps movie and broadcast media soundtracks fuelled this growing aesthetic appetite for music/noise hybridity, or maybe they reflect daily life (more probably it is a circular connection). Cage foresaw it, Schaeffer and the *musique concrète* movement did some early analogue work, but it was digital technology during the 1980s that really made the melody, harmony and rhythm of the noises of modern life available to the musical ear. And it continues to have an impact, as musical effects are engineered in all manner of non-musical contexts and grafted onto non-musical objects. This mashed-up soundscape of possibility is the liquid atmosphere in which the human post-industrial subject is immersed.

CRITICAL PERSPECTIVE

A subjective position of immersion is, however, not necessarily the best position from which to undertake a critical analysis of sound. Those who work with or design sound sometimes need to be able to sit back in their editing-room or studio chairs and think about sound in conceptual models. This is our second way of approaching sound.

When Jean Francois Augoyard and Henry Torgue write about the effect of immersion in their taxonomy of *Sonic Experience: A Guide to Everyday Sounds* (2005), their account is more analytical than subjective:

> The dominance of a sonic micromilieu that takes precedence over a distant or secondary perceptual field. While it is possible that the submerged sound element may be heard temporarily, the dominant effect is primarily perceived as positioned above the background sound. Natural contexts offer numerous examples of this effect: listening to snatches of conversation, a song near the sea, of the music of a carousel on a beach. In this specific context, the murmur of the waves creates a permanent setting that gives the impression of containing a primary sonic situation. The urban drone can also create this structure of a permanent framework over which individual sonic activities are superimposed. (pp. 64–5)

The process of designing sound begins in immersive experience, but involves the abstraction of self from the environment in order to develop a conceptual working model, which is then translated back into immersive experience. One might describe it as a process of *listening/hearing* → *thinking* → *sounding*. Too often though, the first stage is skipped or taken for granted.

Achieving critical distance from which to think about and maybe design sound is difficult when one is continually immersed in a sonic field. I am jotting down thoughts for this Introduction while travelling across London, on a PDA that also plays music. I am immersed in my subject, one might say. I am on the tube, so I have my headphones on. I read somewhere that in-ear headphones saved the hearing of many of the passengers on the trains bombed on 7 July 2005 in London, but this is not why I am wearing them. For some reason I want music in my ears as I travel. I join a carriage full of people with white wires coming out of their ears. I listen to my music and continue to write these words. Each keystroke is accompanied by a little click in my ear. I write in rhythmic counterpoint to the music. I think Einstein once defined the environment as 'everything that isn't me'. In my sonic life, I'm not sure where the line falls any more.

Art traditionally makes it its business to try to manifest meaning in chaotic environments, or at least to inspect them for it. Can this sonic environment be said to have any meaningful coherence? Is there any design to it – or do I bring a 'designer' relationship to it in the way I listen/hear and in the sonic accessories I surround myself with? Designer sound is different, perhaps, to sound design. Post-industrial daily life seems increasingly to be lived in a sonic environment full of designed sonic effects, but the overall environment, from my position of immersivity, seems random, without design or architecture.

Maybe it is for theatre, through its sonic practices, to present the audience with some critical distance; to try to make sense of this strange new world of designer sound, of ringtone bling and mega-bass; of personalized listening profiles; of virtual sonic projections. Sonic magic that would once have drawn vast, astounded crowds to a street conjuror has become commonplace, and the ear grows blasé. Theatre ought to be able to give us some perspective on a world where miniscule disembodied voices seem to speak to me from everywhere and nowhere.

Theatre sound practice has, in the past, shown life played out against vast noisy battles of elemental chaos and cosmic harmony. It has entertained with the melodramatically affective power of sound. It has used sound to show things about reality and dreams, and about silence and existence itself. Each of these manifestations was relevant to its time. This volume will look at this history in anticipation of whatever critical perspective on sound theatre will offer next.

THEATRUM MUNDI

One no longer needs to go to the theatre for theatrical sonic effect. In Oslo airport there are listening points, marked by circles on the floor, where one can step out of the ambience of the departures lounge and into a noise-cancelled zone within which one encounters the sounds of gurgling babies, whispering voices and tumbling surf. What can theatre show us about such times? The concept of 'sound effect' itself now curiously seems to belong as much to daily life as to theatre or cinema. As technologies become ever smaller, consumer products acquire more digitally produced, electroacoustic sound effects to underscore their operational functions or identify their brand. The process of inferring from effect has become less straightforward.

The sound of a camera shutter is now more likely to signify the presence of a mobile phone than a camera. A dog bark might be a door bell. Count the things in your day that beep or otherwise play artificial sound. Birthday cards open on looping samples of well-wishing; the act of remotely unlocking or locking a car involves more waveform synthesis and digital sound processing than Kraftwerk could afford onstage in 1979. Ringtones, alarms and timers on kitchen appliances, fake mechanical clicks and shutter sounds that make electronic products seem mechanical – sonification has gone way beyond user-interface functionality. It is there in the architectural and digitally-emulated acoustics of cars and public 'linger' spaces (lobbies, concourses and malls); in home entertainment systems and in-car audio 'solutions'; in digital phones that sound like old-fashioned analogue ones but with a built in reverb effect to make them sound like they are ringing in a different, more sonically luxurious world. The sum of all this, the everyday life of the early twenty-first-century post-industrial consumer, is already an immersive theatre of sonic ambiguity. What else can theatre show?

For the theatre sound designer, these are interesting times. Each sonification in product design – each beep of a car, bong of a tannoy, sting of audio identifier and squidge or bloop of computer sonic-user-interface – edges sound more centre-stage.

Sound design now seems everywhere, but theatre had it first. In terms of spatial design, when Mr Dolby and Mr DTS were mere twinkles in their ancient ancestors' ears, Greek sound designers were arranging resonant vases around stone amphitheatres to create artificial 'surround sound' resonance. We will read more about that in Part II, and on the way there, we will encounter Mr Jones of Drury Lane and his Shakespearian forebears, with their armouries of noise-making technologies. Brand reinforcement through sonification is something that theatre practitioners have done, in reinforcing stage illusions through sound effects, for millennia.

They now teach it in drama schools and university drama departments, but Sound Design is not a dramatic or a performance art. It is quintessentially a theatre art. It can be dramatic, and it can be performed; but its dramatic performance, in the instant that it is made, also becomes part of the acoustic environment within which drama and audience are performed. A sound is *made* at a point in time and space, but it *happens* all around its audience – resonating in a spatial continuum of sound. *A* sound, the indefinite article, cannot exist without its acoustic environment; without its attendant theatre.

And what would a theatre be without its sound? In the classical analogy of *theatrum mundi*, all the world is a stage and human life is a spectacle for the gods to watch from on high. It is a detached theatre, a silent theatre for spectators, and in my humble, human opinion a visual theatre is less than half a theatre. The original Greek *theatron* meant watching place, but the watching happens within an *auditorium*, the Latin word for listening place, and is done by an *audience*, a congregation of listeners. Watching is subsumed by hearing; *the gaze* is immersed in sound. Audiences inhabit two worlds: they *gaze on* and *listen in* to a detached world onstage,[4] while feeling its resonance within the world of their own corporeal presence. Sound is more than a set of auditory phenomena. According to various cultural traditions, it is the audible manifestation of a binding force that connects our inner world to the external cosmos; it is the universal vibration *prana* in which we immerse ourselves through the sacred syllable OM; it is the constant state of balance between order and chaos that must be sacrificially maintained through performing form, through poetry, music and dance; it is the music of the spheres, Boethius' *musica mundana*, and it is the sonic body – his *musica humana*. The third part of his trinity, *musica instrumentalis*, that which we hear, is merely the manifest symptom of a universe understood through sonic analogy, an analogy encapsulated in the ancient Indian mantra *nada brahma* – the world is sound. If, during modern times, this broader *sound* was temporarily forgotten by some, then it is remembered in post-modern tropes of immersivity, in new conceptual and mathematical models such as string theory, and in theatre production which owns the totality of its soundscape as ontology rather than as effect.

This book is about sound and theatre – the sound of voices, actions, music, machines; the sound of rooms, spaces and places; the sounds of silence and the noises that are not sounds. It is about sound as an effect of flesh coming into contact with air in time; and it is about the things that are communicated within this effect. But it has to be as much about *audience* as sound. Theatre is a place for detached spectatorship and aural participation (although degrees of detachment vary); for critical viewing distance but with audience implication and presence. It is an exposition of objects, but it is also a place where aural subjectivity is re-arranged through the artistry of architecture and dramaturgy.

The audience is partly implicated in theatre by its capacity to make sound. In *The Acoustic World of Early Modern England* (1999) Bruce R. Smith uses the phenomenological concept he calls 'O' to describe a circular connectivity between the body as a resonant instrument of sonic production, the surrounding aural environment, which is a cultural place, and the body, again, as the resonant receptor. All audition and bodily sonic production are transacted within this cycle. When I whisper or talk, cheer or whistle, cough or applaud in the theatre I hear myself and *sound out* my aural sphere, my place in the world, and when I do none of these things, I perform the constraint of sound; I hold my body in a disciplined way to minimize its noise.

As an audience member I radiate sound as well as receive it. My sound emanates spherically, on all fronts, outwards. So too, perhaps, does the aura of my constraint of sound. Regardless of the shape of the building or the way

---

[4] At least in prevalent modern Western theatre conventions.

they have configured the seating, the theatre of sound is round because individual earshot is spherical and because sound ripples outwards on all fronts. In our clapping, cheering, laughing and booing, but also in our constrained sound, we come to the theatre both as performers and audience. We come as dramaturgs too.[5] We make theatrical sense of the events unfolding on the stage by the way we infer things from the total environment; through the things we deem important and the things we choose not to hear.

---

[5] By referring to *dramaturgy* here I mean the overall process of making *sense* in theatrical production. *Sense* both as *intelligence*, but also as *sensation*. Dramaturgy brings theatrical intelligence to literary drama, while also delivering text from the abstract into the realm of the senses. Any conversation, decision or thought process which helps make sense of a theatrical production is dramaturgy, in any department. Sound, lighting, costume or set designers; stage managers, actors, writers and prop-makers: in their conversations and negotiations, each is a dramaturg.

Dramaturgically Organized Noise

Be not afeard; the isle is full of noises,
Sounds and sweet airs, that give delight and hurt not.
Sometimes a thousand twangling instruments
Will hum about mine ears, and sometime voices
That, if I then had waked after long sleep,
Will make me sleep again: and then, in dreaming,
The clouds methought would open and show riches
Ready to drop upon me; that, when I waked,
I cried to dream again.

(Shakespeare, *The Tempest*, Act 3, Scene 2)

Defining Theatre Sound Design

DESIGN

This chapter and Chapter 2 look at how sound design is defined by its practitioners and by the specialist literature and discourse that surround a comparatively new term in the glossary of theatre practice.

Many professional theatre sound designers will have stories to tell of how directors and producers have either misunderstood, or simply not understood at all, what sound design is. A common source of this perplexity has been the association of the term 'design' with the visual. The production of sound effects (formerly known as *noises off*) was understood to involve artistry of a kind, but in terms of the organizational structures of theatre practice it belonged in technical (props, stage-management or electrics) not design departments. Moreover, a design was something static, something fixed in time; time-based designs had other names: plays, compositions and so on. Sound design challenged category and terminology. Sound effects fitted into and around the text – so if there was design there it surely was done by the author and the director. Whereas the concept of sound *system* design was acceptable, there was considerable cultural resistance to allowing the word design to be used in relation to what we might call the sonic 'content' or 'programme' of theatre. And yet, by the turn of the millennium, *theatre sound design* had become an established term in theatre programme credits and drama curricula. However, its uneasy beginnings are not far behind, and still resonate in this current *wiki* definition:

> Currently it can be said that there are two variants of Theatrical Sound Design. Both are equally important, but very different, though their functions usually overlap. Often a single Sound Designer will fill both these roles, and although on a large budget production they may work together, for the most part there is only one Sound Designer for a given production. Where such distinctions are made, the first variant is "Technical Sound Design" (which has also been termed Theatre Sound System Design by the United States Institute for Theatre Technology's (USITT) Sound Design Commission), which is prevalent on Broadway, and the second "Conceptual Sound Design" (which has also been termed Theatre Sound Score Design by the USITT), which is prevalent at Regional Repertory Theatres. Both variants were created during the 1960s. These terms are really examples only, and not generally used in practice since most Sound Designers simply call

themselves Sound Designers, no matter which role they are filling primarily ('Sound design', *Wikipedia, the Free Encyclopedia*. 2 Mar 2007, 17:12 UTC. Wikimedia Foundation, Inc. 4 Mar 2007, h*ttp://en.wikipedia.org/w/index.php?title= Sound_design&oldid=112107638*)

While some sound technicians fought hard, in the 1970s and 1980s, to be credited as designers – on a par with set, costume and lighting designers in terms of billing and pay – others did not want to go where that that term seemed to lead. They were happy to be the technical facilitators in the traditional creative hierarchy where the 'creatives' were not specialist in production, but realized their vision through explanation to, and discussion with, technical specialists who would argue that they found their creativity in fulfilling a brief or in engineering elegant technical solutions. This might seem like a kind of design, but in theatre terminology, the term 'design' brought with it conceptual responsibility. A technician could disown an artistic failure and still be satisfied that they had done their job well.

Digital technology played a part in the establishment of sound design. The near-instant fingertip access to sounds afforded by samplers in the rehearsal room seduced influential directors, such as Peter Hall in his latter years at the National Theatre and in his commercial ventures thereafter. In order to play with these toys, directors needed people who could programme them, who also understood theatre (which people from the music industry where this technology originated, tended not to). So it was, therefore, at the insistence of 'big name' directors that producers granted the term 'sound designer' to those who were ambitious for it, and before long it became firmly established. Producers took some convincing. Here was a new 'creative' fee, and here were new hire costs. Many a showdown between director, sound-designer and producer centred on the rationale for an operator fee, an auditorium mixing position or the hire-charge of an unfamiliar-sounding digital sampler or processing unit.

Sound, unlike lighting, was not generally considered to be a base-level technical requirement of theatre other than in musicals. Producers were initially (in the 1980s) resistant to incorporating any sound that a stage manager was incapable of operating from the wings. Even worse, from the producers' point of view, sound designers, backed up by their patron directors, started insisting on four or five weeks additional hire budget so that they could have a sound system to play with in the rehearsal room!

Gradually producers were persuaded by the insistence of the directors who wanted to 'go further' with sound, that sound was something worth paying a little more for. Sound design for non-musical theatre gradually became a (barely) viable profession for a handful of people by the late 1980s and even today I would estimate that there are no more than 30 sound designers in the UK making their living solely from theatre sound design.

Things have changed. The West End and Broadway now have awards for theatre sound design. Paul Arditti, who has won several of them, does not have to battle so much these days to have his name on the poster. The cross-influence of cinema, home entertainment and other theatrical forms, for example the hi-tech spectacular of Cirque du Soleil, has raised audiences expectations of whizz-bang, swirlingly immersive surround sound. Theatre sound design has become a bona fide specialist area of training and degree-level study.

Outside of the commercial mainstream, and even within it, hierarchies and models of theatre production are also changing. Sound designers are forming their own companies and becoming the instigators of theatre. They are branching out into audiovisual design; finding new ways of collaborating and making theatre; diversifying their creativity by making sonic art, teaching, writing and making creative use of the Internet.

THE SOMEWHAT RELUCTANT DISCOURSE OF THEATRE SOUND

In 2002, assisted by my former graduate student Gregg Fisher, I convened a conference on behalf of the Central School of Speech and Drama, at the National Theatre in London to discuss the art and dramaturgy of theatre sound. To our knowledge, this was the first conference for professional practitioners and theatre sound educators that focused exclusively on creative processes and discouraged the alphanumeric technical jargon into which sound practitioners so easily slip when in each other's company. We were amazed and delighted by the positive reaction this proposal received. Practitioners travelled from around the world for an opportunity to discuss their creativity with others who, like themselves, felt insecure about discussing processes which they normally undertook as the sole member of the sound department. Many were fed up with being characterized as techies or 'noise boys', and wanted to engage more with the kinds of discourse enjoyed by scenographers and theatre architects through international organizations like the International Organization of Scenographers, Theatre Architects and Technicians (OISTAT). 'When set designers get together they don't just discuss the latest power-drill or paintbrush on the market: why is it that sound designers are obsessed with their kit? We complain about not being taken seriously as artists, and yet we conform to the technician stereotype. We don't do ourselves any favours', it was said.

And yet, despite the overall feeling that sound designers really ought to talk together more, there was also a sense that theatre sound seemed to lack the critical vocabularies or theoretical frameworks that other artists seem to have. Short-hand vocabularies would develop with particular collaborators, but discussion of sound generally was awkward.

I expect this will change as graduates of sound design degree programmes, which began to appear in America and the UK in the mid 1990s, enter the arena, although even now the literature of theatre sound design is remarkably limited for such a key area of theatre practice, and to this point comprised almost entirely of 'how-to-do it' books. The English language canon is so limited that it can be listed here in what I believe to be its entirety:

Frank Napier (1936) *Noises Off* (London: Muller): Aimed at the amateur market: Napier is exceptional in that he does allow himself to theorize as well as giving 'recipes' for practical noises off. Describing himself as a noise-maker, his career at the Old Vic straddled the advent of modernity.

Michael Green (1958) *Stage Noises and Effects* (London: Jenkins): Aimed at the amateur market, recipes for practical noises-off but without the opinion and analysis of Napier.

Harold Burris-Meyer, Vincent Mallory (and Lewis Goodfriend) (1959) *Sound in the Theatre* (Mineola, NY: Radio Magazines): The first 'handbook' of the professional, electrical theatre sound era co-authored by the influential pioneer of electroacoustic theatre sound, Burris-Meyer.

David Collison (1976) *Stage Sound* (London: Cassell): Introduction by Sir Peter Hall. Collison is thought to be the first sound engineer to be credited as *sound designer* (in 1959). Includes a brief, well-illustrated history of practical noises-off. The second edition (1982) extends the technological scope, from the dropping of styli onto gramophone records through to electronically automated mixers, showing how rapidly technology had revolutionized hundreds of years of sound practice.

Carol Waaser (1976) *The Theatre Student: Sound and Music for the Theatre* (New York: Richard Rosen Press): From the same period as Collison but aimed at the theatre student who knows very little about sound rather than the specialist.

Graham Walne (1981) *Sound for the Theatre* (London: A&C Black): The standard stage management sound textbook in the UK until superseded by Leonard.

Patrick Finelli (1989) *Sound for the Stage*, (New York: Drama Book Publishers): Basic technical manual on how to design and install theatre sound systems.

Deena Kaye and James Lebrecht (1992) *Sound and Music for Theatre* (New York: Back Stage Books): Aimed at technical theatre students. Some contextual analysis and a powerful foreword by Peter Sellars. More widely available than Bracewell but not as detailed.

John Bracewell (1993) *Sound Design in the Theatre*, (Englewood Cliffs, NJ: Prentice Hall): The definitive American college theatre sound design text by Dr Bracewell (a student of Burris-Meyer), probably the most comprehensive book on theatre sound, including chapters such as Psychological Basics of Auditory Aesthetics and Creativity.

John Leonard (2001) *Theatre Sound* (London: A & C Black Ltd): Comprehensive guide to theatre sound in the late twentieth-century mixed digital/analogue ecology, by one of the UK's most experienced sound designers.

With the exceptions of Napier, Bracewell, and Kaye and Lebrecht, there is very little space in these books given to what we might call the dramaturgy of sound. Each of them, understandably given the dates of publication and their intended readerships, assumes that the sound practitioner primarily provides a service to a director in relation to staging a literary text – there is no mention in any of these books of collaborative, devising practices or of 'alternative' forms of theatre. I expect that those books will eventually appear. I should, at this point, mention, as an addendum to this list, various websites and internet forums that have grown up around theatre sound. The most prolific and important of these is the *Theatre Sound Mailing List*, a forum which claims to be for those who 'do audio for musical theatre or plays, concerts, worship services, etc'. The list's archives are a tremendous resource, created by the list members and can be accessed at http://www.brooklyn.com/theatre-sound/archive.

CONCLUSION

Theatre sound design is now an established profession of the theatre, but those studying theatre sound design should not be guided solely by professional practice. In the introduction to this volume, I talk about theatrical immersion in the everyday, and immersivity is a trope which permeates new thinking in relation to subjects as diverse as cultural studies, anthropology, archaeology and law. Theatre academics too, are starting to think about theatre as an ecology in ways that I would suggest are aural. Theatre sound designers do not have to be interested in these things in order to do their job, but they should at least be aware that there are other theatres of sound. At the very least they should recognize the fact that, as people who spend most of their working lives listening and hearing in a theatrical environment, that there are probably people out there who would be interested in what they have to say.

The remainder of this Part reproduces extracts from some of the texts mentioned above in order to describe the orthodox pedagogy of theatre sound.

Chapter 2

What the Textbooks Say

Within the theater, auditory space consists of the performers' voices, footsteps, music and the natural and synthetic sounds completing the imagined environment. Although sound effects from property devices are still viable (especially the use of theatrical bomb tanks), today's sound designers usually work with an electronic playback and sound reinforcement system. (Bell, K., 1997)

This chapter looks at the history of this 'imagined environment'. It presents a journalistic article on theatre sound from 1904 followed by a series of brief extracts from some of the major textbooks on theatre sound. Taken together, they document the changing role of theatre sound and those responsible for it during the twentieth-century. They show how 'Theatre Sound Design' acquired an orthodox definition from practices and assumptions which happened to be prevalent at the time of the conception of the term. In Chapter 3 we will go on to put this into the context of a longer theatrical history. The remainder of the volume, in various ways, raises various questions about the assumptions represented in this chapter.

STAGE SOUND IN 1904

An Ancient Tradition

In the journal article *Stage Sounds* from 1904, Harley Vincent seems to assume that his readership knows nothing at all about the subject. This may be his journalistic device, although it is quite possible, in an age before professionally-modelled amateur dramatics, that the readers of *Strand* magazine may indeed not have ever encountered terms like 'wind machine.' One gets the sense that the article is occasioned almost entirely by an interview with one Mr Jones, the Theatre Royal Drury Lane property-master. Vincent describes standard ways of realizing the scripted sound effects of the repertoire, much as a percussionist might describe the methods employed to meet the precise needs of the classical repertoire. Jones is a craftsperson: creative, ingenious and traditional. We can get a sense from this article that these techniques have probably stood Jones' predecessors at Drury Lane in good stead

16

for centuries. The 'repertoire' of sounds described might be described as a classical *acoustemology*[1] of theatre – that is to say, a repertoire of sounds which are culturally defining. As such, they are non-musical: they tend to represent worldly activity: 'natural' sounds, often of storms or other turbulence within the ecological balance of the cosmos, that may have some supernatural significance or portent but which are categorically different from musical sound, which is supernatural. Jones was operating during a period when extra-diegetic[2] melodramatic underscoring of drama was still common, although dramatists such as Ibsen, Maeterlinck and Chekhov were leading the process of abandoning it.

The Advent of Phonography

And then ... the ominous mention of the first theatrical use of the phonograph in a recent (1902/3?) production of Henry V in Berlin ... 'The innovation is likely to spread' says Vincent 'and will surely prove a considerable economy for the smaller theatre, where the outlay on stage noises of the human and musical sort is no trifle.'

This mention of the phonograph in 1904 predates Piscator's production of *Rasputin*, which is commonly held as the first use of recorded sound in the theatre because Brecht claims it as such in his 1935 *Notes to Die Rijndkoepfe und gie Spitzkoepfe*.

> Recently the gramophone industry has started supplying the stage with records of real noises. These add substantially to the spectator's illusion of not being in a theatre. Theatres have fallen on them avidly; so that Shakespeare's Romeo and Juliet is now accompanied by the real noise of the mob. So far as we know the first person to make use of records was Piscator. He applied the new technique entirely correctly. In his production of the play Rasputin a record of Lenin's voice was played. It interrupted the performance. (Brecht, in Bentley, 1978, p. 103)

Brecht, it should be noted, worked on the Piscator production – so his claim that the gramophone had been used 'entirely correctly' cannot be taken to be completely objective! Later in this volume, John Levack Drever refers to an even earlier documented use of a phonograph, to reproduce the sound of a baby crying in Arthur Law's *The Judge* in 1890. Neither Vincent, writing in 1904, nor Brecht writing in 1935 seem aware of *The Judge* – which given the enormous number of theatre productions at the time is hardly surprising, but it does suggest that this new technology was not an overnight sensation.

---

[1] *Acoustemology* is a term, originally coined by Stephen Feld, which originates in anthropology, but which has been adopted more generally in acoustic ecology and other fields of sound study.
[2] Diegetic means located within the visible scene, extra or non-diegetic, therefore, means located outside or beyond the visible scene.

2.1   Harley Vincent (1904) 'Stage Sounds', *The Strand Magazine*, vol. xxviii, pp. 417–22 (Photographs by George Newnes, Ltd)

Suppose some reader of The Strand were to ask, 'What is a wind-machine?' how many persons in an intelligent audience would be able correctly to answer the conundrum? Yet how often have they, in some thrilling drama at Drury Lane or one of the great London theatres, listened with sympathetic anguish to the heroine's tearful ejaculation, 'Oh, what a night! Hark to the fearful wind as it beats on yon desolate moor!' And what if, after all our straining of ears to hear the wind beating on the desolate moor (the scene, by-the-bye, of the heroine's desertion by the villain of the play), there were nothing more realistic to reward us than the scene-painter's gorse and heather and the proscenium lights turned low?

What would the murder scene in 'Macbeth' be without wind? Macbeth and his consort might act for all they were worth, if the storm didn't 'whistle' – and here is just the manager's difficulty – round the battlements of the castle. Failing the wind the most realistic part of the spectacle would be wanting.

Of all sounds behind the stage wind is the easiest to represent. The wind-machine is the most reliable of all the complicated 'theatre machinery.' In little theatres, whose audiences are wont to be highly imaginative, there are generally no wind-machines at all. The stage-manager simply goes behind and works with a big bamboo cane on the back of the curtain. The result is a sound which fairly well represents wind; that is, of course, to say if a deep howling and sobbing be not wanted.

For this latter purpose bigger theatres have their wind-machines or barrels. Just picture a huge coffee-roaster, whose sides are not 'entire,' but consisting of single laths of wood, with strong silk rep bound round it. You have then an exact idea of a wind-machine. The roaster is turned and the laths stretch the silk, thus producing a rushing, whistling sound. If the silk is stretched tight the noise becomes clearer. This simple apparatus answers its object very well, if the handle is turned skilfully, first quickly, then gently, just as the wind is wont to whistle.

So, then, we will suppose that when the cue is uttered, 'hark to the fearful wind!' the property-master or his assistant takes his place at the 'wings' with the machine shown in our first photograph, and works it with such *verve* and vigour that the house fairly shivers with cold and instinctively redoubles its commiseration for the unfortunate heroine, whose scanty raiment scarce tempers the force of the icy gale. But there are various kinds of wind. The scene may be a shipwreck, where the lad or lassie in whose fortunes the house is interested is rescued in the very teeth of a salt gale. In such a case the stage-manager will take the property-master aside and tell him that the ordinary Dartmoor breeze will not do.

'The gale I want,' he says, 'must have teeth, or how is the hero to be rescued in them? I want roaring and pelting and smashing and clashing. None of your land zephyrs for me. I must hear the dolphin howl and the shark shriek!'

Whereupon the obliging and ingenious property-master, instead of tearing his hair and becoming a prey to melancholy, proceeds instantly to work to construct a wind-barrel which will imitate the kind of wind demanded by the exigencies of the piece. A bag of rice will imitate a downpour of hail.

There is, in fact, no sound which a competent property-master, such as Mr. Jones, of Drury Lane Theatre, is not prepared to imitate. Some stage sounds are, of course, quite outside his domain. And the responsibility is all upon the shoulders of the stage-manager.

The poor stage-manager! As if he hadn't enough care with what the audience hears actually on the stage without attending to so much that must be heard from behind the stage! And it must be borne in mind that in this respect nothing is unimportant and merely secondary, and also that it is a difficult business to find the best manner of adapting sounds behind the stage to what is transpiring before the eye of the audience.

Only the theatre-world knows that rhubarb has a place in the domain of stage sounds. It is traditional that the inhabitants of Meiningen, who brought stage sounds, like so many other matters, to a high degree of perfection, discovered a special use for the word 'rhabarber.' For example, when a number of human voices uttered this magic word 'half aloud,' the result was the most perfect representation of the murmur of a multitude conceivable.

Closely allied to wind, and as commonly demanded on the stage, is the sound of rain. Roughly, rain may be said to be represented by dried peas. A handful of these are put into a monster wire sieve, which is then swung slowly to and fro. But the Metropolitan play-houses are, as a rule, better equipped. At His Majesty's the rain machine takes the form of a very long, narrow box, within which little ledges are nailed. If this apparatus be lifted slantwise, as is shown in the accompanying illustration, the peas roll slowly over the ledges. Thus, at the cue, 'You must not stir out to-night; the rain is coming down heavily!' a rattling sound is produced very fairly representing rain. The roaring of the sea is usually a combination of rain and wind machines. But in a recent production the stage-manager was more particular. A

Figure 2.1 Wind machine 'Hark to the fearful wind!'

Figure 2.2 The rain box 'You must not stir out tonight; the rain is coming down heavily!'

Figure 2.3 The Rain-barrel, containing dried peas

number of 'first-nighters' may recall the fiasco which occurred when the management tried to represent the roaring of the sea. Sounds issued forth which no one recognised, and the result in the long run was comic. It would have been better to forego the attempt and leave things to the imagination of the spectator. In spite of the great improvements in stage-management a great deal must yet be left to the imagination, and no one must feel aggrieved if, in the most violent storm, the leaves of trees on the stage remain unmoved. All the same, stage-management has learnt fairly well to imitate elementary sounds. Another kind of rain-machine is the rain-barrel, also used at some of the leading theatres, whose principle is the same as the one already described.

Moreover, animated Nature must also be considered. Shakespeare's 'Hamlet,' for example, requires a cock-crow. This effect has up to now been produced at one theatre by an intelligent stage workman, an excellent imitator of animals, whose cock-crow was very cleverly done, sounding as if from a long distance and producing a good effect. Cock-crowing is, moreover, now regularly paid for as a 'special' musical performance. Parrots talk in several plays, and a 'full-voiced' chirping of birds occurs in one comedy. A concert of feathered songsters occurs in the second part of 'Faust,' where the well-known 'water-whistles' which so delighted us in our childhood are used, mingled with notes from the flute, and the imitation was very natural and life-like. In 'A Midsummer Night's Dream,' Shakespeare treats us to the lowing of the cattle. Whether this is suited by the sweet strains of Mendelssohn accompanying the representation of this scene is doubtful; at any rate, the effect is curious. In the second part of 'Nibelungen' there is scarcely need to signalize Siegfried's words, 'Thou hearest the dogs will not be held in leash,' with a baying pack of hounds. The receipt for the latter is very simple. On a big wooden table, big wooden spoons are drawn to and fro. The spoons are rubbed with chalk, and must be pressed fairly hard. This is said to have originated with a gentleman whose huntsmen used to practise the trick as a hunting joke. The roaring of a lion can be imitated by a large drum, one of whose sides has been perforated and a large piece of rope introduced. The rope is then operated upon with a well-resined glove. Basses and 'cellos represent, with deft manipulation, the effect of the 'Dragon's Den' or 'Witches' Cave,' and with this remark we come to the important part played by music *behind* the stage.

What is the use of music *behind* the stage? The first reply is that, in melodrama, it gives results unobtainable through the orchestra. Sometimes the object aimed at is to present to the audience sounds which travel from a distance. At other times the audience is made to believe that sounds really executed *behind* the stage proceed from a dummy instrument in the hands of an actor, the necessity in this case, of course, arising from the fact that the actor cannot play the instrument in question. Of course, if every minor character on the stage who carries a musical instrument could play the same there would be no difficulty, whereas the fact is that numbers of characters who come before the footlights with musical instruments are merely supers, or theatre-workmen with insufficient musical ability. The instruments, too, range over periods of almost infinite remoteness, such as in the plays of 'King Lear' and 'Coriolanus,' and anachronisms must be avoided at all costs. In 'King Lear,' for example, a jovial modern trumpeter, even although able to blow his own modern instrument, is a sheer anachronism. Hence it comes to pass that the manager with an eye to artistic effect puts a properly-costumed super, with a dummy instrument of the right period, on the stage and produces the actual musical sound from *behind* the wings. In the case of a musical procession with dummy instruments moving to and fro on the stage, of course the real players *behind* the stage keep moving in similar directions, though, in this case, the result is not perfect. Fortunately, many spectators do not trouble themselves much about these little inconsistencies.

Few sounds on the stage, especially in farce and farcical comedy, are more familiar than the crash of broken glass. There are doubtless many charming ladies extant who fondly believe that the cost of window-panes to the management must be a serious item when the low comedian and his victims have to be ejected *viâ* the window many times in the course of an evening. As a matter of fact, two baskets, one half full of broken china, are usually all that is required, the contents of the one being poured into the other. If a dreadful crash is demanded, a sackful of scollop-shells will represent it with most alarming accuracy. But theatrical science at Drury Lane goes farther than this, and we have a 'crash' machine, fitted with ten resonant slats actuated by a cogged cylinder. Our illustration shows the machine and the manner in which it is worked at the wings whenever a scene of stage violence takes place which calls for its employment.

In plays of the 'Miss Elizabeth's Prisoner' type, where the clatter of a horse's hoofs is demanded, the effect is realized by two hoof-shaped blocks of wood struck upon a slab of stone. The blocks are fastened to the wrist, and if several horses are to be represented two supernumeraries or stage-hands are called into requisition. Another form, used at the Alhambra Theatre, for example, is also shown in the illustration reproduced [below]. This instrument somewhat resembles a pair of compasses, but the effect is highly realistic.

'Good-bye, Kate!' 'Good-bye, Jack, and God bless you!' 'Right away, there! Stand back, please!' The last carriage door is closed with a bang, there is a burst of

Figure 2.4 'Crash! The villain's neck is broken!'

Figure 2.5 Imitating the clatter of horses' hoofs

Figure 2.6 'Horsemen approaching – let us conceal ourselves!'

cheering from the crowd, a little strip of scenery begins to move, a light puff of smoke is seen, and the Dover Express is off. But these details would be nothing if we did not *hear* it speeding away. Invisible to the audience sits the inevitable stage-hand with two pieces of glass-paper, working them diligently. 'Puff-puff, puff-puff!' and so the effect is produced.

For thunder there are four arrangements. The primitive one is the 'thunder-plate,' a very long and slender plate which hangs loose on a string and is set work-ing at the lower extremity. The rattling noise which immediately follows a flash of lightning is thus fairly well produced. For rolling, distant thunder there is a gigan-tic kettle-drum covered with an ass's skin, and worked with two vigorous beaters. In the older theatres a 'thunder-carriage' is still met with; that is, a cart loaded with stones, and drawn this way and that over the floor. The 'thunder-clap,' however, is the *chef d'œuvre*. This is produced by a rectangular wooden pit reaching from the 'loft-of-the-stage-for-scenic-machinery' to the podium. The inner sides are provided with irregularly constructed cross-laths, over which stones thrown down from above clatter. If the manager desires a specially severe storm he gives a vigorous turn to the huge rattle at the same time, thus representing the crashing of broken-in doors, whilst if the rattle is turned slowly the effect is that of far-off musketry fire.

Amongst the apparatus for imitating music in general use is the 'distant chime machine,' which consists of a set of pine spindles worked upon by resined fingers, producing a realistic chime. Another is the 'wedding bells machine,' or 'peal of bells,' operated as shown in the illustration below.

It is inconceivable how difficult it is to regulate stage music; how often the tones must be modulated or, to render this easy, the positions of the 'executants' must be changed; for example, when blowers of instruments, even with the best will in the world, cannot go on playing everlastingly.

Figure 2.7 Glass-paper imitates a railway engine – 'Puff-puff–puff-puff!'

Figure 2.8 'The chimes! Are they not beautiful?'

Figure 2.9 A peal of wedding bells

And then the poor musicians are jostled to and fro. They are liable to be hunted with their instruments and desks through every conceivable nook and corner. 'It sounds better in that other part,' exclaims the manager; 'why on earth aren't you there?' And before there is time to reply the 'property-man' comes along and declares they must move somewhere else, since the place where they now are is wanted to put things for the next rapid change of scenery; or the assistant manager asks whether the next great procession must come through another wing, as the desks of the musicians are a complete barrier in the wing originally chosen.

But all these difficulties are nothing compared with those which arise when a distant insurrection, a roar of the crowd, or the din of arms on a battle-field is in the scene. The position of the executants is in this latter case no less important, but it is, of course, more limited, since those whose business it is to produce the sounds naturally cannot retire very far, owing to their return being necessary at any moment. That, however, is a comparative trifle. The real difficulty is owing to the vagueness, the want of something definite in the duties of this class of executants. The musical artists have, as we have shown, great difficulties, but, at any rate, their work is definite, since they have both musical notes and instruments, whereas their colleagues who 'represent' the clamours and murmurs of the multitude have none. The repetition of the word 'rhabarber' to imitate sounds we have already alluded to, and, moreover, the attempt has been made to adapt certain sounds and sentences to express such sensations as rage, vengeance, excitement, and so on. No striking success, however, has followed this attempt, as one or other of the executants is very liable to fail in speaking in suitable tones to express the various emotions, owing to a lack of motive, such as inspires the actor who plays his part in the full excitement and glare of the footlights. Supposing only *one* voice appears to come from too near a distance, the general effect is totally marred. Next comes the real tug-of-war, for one of these distant roars of the multitude is liable to last five or even *ten* minutes, an unheard-of length of time for the poor executant to keep on murmuring accents of rage and scorn! Considering, too, that the executants consist merely of supers and stage-workmen, the leading actor is wont to be put out by the cries and interruptions of the former whenever the play demands their actual appearance on the stage.

The latest recruit to stage mechanics is the phonograph, which has recently been introduced in Berlin. It proved a grand success, the first attempt being made in Shakespeare's 'King Henry V.,' a drama in which the din of battle is especially prominent. One who was present declares that not a soul noticed that in place of human voices a piece of pure mechanism was at work. Instead of thirty 'supers' crowded together and blocking up each other's way behind the wings there was a little table with an apparatus which could be shifted from one place to another at a moment's notice. And how faithful to his task was this new colleague! No disturbance now would arise owing to awkwardness or to the fault of some malevolent super or untimely wag. The innovation is likely to spread, and will surely prove a considerable economy for the smaller theatre, where the outlay on stage noises of the human and musical sort is no trifle.

THE 'BUSINESS OF MAKING NOISES'

Tradition Meets Modernism

Frank Napier's 1936 book *Noises Off*, aimed at the now burgeoning amateur dramatics market shows Jones' ancient craft some 30 years on and in a state of transition. Modernism has had an effect in a number of ways. The music of the melodrama, already being abandoned by some dramatists in 1904, has by now fallen silent, and 'new dramatists' are scripting sounds which stand out against a backdrop of brooding silence in a way that demands new subtlety and new ingenuity of the 'effectsman'. While he still provides instructions on how to produce elemental and animal sounds, there are also sections on electrically produced and industrial machine sounds as well as sounds of modernized warfare. Gramophone records are starting to have an impact, although Napier does not give a sense of theatres embracing them as 'avidly' as Brecht had claimed in his essay of the previous year. Napier rigorously promotes the human qualities of the 'effectsman'. He uses references to *The Cherry Orchard* to establish the tone of the book and to make the point that modernist plays – he cites productions of Obey and Čapek among others – are demanding more innovatory textual analysis and 'psychological' interpretation.

The 'breaking string' effect in *The Cherry Orchard* has been the subject of many a sound design project for stage management and sound design students over the years, and might be considered the 'keynote' sound effect of the twentieth-century. We shall discuss it more later. Napier gives a detailed description of how he realised the effect in the 1934 Old Vic/Sadlers Wells production, with the aid of a musical saw (for which instrument he also composed a musical part in *The Tempest*, and used for 'spook' sounds in *Macbeth*).

Napier is insistent that the specialist noisemaker needs a rare psychology and creative genius as though he is justifying his institution against some perceived threat from those who would run gung-ho into a brave new world of electroacoustic sound (George Devine perhaps, who demanded multi-channel 'surround sound' at the Old Vic as early as 1940, in his experimental production of *The Tempest*, see Irving Wardle, *The Theatres of George Devine*, 1978, p. 86). This may well have been the case, although he may also merely be saying to his amateur readership 'this may look like messing around with musical saws but it is serious, grown-up stuff you know'.

Nevertheless, something akin to a philosophy of noisemaking emerges from his enthusiastic prose. We can clearly see that he is talking about complex, specialist embodied knowledge handed down through a long if obscure tradition, and we can see that the traditional 'effectsman' took pride in being a stage performer rather than a stage manager. The same seems true in the previous extract concerning Mr Jones.

The notion of sound operator as performer is one that Arditti echoes later in this Part in relation to randomly accessible digital sound in the 1980s. Napier calls for sound effects and underscoring to be established in the rehearsal room and practised in rehearsals from their commencement, which is something sound designers still argue for today. Napier is at pains to emphasise artistry. Technical or engineering ability is acknowledged merely as 'another useful, though subsidiary, talent for an effectsman'.

Note his emphasis on being able to 'hear sound in the brain' – the phenomena known as phonomnesis, imagined sound or 'auralized' thought.

2.2   Introductory Chapter From Frank Napier (1936) *Noises Off: A Handbook Of Sound Effects* (London: Mueller).

In spite of the very considerable number of books on the theatre and theatrical matters, nothing seems to have been written yet about off-stage sound effects. At any rate, no comprehensive book has been produced which is devoted to this branch of theatrical technique alone. This omission leaves a gap, which should be filled, for the subject is one that needs attention. It may safely be said, that noises off occur in most plays, which is by no means true of period costume. And yet the bibliography of the latter subject is extensive, not to say voluminous.

The discrepancy is doubtless due to the fact that, whereas the design and execution of period costume is guided by rules, which are to be ascertained from the study of historical data, there are no rules, but only a few principles, involved in making noises off, for the problems differ with every play and every theatre: Moreover, period costume can be recorded by description and pictures, but there is no way of writing or drawing an unmusical sound. The data must be collected by the ear and stored in the brain.

The subject of noises off is in itself a fascinating one. It leads the eager practitioner into such varied fields: from the home to the workshop; thence to the aerodrome, and back to the farmyard by way of the battlefield; from the present backward or forward in time; from the commonplace to the fantastical; from the sublime to the ridiculous.

Almost any sound may be required in a play. 'There's John now. I heard his key.' Simple. Or, in 'The Cherry Orchard,' – 'A sound is heard that seems to come from the sky, like a breaking harpstring, dying away mournfully.' Not quite so simple.

To be a 'Public Noise-maker No. 1', therefore, very diverse qualities are needed, and there is practically no end to the studies that will extend the knowledge and improve the technique necessary for this master craft. It shall not be called an art, for that might lead us into attempts to define that provocative word. Thought, however, is free.

In view of the growth of the Amateur Theatre in this country, and since there is no other book on the subject, I hope that this fruit of my somewhat peculiar labours will be of service to many.

As the title implies, this book deals only with sound effects produced off-stage. Music will be excluded, except for passing references, because it does not, or at any rate should not, fall under the category of 'noises off". Nor will vocal sounds made by characters, while invisible to the audience, such as sneezes, hysterics, death-cries, and other emotional exclamations, be discussed. These should be classed as 'acting', the business of the performers in whose parts they occur, notwithstanding the fact that, upon one occasion, I was called upon to register sudden death for three different characters at a matinee performance, while at another performance that evening I had to produce simultaneously the growls of a bear devouring a gentleman, the cries of the gentleman being devoured, and the yells of an eye-witness, whose upper registers had temporarily deserted him.

Now, there is one obvious aspect of this business of making noises. When the script of a play specifies that certain sounds, germane to the plot, are heard, those sounds must be heard. They have, of course, varying degrees of importance, and should be treated accordingly, just as lines of dialogue are treated, for they are as much parts of the play as are the lines. A knock at the door, or the ringing of a bell, which interrupts a scene, or to which the characters refer, must come as smartly on their cues as the spoken word, or the progress of the play will be held up. The point is obvious and needs no stressing.

But there is another type of sound, which, though asked for or implied in the text, is of such minor importance, such undramatic value, that it may be omitted, if it cannot be successfully produced. Better no sound than a bad sound. For instance, a character may say, 'John'll be here in a moment. I heard the car.' Now, it is quite conceivable that that character has heard a car, which the audience have not heard, particularly if there has been loud conversation on the stage just before the remark, and if the character acts as though he has heard a slight sound. In such a case, there being no other car effect in the play, it is better to make no sound, when it is considered that the production of a good car effect costs money and/or time and ingenuity. Suppose, on the other hand, that the stage-management makes a noise like a lorry arriving, and John has to enter and say, 'Darling, the new Rolls is a dream!'

There are occasions when it is extremely difficult to decide whether to have the sound or not, but that is where the fun comes in.

In a third class of sounds are those which, whether specified by the playwright or not, assist the atmosphere of the play, such as wind, sea, machinery, and the like. These are of tremendous value, but again must be well done or omitted. A producer who takes trouble over such effects is amply repaid for his efforts, for they act, to some extent, as a compensation for a small stage and indifferent scenery. A wonderful illusion of space can be obtained by arranging sounds of the right pitch and volume, and by paying attention to the balance of foreground noises with those at a distance. It often happens that a producer has no suitable backcloth, and is compelled to cover the deficiency by setting his window in the side-wall of the set. This device does nothing, however, to assist him in his task of conveying to the minds of the audience the locality of the play. Let him study the details of the noises off, therefore. For instance, round a lonely house in open country the wind howls and whistles, but to a house in the woods it is like a roaring roof overhead with the creakings and sighings and flutterings of trees added. The locality of a town house can be indicated very well by the type of sounds audible. Even the size of the house itself, in whatever locality, can be determined by the noise of the front door, or the distance of the bells from the sitting-room.

In these matters producers, who mourn for the smallness of their theatres, are in reality fortunate, for sounds that will tell the same story to the whole audience in a small hall, will in a big theatre be inaudible to half the audience, or deafening to the other half.

If we are agreed that sound effects are necessary and valuable, the next question to discuss is, what sort of persons are best fitted to produce them? Experimental psychologists divide individuals into two main types, the visual type and the auditory type; those who do the bulk of their observation and memorizing through the senses of sight and hearing respectively. Clearly, an individual of the latter type is required, for he must be able to observe sounds minutely and remember them exactly. He must have a good ear. No one can whistle a tune unless he can *hear it in his brain*. The same is true of sounds of any kind. If a person of the visual type be let loose with bass drum and a thunder sheet, he will beat the one and rattle the other, whereas a person of the auditory type will hear a real thunderstorm and reproduce it. The difference in result will be most marked.

Another point of the greatest importance is that, when an effect has been rehearsed and the producer has pronounced it perfect, the effectsman has to be able to remember the exact volume of sound necessary, and that is very difficult, even for the auditory type. Consequently the effectsman must be capable of intense concentration. This refers not to sounds produced by electrical or mechanical means, with which it is always possible to measure and record sound volume, but to those produced vocally, or by muscular action, when it is not possible.

In these cases even the auditory memory is not reliable, for when a man is actually making a noise, a large part of his attention is directed to the process of making it, leaving less to be focused in the sense of hearing. And the louder the noise, the greater must be the difference between two volumes to become perceptible. The ear of a man in the centre of a loud noise is satiated, and becomes incapable of appreciating nice distinctions. Thus then, the ear being handicapped by the lack of attention focused in it, that part of the attention which is directed elsewhere, can be made to furnish compensation. The auditory memory retains its part of the total impression, while the balance is made up by the tactile memory, if we may so call it, the memory that treasures sensations of touch.

For example, a man is required to imitate gunfire by striking a bass drum. To achieve the right volume of sound, he must strike the drum with exactly the right amount of force. He must concentrate, therefore, on that aspect of the matter, the exertion of force. When exerting force, no matter how slight, we can tell how much we have exerted, not in terms of pounds per square inch perhaps, but by the 'feel' of it, transmitted to our brains through the sense of touch seated in the joints, muscles, and skin. This 'feel' is retained by what I have called the tactile memory. *Let the man rehearse his gunfire, therefore, often enough to impress the correct 'feel' on his tactile memory*, and he will be able to experience it in his brain, just as he can hear the sound in his brain. The combined operation of his tactile and auditory memories, each contributing their quota of recollection, will then enable him to reproduce the required sound at will.

Producers would do well to grasp this point. Usually they rehearse an effect until it has been done correctly two or three times only and then pass on to something else, forgetting that it is infinitely harder to learn a sensation than to learn dialogue. And again, effects are seldom rehearsed at all until shortly before the first performance, whereas they should be tackled at the beginning and rehearsed as much as the other parts of the play. It may be objected that, because conditions at rehearsal and at performance are very different as a rule, it is better not to practise effects until performance conditions are obtainable, so that the right effect can be gained at once, and the effectsman will not have to unlearn a wrong sensation. But a wrong sensation does form a basis on which to found a right one. Our gunfire man, finding that at rehearsal he has been making less sound than is needed, when the scenery has been interposed between him and the audience, having learnt a wrong sensation, can easily increase his sound proportionately. His wrong sensation forms a standard of comparison. But if he has no chance to try, until the scenery is up, which with costumes, make-up, lighting and properties will be harassing the mind of the producer, he will clearly have insufficient attention paid to his efforts, and will only get comfortable and sure in his job by the time the show is due to come off. And the Press and notables come on the first night.

An effectsman, then, must have a good ear, the ability to concentrate, and he must be sensitive. Yet another indispensable quality is a well-developed sense of rhythm. Suppose that a person is engaged in making sounds to suggest running machinery. He must be able to select the rhythm of the particular machine he is imitating, and stick to it for any length of time without hastening or slackening the pace. With more complicated machinery it may be necessary to have three people engaged, A working at a slow speed, B at a speed twice as fast as A's, and C at a speed that bears no obvious relation to either. A and B must be able to work together, and C must be able to shut his ears to A and B, and stick to his own speed with absolute precision. Any divergence from their given speeds will ruin the effect, since regularity is the essence of machine sounds.

Suppose, further, that the play comes to its climax when the machinery gets out of control and gathers speed, until it jams from overheating. Each of the three will have to increase their speeds, while retaining the same inter-relationship. Poor C!

Under the heading of rhythm-sense the ability to judge intervals between the components of complex sounds must be placed. And it is most important that an effectsman should have this ability, since it is often the correct spacing of the components that gives to the complex sound the characteristics whereby it is recognized, the falsifying of which will render the sound unidentifiable. Or another fault may be made. Though the relative intervals between the components are correct, and the total sound is recognizable, the entire combination may be speeded up, or slowed down, giving the wrong emotional value for its context. A complex sound, supposed to be made off-stage by a character, must have the emotional value of that character at that moment. Undue speed may suggest haste or anger at a moment when laziness or indifference is required, and vice versa. From this we learn that an effects-man, besides having rhythm-sense, must also be something of an actor, since he has to be able to assume, if only momentarily, the mood of any character.

And this fact leads us on to the consideration of how much stage sense is neces-sary. We may define 'stage sense' as 'the knowledge of what is dramatically effec-tive'. This knowledge may come either intuitively or by experience, but, clearly, the more of it an effectsman has the better, as a general principle. More particularly, cases often occur when he has to exercise dramatic judgment. He has to choose the psychological moment for his noise, and make his noise before the moment gets away. One very frequent example of this is when the word-cue for an effect gets a laugh. And as the length of laughs vary with every audience, the effectsman has to judge the laugh at every performance, in order to select his moment. If he functions too soon, the noise of the laugh will kill his effect; if too late, there will be an undra-matic pause, during which the play will be 'dropped on the floor'.

More difficult problems arise sometimes in serious plays, when degrees and durations of emotional tension have to be judged. It will help a player enormously to hear a sound, to which he has to react, at the exact moment that he is emotionally ready for it. To do this an effectsman must be able to put himself in tune with the player. He needs for such occasions, and indeed for the whole business, great sympathy, using the word in its true meaning, sympathy not only with his fellow men, as men and as the characters they are portraying, but with all nature. He is produc-ing sounds representing those made by various forces; he should be able to assume, at any rate in part, the nature of those forces, just as a player tries to assume the nature of the part he is playing. So far as the player succeeds in taking on the mentality of his role, just so far does he succeed in convincing his audience. The same is true of the effectsman. Both jobs are fundamentally of the mind. We direct our bodies from our brains, so that, if we think rightly, the right actions will follow, and the tight impression will be created in the minds of the audience. Therefore *Be* a thunderstorm. *Be* the lazy surf. *Be* a galloping horse, tearing down the forest ride with a hero on your back; shrink from the jarring cobbles in the court-yard, and, when the hero thoughtlessly wrenches your mouth in his haste to dismount, stamp and snort with pain. Anything else will be monotonous, if not wrong, and unworthy of an artist.

There is one quality, one key-quality that an effectsman *must have*. Without it all other qualities are as sheep having no shepherd. It is utter, absolute, cosmic relia-bility. Nothing make's acting such a nerve-wracking occupation as being unable to rely on the effectsman, and there is probably no actor, professional or amateur, who has not suffered from this particular form of torture at some time. We may take it, therefore, that agreement, on this point is unanimous. An actor, who is late for an entrance has at least to appear and face the music; the crime carries its punish-ment along with it. But a defaulting effectsman puts his fellow performers to public shame, while himself lies hid in anonymity. He should be made to take a curtain call, in chains.

This risk of missed cues is lessened greatly if the effectsman is properly rehearsed. He learns his part in the same way as do the rest of the company. The order of cues and the length of the waits between them sink into his brain and become a unified performance, as opposed to a string of isolated anxieties. As a rule, the stage-manager and the effectsman are one and the same, and it is of the greatest assistance to a stage-manager to be able to rehearse sufficiently, to know his part, so that, even if his prompt copy were lost or destroyed, he could conduct a performance with confidence. *Stage-managerial confidence is the foundation of successful play-production.* Too many producers make drastic changes at the last moment, being unwilling, or unable, to do their thinking at the proper time, namely, before the play goes into rehearsal. As a result, unnecessary strain is put upon the stage-manager, whose first night becomes a first nightmare, instead of a calm, straightforward piece of work.

Another useful, though subsidiary, talent for an effectsman is to be 'good with his hands'. Ability to work in wood, metal, leather, etc., is a great assistance, because he can then make for himself any necessary contraptions, and experiment with them, and alter them, until they are perfect. If he has to have this part of the work done by somebody else, it is often extremely difficult to describe exactly what is wanted. A great deal of time is wasted in explanation and argument, and he is hand-icapped by lack of knowledge of the possibilities of various materials. But, if he does the work himself, these handicaps are removed together with certain other difficul-ties. If with infinite patience and labour he has half-completed a contraption, and, he then has a very much better idea, he can quietly scrap the one and start on the other, working, if necessary, all night. When another man is making the first contraption, however, it all becomes very difficult, and the effectsman has either to put up with second best, or go through the whole process of explanation and argument again in circumstances that are much less comfortable.

So then, for a good effectsman we have to find a person of the auditory type, having a sense of rhythm, as much stage sense and experience as possible combined with acting ability, sympathy, and sensitiveness. Add to these utter dependability and handiness with tools, and season the whole mixture with patience and humour. If he is also a singer, a harpsichord-player and a certified plumber, so much the better.

When a company has discovered such a god-like mortal, their only other difficulty will be to resist the temptation to cast him for the leading part and let the noises 'go hang'.

THE SCOPE AND LIMITATIONS OF THEATRE SOUND

The Intermediate Theatre Soundscape

Burris-Meyer and Mallory's *Sound in the Theatre* (1959) was seminal within American theatre practice. In it we see the impact of radio on theatre, in audience expectations of modern-sounding, electroacoustic (amplified or reinforced) sound, and in the stylistic conventions such as the disembodied voice employed in Living Newspapers. *Sound in the Theatre* was aimed at the high-end amateur, the student, or the theatre electrician or stage manager in need of professional development. It set a template for later textbooks.

Where Napier, with his physical interface with practical props, talks about 'performance' Burris-Meyer and Mallory talk about control. The equipment and techniques they list are presented as tools for controlling sound in order to achieve a defined list of functions within a scope they establish at the beginning of the book. *This* is what sound *does* in theatre, they say matter-of-factly. Like Mr Jones at Drury Lane and Napier at the Old Vic, they worked within a theatre where sound's function was partly prescribed by tradition, but which was also alert to cultural and technological changes going on outside its walls.

Despite a somewhat dry approach compared to Napier's there is nevertheless a clear sense that they understand dramaturgy and share Napier's view that a sound operator must perform – although they put a higher premium on technical ability, calling for 'technically competent showmen'.

Their take on the scope of sound conforms to the familiar orthodoxy. There are some interesting variants: they differentiate between locale and atmosphere, but make no mention of what Collison, 17 years later, calls 'spot' effects (interpolated effects in the midst of dialogue). Perhaps this is because they are concentrating on electroacoustic sound and are writing at a time of transition when the sound effects gramophone records have limited application because they are difficult to cue and deteriorate rapidly with repeated, nightly use. So 'spot' effects, which needed to be cued precisely in relation to action or dialogue, or which needed to sound as though they came from within the stage space, were still mainly made with practical props (as 'noises-off').

The audience, therefore, had to accept three sonic 'worlds': the 'real' world of actor's voices, stage movements and the audience's coughs, the world of the 'live' *noises-off* – the thunder sheet, the 'practical' telephone or doorbell and the coconut shell, which the audience accepted by convention but which were obviously *live* but not 'real', and a separate, mediatised electroacoustic world of replayed sound, which was 'realistic' but not 'real' or live. This kind of mixed aural-ecology still exists in theatre today, where even the most lushly produced electroacoustic sound design sounds different to the acoustic sounds of the stage and auditorium. The audience expects to encounter different degrees of artifice within the theatre: some props are real, some are mimed; some scenery is explicitly represented, some is implicitly suggested. Nevertheless it is historically noteworthy that during the course of Burris-Meyer and Mallory's careers, the auditory sphere of theatre developed two separate 'registers' – the acoustic and the electroacoustic. While both were experienced as part of the same local sonic environment the cultured ear easily recognized two distinct realms of sound: one *immediate* and the other *mediated*. The aural experience of theatre thus became what we might term *intermediate*.

This bifurcation of aural experience was not confined to theatre. Between the 1930s and 1950s the development of radio, film and television brought immediate and mediated space into coincidence in daily life. Orson Welles' documentary-style *War of the Worlds* adaptation, broadcast live in 1937, created such confusion among those who missed its beginning, that people took to the streets in Martian hunting posses. More commonly, the experience of going about one's daily business and hearing the same radio programme playing in shops, in cars and from open windows, became commonplace and created a new community among people who existed somewhere between the immediate noise of their daily lives and the mediated narratives of broadcast news and soap operas. The knowledge that one might *share audience* of a live radio broadcast, in time but not in place, with unseen strangers across the nation, changed the premise of *audience* itself.

Acousmatic – or displaced sound – which might in the past have automatically signified supernatural activity, now became mundane, and acoustic space gained potential virtual dimension.

Aside from this spatial change, the acoustemology of everyday life now also acquired acousmatic sounds and sound qualities. The disembodied, close-miked voices of continuity announcers and newsreaders presented the ear with an intimacy previously only associated with physical closeness. Music became part of the background of daily life without the presence of musicians. Mediatized voices and music entered the home, the urban street and the car and connected such diverse locations within a new continuum. Among all of the arts, theatre, with its intermediate soundscape, was best placed to explore the dynamic effects of these new intermedial juxtapositions of real, realistic, live, present, virtual, placed, displaced, synchronistic and anachronistic.

2.3   Extracts from Harold Burris-Meyer, Vincent Mallory (and Lewis Goodfriend) (1959) *Sound in the Theatre* (Mineola: New York, Radio Magazines).

Scope

Sound in the theatre has the following functions:

1. To transmit the human voice in speech or song; (adequate audibility is always the first requisite).
2. To establish locale; (bird songs, traffic noises).
3. To establish atmosphere; (wind and rain).
4. To create and sustain mood; (combinations of devices used for locale and atmosphere; distortion of speech; soft music).
5. As an independent arbitrary emotional stimulus; (music).
6. As an actor; (the voice of the LIVING NEWSPAPER).

7. To reveal character; (the unspoken aside).
8. To advance the plot; (sound bridges between scenes or episodes).

These functions may be undertaken singly, in combination, independently, or counterpointing or reinforcing their equivalents in the visual component of the show. Their full accomplishment requires that it shall be possible for the audience to hear *any sound from any source, or no source, or a moving source with any frequency spectrum or intensity from any apparent distance, in any apparent direction, and with any desired reverberant quality.*

Limitations

Traditional forms of presentation undertake no such elaborate control of sound as is here listed. This circumstance is not the fault of the playwright; Shakespeare demands all that the best modern techniques can provide. It comes about basically because the showman is seldom technically competent, and the technician often does not know show business.

Only a few of the theatres built in this country before World War II were designed with any thought of acoustics. Very few turned out to be better than acoustically tolerable. Many have undergone various types of architectural alteration to overcome acoustic limitations. No attempt to improve a bad structure has produced as good a theatre or as cheaply as can be achieved with integral acoustical design. The public address system too often is used as a crutch, with which an attempt is made to compensate for bad theatre planning. In this use, the public address system is never quite successful, and the performance suffers.

In that part of sound control that is electronic, Radio Broadcast is the parent art. As a result, much of the sound operation in the theatre is a recognizable offspring. Many practices have been developed in broadcast which are not suitable to sound control in the theatre.

One such practice is that of secondary monitoring, in which audible material projected to an audience is monitored by means of headphones or a loudspeaker backstage or in an acoustically treated room. A cardinal rule of sound control is that the operator must be so stationed that he hears what the audience hears – directly.

Another such practice, however, which is no longer respected in broadcast studios, is wrong microphone position and distance. The layman believes that the microphone is to be treated as a telephone. This misconception is fostered by press photographs showing announcers massaging their tonsils with the instrument and crooners hanging for support upon the microphone stand. Most microphones distort badly when a respectful distance is not maintained.

On the current vestigial vaudeville stage, subtle and delicate reinforcement is often neglected and the voice of the soloist is merely increased in intensity. This is readily understandable as a necessity for the spent young ladies who sing with dance bands. In the case of the trained singer or speaker, inappropriate loudness and disproportionate emphasis of low frequencies results in an unreal stentorian voice, when suave, understandable speech is required.

Arising from that same radio-mindedness is the limitation imposed by electronic equipment of inadequate response and power. Perhaps deceived by radio clichés about what the public wants in radio quality, the sound technician in the theatre has usually used equipment which might be all right in the home for an uncritical radio listener, but is woefully inadequate in the theatre. If the audience accepts electronically reproduced sound as real, the equipment must reproduce and project undistorted all it receives.

Styles of acting have changed. Since Nazimova played an entire scene with her back to the audience, (in *Belladonna*) less accomplished players have cultivated an intimate style while neglecting the development of adequate skill in voice projection. Speech and song whose intensity and definition are adequate in motion pictures and radio will often not get beyond the sixth row in theatres. Electronic devices cannot compensate for lack of training and discipline but are, and will probably continue to he, used to prop up the mediocre performer.

On Sound Effects

Effects include all sounds required by the production other than speech, song, or instrumental music. They are potentially important to the production in that they create, reinforce, or counterpoint the atmosphere or mood; reveal character; or contribute to the advancement of the plot. In a sense they fulfil the function of music as illustrated by the fact that musical figures can often be substituted for effects and serve as background music. In conformity with the principle that music is a way of handling sound, effects treated according to the principles of music composition can achieve emotional response as does music. Sound effects need not be faithful reproductions of the subject concerned. It will often suffice if only some of salient significant element of a sound is reproduced. Some effects have significance on the basis of their sheer psycho-physical impact, as the bombing in *Idiots' Delight*, and the drum in *Emperor Jones*.

THE USE OF SOUND

Theatre Sound Tracks

Between *Sound in the Theatre* in 1959 and David Collison's *Stage Sound* (from 1976) we get more of a sense of the impact of mediatization on auditory culture and the way in which theatre, while ostensibly presenting its audience with a live experience, was not entirely a 'live' production. What is clear from Collison's book, however, is that the adoption of multiple-source sound playback did not change the need for the operator to be an adept and instinctive theatre performer, and nor did it make their role any easier.

In 1959 David Collison was credited as a 'sound designer' for the repertory season at the Lyric Hammersmith, London in what may well have been the first published use of the term. By 1976, he was writing about a theatre whose practices had become invaded not merely by the 'radio clichés' which had irked Burris-Meyer, but by pressure to emulate, in relation to live, acoustic voices, the pre-recorded soundtrack mixes of TV and film, comprising spot effects, incidental music and background, 'wild track'-style atmospheres. Practical sound effects had more or less disappeared bar the use of pyrotechnics and practical telephones and bells. Spot effects were now ordinarily cued from reel-to-reel tape recorders.

The challenge, for sound operators, was in achieving this filmic 'soundtrack' effect in relation to unmiked, acoustic voices. In film, the human voices are on a separate 'channel' in the mix and can be lifted over the ambience, Foley effects and music. In theatre, the operator needs to make sure that any sound heard concurrently with the human voice 'sits' just under the threshold of distraction or unintelligibility. In practice this often means that the sound/music has to be so low that it is ineffective or annoying.

Theatre sound designers (and operators) needed to develop techniques to approximate, or 'cheat' this effect. Indeed, the word 'cheat' entered the sound operator's vocabulary around this time. *Cheating out* or *in* are techniques either of establishing an atmosphere at a noticeably loud level, and then very slowly fading the level down until it disappears without the audience consciously noticing the moment at which it disappeared, or of imperceptibly bringing an atmosphere or piece of music in. The word 'cheat' is interesting as it implies that the more honest thing to do would be to leave the sound 'in' for the duration of a scene, as though it really were the sound of that scene, even if it drowned out the words or became tiring on the ears.[3]

As well as cheating, operators 'rode' the faders, 'ducked' the level down under lines of dialogue and 'poked' it up in between. A whole new glossary of operator-speak emerged. The new generation of sound technicians and operators tended to come from music or lighting backgrounds, because of the technical knowledge needed to rig sound equipment. Whereas effectsmen like Jones and Napier had honed their performance craft and worked in a theatrical tradition, the new breed often did not, and needed to learn about theatre sound's subtle balance with the acoustic voice, and about the rhythms of cueing. Knowing how to anticipate a cue, or how to leave a beat or two after a cue line in order to achieve theatrical effect are dramaturgical decisions.

The intermedial relationship of recorded sound to acoustic voice made 'articulating' mediatized effects with the dialogue more challenging. The noisemaker in the wings, with his battery of percussive instruments, worked

---

[3] In the early days of what is now known as 'verbatim' theatre, the director Nicholas Kent asked me to design the sound for one of his Tricycle Theatre productions. He said he wanted recordings of actual location sound to run under whole scenes. I declined the gig because I thought this approach was theatrically naïve. With hindsight I regret not taking the job – I think he was actually suggesting something daring and innovative which was consistent with the emergent premise of verbatim theatre.

in the same aural environment as the voice, whereas recorded sounds existed in an electroacoustic 'plane' within the theatre acoustic, like an orchestra in which the violins are live, but the woodwind are recorded.

A New Order

The acoustemology – or culturally-defining repertoire – of sound effects characteristic of the drama of the time (the doorbells, cars pulling-up, dog-barks, phone rings, birdsong, crickets, incidental music and so on) continued to adapt to the mediatized times. The traditional role of theatre noises was largely symbolic. Elemental noise such as rain, wind and thunder, in classical tradition, were a sign of something being wrong in the cosmos. 'Natural' sounds still tended to figure prominently, recalling this classical tradition (the ominous thunderclap, the idyllic birdsong) but were augmented by equivalent sounds from the industrial or urban soundscape (the thunderous machine). But sounds were increasingly used to set the scene as well as make significant announcements or describe unseen events (not necessarily for the first time, we shall read later about nineteenth-century use of picturesque sound).

In the following extract, Collison begins with *his* version of the functional 'scope' of theatre sound, and then discusses two examples which clearly show cinematic influence: a Tennessee Williams play which employs a classically symbolic acoustemology in the form of a 'wild track' (crickets, birds, frogs and so on), and a production of Macbeth which uses a stylized human heartbeat, implying a subjective perspective on the scene.

Classical contexts then, but a modernist method: that of montage. His approach is that of the post-production editor, building a total soundtrack in the counterpoint of musical, sonic and vocal elements. But of course, this is not a post-production mix, but a live contrivance. The live operation – the performance – of these complex sequences required the combined skills of orchestral conductor and mad scientist.

Note the mention of the 'continual racket of birds, bells, traffic, radios, etc.' – the old acoustemology mixing riotously with the new.

2.4   Extract from David Collison (1976) *Stage Sound* (London Cassell)

The Use of Sound

Sound effects may be used for a variety of reasons:

> To establish (a) locale, (b) time of year, (c) day or night, (d) weather conditions.
> To evoke atmosphere.

To link scenes.

As an emotional stimulus.

To reproduce physical happenings: spot cues like cars arriving, babies crying, clocks striking, elephants falling out of trees, etc.

Background effects

Let us take background and atmospheric sounds first. Just pause for a moment and listen ... I guarantee you are now aware of a whole spectrum of background noises of which you were not fully conscious a moment ago. These are the reassuring and comfortable sounds of life, of people, of things going on.

I am not, however, advocating a continual racket of birds, bells, traffic, radios, etc., running throughout the play. Far from it. Much thought must go into a good background sound track which should, as in real life, register for the most part only on the subconscious level.

In the theatre we have the tremendous advantage of being able to add to and subtract from the background at will; at one moment strengthening a dramatic pause, at another adding to a confusion, thereby giving depth, life and atmosphere to the whole.

A sudden silence or absence of sound can be just as disturbing as a sudden loud noise. This artifice was used to great effect by Peter Hall in his original London production of *Cat on a Hot Tin Roof*. The hot still atmosphere of the deep South was created by using a combination of continuously cheeping crickets and various croaking frog noises with occasionally, during a pause, the harsh squawk of a bird.

The method was, for example, to start a scene with a cricket chirping slowly and repetitively out on the verandah, then when the action was under way very subtly to add some deeper frog noises; a couple of pages later these would be supplemented by the high-pitched and continuous sound of cicadas. Having built up the background over quite a long period in order to achieve total acceptance by the audience, dramatic moments could be heightened by merely subtracting one or more of the elements. At one moment I had two types of cricket and three different frog sounds all going at once until, in the middle of the last line of a tense exchange, they all abruptly disappeared. The ensuing pause was electric.

Although there must have been well over 70 sound cues in that production, including plantation workers singing, a distant church bell, an offstage party, children shouting and several radio sequences, many friends who saw the show were unable to remember sound effects at all. That kind of total integration of effects in a production is the essence of a good sound track.

One of the real cliché effects for creating tension is the heartbeat, and under the right circumstances it really does work. We have noticed even in our own sound-effects department that when working with music or effects which have a slow rhythmic beat everyone tends to work more slowly than if the beat is fast. The pulse rate changes. This phenomenon can be applied to an audience.

In a production of *Macbeth* I once used a very low frequency drumbeat during the scenes leading up to the battle. It started at a little below the speed of a normal heartbeat and was played at a very low level, with the gain being increased imperceptibly over a long period during which the speed of the beat was also gradually increased, the idea being that it would carry the audience's pulse rates with it. During some final frenzied activity on stage a few moments before the start of the battle the drumbeat which was by now quite loud and fast was suddenly cut. There was a pause … the audience were on the edges of their seats … then crash! Trumpets, shouting, swords clashing and all hell let loose.

This sequence used the increasing heartbeat effect, the heightened pause and the shock of a sudden loud sound.

It often happens that a continuous background sound creates a distraction. This is especially true in a large theatre where intelligibility is a problem. In all too many places of entertainment one has difficulty in hearing the proceedings because of the hum of an air-conditioning plant or the rumble of traffic. Because this low frequency sound is constant it tends to be discounted, but the effect is of an aural barrier between the actors and the audience.

To run a wind or rain effect, for example, throughout an entire 20-minute scene at a fixed volume level is seldom a good idea. Maybe it is supposed to be raining but it is not necessary to hear it all the time. When it rains in real life we hear it usually when it starts (change of background) and then only become aware of it spasmodically, particularly during pauses in concentration.

In a theatrical situation the rain would either be brought in suddenly to denote a downpour or would be faded in under dialogue some 30 seconds before it was actually required in context … The audience should register the fact that it is raining and then turn their concentration back to the action (if they do not, then we are all in trouble). The level can now be adjusted so that the effect is gently lost under the scene. In other words, we are assisting the concentration process and moving the focus back to the actors. The rain should then occasionally be brought back to be registered during pauses. The reasons for bringing it back are as follows:

Because the text calls for it.
Because the director wishes to remind audience of the world outside.
Because the scene requires punctuation.

An obvious place to bring back an effect is when someone enters or leaves the stage setting; not only does this action relate to the world outside but it is usually a punctuation point in the scene.

A sensitive use of background sound can add an interesting and important dimension to the setting.

Spot effects

Specific spot effects can also do a great deal to help atmosphere. They should, however, be used sparingly and always to some purpose, such as the aforementioned three reasons. They should be cued-in accurately at every performance just as a film sound editor will precisely position his various voice, music and effects tracks. Good spot effects can assist the actor by giving him another element against which he can react. For example, a scene with a period setting inside a house: at a suitable moment the distant sound of a horse and carriage or a street seller shouting his wares is heard. The actor, without necessarily even pausing, gives the merest glance towards the window and the reality of the situation is immediately enhanced.

SOUND DESIGN AND CRAFT

Orthodoxy and Innovation

John Bracewell's *Sound Design in the Theatre* is considered by some to be the definitive American textbook on the subject and became a set text on many college sound design syllabuses. His approach to sound design assumes that the sound designer would be working within a standard production hierarchy, on a familiar repertoire of plays, with technical resources of a certain standard configured in standard ways. In the UK, as alternative forms of theatre began to proliferate in the 1990s and the demand for sound design increased, young sound designers were as likely to be doing professional or semi-professional work on 'the fringe' using domestic hi-fi equipment.

Collaborative models of theatre production; methods of collaboratively devised authorship; *physical* and *visual theatre*; 'sound-led' theatre even: such forms began to emanate from the American and British theatre Fringes, centred around New York, London, the Edinburgh Festival and the British Arts Council small-scale touring circuit, in the late 1980s. By the early 1990s they had begun to infiltrate arts-council funded Repertory producing houses in the UK.

Théâtre de Complicité's *Street of Crocodiles* started as a workshop at the National Theatre Studio in 1991 and was produced in the Cottlesloe in 1992, involving sound designer Christopher Shutt within an inter-disciplinary devising process of structured 'play'. Similar methodologies, which involved composers, sound designers, musicians and operators at a far earlier, authorially-creative stage than before (as far as the budgetary constraints and traditional four-week rehearsal processes would allow) began to be used in UK theatres such as the Glasgow Citizens, Derby Playhouse, West Yorkshire Playhouse, Birmingham Rep and even at that bastion of the written play, the Royal Court. New approaches to sound design that worked within a process of *devising* rather than *staging* or *realizing*, required new skills – particularly of communication and collaborative creativity. This kind of creative involvement in theatre was attractive to composers and some student sound technicians, but there was concern among established industry practitioners at the time, that a new generation of sound practitioners emanating from colleges and university drama departments called themselves sound designers with little training in, and scant regard for, basic engineering skills.

Bracewell is representative of a prevailing wisdom of the time that put technical basics of sound engineering before creative strategies or innovation. There is a firm sense of 'know your place' throughout, and 'don't get carried away'. At that time, it was inconceivable that a theatre sound designer might be able to get by professionally on compositional flair or skills of collaborative creativity, or an operator on a musician's sensitivity of touch or an actor's sense of timing and response to the rhythms of performance, without also having the ability to wire up an XLR plug or tail-in a power-supply to a three-phase mains supply.

That said, Bracewell's book is probably the best and most complete iteration of this orthodoxy, and is excellent in its way. If its approach to creativity seems somewhat formulaic by today's standards, then it should be remembered that most sound literature did not even venture near the subject and concentrated wholly on technical equipment and processes.

It is worth remembering by the way, that in 1993 most people still had no access to the Internet, and computers were still considered too unreliable for live theatre use.

Like his erstwhile mentor Burris-Meyer and like Collison, Bracewell (1993, p. 207) begins with a definition of functional scope:

Audibility
Motivation
Music
Vocal alteration
Vocal substitution
Extension of dramatic space/time
Mood

He arranges these seven functions into three categories: the *practical* ('necessary considerations for audience comfort in perceiving the vocal component of dramatic production' – i.e. *audibility*), the *dramatic* ('those things that directly advance or condition the progress of the drama or the environment within which the dramatic action takes place' – i.e. *motivation* and *vocal alteration/substitution*) and the *aesthetic* ('matters that have to do with personal interpretation of the immediate *emotional* character of the drama and with the long-term development of feelings and attitudes as modified by the dramatic experience' – i.e. articulation of *dramatic space/time* and *mood*). Audibility is in the *practical* category, and music overlaps *dramatic* and *aesthetic*.

2.5   Extracts from John Bracewell (1993) *Sound Design in the Theatre*
(Englewood Cliffs, New Jersey: Prentice Hall)

On Design

The primary difference between art and design in general is that design is art limited by a function other than its own. The designer as an artist is not free to enter into a state of engaged perception with just any set of possibilities in space and time. The focus of perception and insight must adhere to one particular object – the thing to be designed. That object to be designed is usually specified by some function other than the designer's own immediate interests. A designer, therefore, needs to be a person who can easily become actively involved with objects or functions for the immediate challenge that those entities present.

The object to which the theatrical designer's creative engagement is directed is the idea or ideas expressed in the playwright's script together with the director's interpretation of what that script means. The designer's function is to create, within the range of ideas expressible within his or her medium, a set of conditions that will promote the insights and the emotional character implicit in the script and the director's interpretive purpose. Those conditions may be the color and shape of the clothing worn by the characters; the depth, texture, color, and form of the surroundings in which the characters act; or the qualities of the auditory environment and/or the musical analog of the characters' feelings and interactions.

For the sound designer, the object of an engaged perception with the playscript is the auditory world of the drama. In order to perceive that world, and to be able to focus a heightened awareness on the interrelationships of that world, however, the initial engagement must be with the entire drama, not just its auditory surround. Recall that this world in the drama is the playwright's creation, that everything within it is there for a reason, and that the changing relationships in the dramatic space operating through dramatic time imply the necessary characteristics of this imagined world. The auditory characteristics of this world are what the sound designer must intuitively find. He or she must explore the possible relationships of those characteristics and find the set of sounds (and musical qualities, if needed) best suited to enhance the meaning and emotional dynamics of the playwright's intentions.

The result of the creative process for the sound designer is, of course, the assemblage of music and/or sounds that will be used to realize the auditory world of the production. That auditory world will be successful, in part, insofar as it functions as a useful metaphor for what the designer and director believe to be the meaning (the original insight and its emotional concomitant) intended by the playwright. The sound, along with all other aspects of production, must contribute to building for the audience the emotional structure that will lead them back to insights and feelings similar (in kind, if not in fact) to those experienced and communicated by the playwright.

On Craft

Sound in the contemporary theatre has three aspects each of which could be considered a separate craft: environmental ambience, music, and electroacoustic reinforcement. Environmental ambience is an all-inclusive term encompassing atmospheric noises and the sounds of the dramatic environment (including the obligatory sounds called for by the script), vocal assistance for the actor (meaning alteration and/or substitution of voice, not acoustic reinforcement), and the symbolic shaping of sound to imply extensions of dramatic space and time. Music involves the determination of the character and kinds of music to be used as incidental music to provide introductions, bridges, and closures for scenes and acts, as integral music used within a production as part of the dramatic action (usually but not always specified by the playwright), and as underscore music to help enhance and reinforce the dominant mood and character of a scene or to provide dramatic counterpoint to the immediate action within a scene. Electroacoustic reinforcement is the use of audio to improve the audibility of actors' voices by simple amplification, by corrective action to overcome acoustic deficiencies of the theatre or auditorium, or both.

ART AND CRAFT IN THEATRE SOUND DESIGN

I include the following extract from Mic Pool's self-published *Manifesto* on theatre sound for two reasons: it provides an interesting UK perspective alongside Bracewell's views on the Art and Craft of sound, and it also represents the first use – in 1993 – of a personal website to publish what we would now know as a 'Blog' on sound.

2.6   Extract from the website 'The Aural Imagination', http://www.micpool.com

---

What is Craft?

Before we examine the art of sound design lets consider what might constitute a good example of craft. It might be helpful to consider equivalent visual craft examples.

Consider the requirements of a definitive photograph of a discarded coke can, as a representation of urban angst, and a sound recording of the same subject.

First imagine an instamatic snapshot of the can. Now think of the equivalent sound recording. Perhaps it was tossed in the air, the sound of it landing recorded with a single microphone. It probably has some unwanted background sounds and fails to capture the excitement or threat of hearing a can falling in the dead of night. The sound fails to generate any response from the listener; 'It's a can so what?'

Now visualise the photograph as executed by a top photographer for a magazine

assignment. The coke can picked from hundreds because of its unique deforma-
tions. Many light sources skimming the concrete on which it rests to bring out its
pitted texture. Its placement on the magazine page framing it and giving it an enclos-
ing context. The viewer finds the photograph fascinating; there is a resonance which
stirs memories of the viewer's experiences.

Consider how we might set about utilizing the craft of sound recording to elicit a
similar emotional response. The choice of acoustic and microphone placement
chosen with as much care as the photographer took with the location and lighting
of the subject. Aluminium cans, steel cans, cans thrown from balconies, rolled down
stairs or crushed by feet. And a framing context, perhaps a fast rhythmic pulse
running under it.

And what else will we put on our aural page. Footballs hitting shutters, a hand-
brake turn or a wheelie, all recorded with skill and craft as a distillation of the sensation of hearing those sounds for real. The sensation enhanced by the intensification
of their defining features and finessed through the framing device.

As a by-product of our consistency and attention to detail we have created a
cohesive logical soundworld which is the foundation of all good sound design.

Manifesto: What is Design?

I would define design as:

A process of organised creativity with defined goals or functions.

Design is distinct from fine art; its main role is to serve functional purposes. In the
context of the theatre these purposes might be defined as:

Enabling the play to be performed
It is amazing how often this is neglected. Many designers seem content to present a superficial setting and leave the solution of the real design problems of a
play, without which it cannot be performed, to others. The designer's primary task
should be providing solutions which aid the presentation and understanding of the
piece.

Providing fluidity to the dramatic action
The action of a play must flow from one situation to the next in a manner appropriately paced and styled. Sound design has an important role in this process. Too
often though it is used to cover the set designer's neglect of this area by providing
covering distraction for ill designed stage mechanics. A linking design element
should be a journey. The scenic elements should be choreographed at the pace the
drama requires not that dictated by the mechanics. The sound design should travel,
trailing ideas from the preceding scene, introducing new elements relevant to what
is to follow. The most basic form of this is the cross-fading of music from an abstract
link, replayed on the theatre's front of house speakers, to a radio on the set which
forms part of the actuality sound for the following scene.

Providing a physical reality for the production
Essentially an environment, a cohesive logical world, real or imagined for the play to inhabit. Often the sound will define the area bounding the set. The sound of approaching and departing vehicles could establish the geography of a remote farmland setting or complex rain effects might breathe life into a setting by presenting the sounds of different surfaces being struck by rain, corrugated tin roofs, drains, windows, etc.

Enhancing the depth and meaning of the play (contextualisation)
Perhaps by creating a parallel internal logic in the arrangement of music and sound effects. Two case studies might better illustrate this. A Shakespeare play, *The Taming of the Shrew* uses music to define the essential social stratification of the characters represented and provide commentary which advances the director's vision of the play. A modern play, *Fathers Day* by Maureen Lawrence, uses sound to present aspects of the recollections of a failing memory.

Enhancing atmosphere and mood
The last function should be arrived at through attention to those preceding. Do not have as a primary goal in design the manipulation of the collective audience's emotional response through the creation of so-called atmosphere.

Common Elements of the Theatre Design Disciplines

The important common thread between theatre design disciplines is they deal with the journey from an abstract idea or imagining to a physical reality.

A lighting designer, when watching a run of a play, sees visual images of what the production might look like when lit and would arrange his equipment to be able to achieve the transfer of imagery from the mind to the stage. In the same way a sound designer is concerned with replicating the sounds he hears in his head in a form that can be performed in the theatre.

The technical advances in sound technology now allow the level of control necessary to allow sound designers to achieve this translation from imagination to reality.

Theatre sound technology is the tool that enables a sound design that exists only in the imagination of the sound designer to be shared with an audience.

SOUND VERSUS MUSIC, AND PETER SELLARS ON THE ONTOLOGICAL AURALITY OF THEATRE

At around the same time as Bracewell's book, Kaye and Lebrecht published a concise 'how-to-do-it' book, aimed at 'designers who desire both a greater knowledge about the aesthetics of their work as well as a practical approach to the design process.' (1992, p. iv)

If Bracewell's book provided an orthodox grounding for aspirant 'creatives', Kaye and Lebrecht's book seems to be aimed at sound technicians and operators who are asked to design but do not know how to generate creative ideas. This is a sign of the times in which it was written: design is by now in some demand, and those technically responsible for theatre sound require tuition. In their *Preface*, Kaye and Lebrecht write, presciently:

> Ultimately, the stature of the sound designer will be acknowledged to a greater extent by directors, producers and general managers. Budgetary considerations will not always be an obstacle. We hope that sound design in theatre will continue to develop as an accepted and essential design element. (p. v)

On Music

Sound and Music for Theatre differs from other works discussed previously in that it includes musical composition within its scope. This is a departure from tradition: in his introduction, Frank Napier made a clear demarcation, long understood in departmental theatre culture: 'Music will be excluded, except for passing references, because it does not, or at any rate should not, fall under the category of "noises off"' (Napier, 1936, p. 2).

The development of the integrated film soundtrack, in which sound and music fused, and the development of digital sound storage and Musical Instrument Digital Interface (MIDI), led to the blurring of this distinction. First, sampling technology (appropriated from Hip Hop/Rap music production) allowed sound to be digitally recorded in short snatches and replayed instantly from integrated-circuit Random Access Memory (or RAM) through the use of a MIDI instrument (usually a keyboard, but occasionally a percussion instrument). Sounds could be played in chords and pitched according to octaval scales. While sample length was limited in early models, it was possible to 'loop' sounds (join their end to their beginning). A repetitious sound such as a clock, or a noisy effect with little perceivable linear development such as rain could thus be made to sound continuous, but the looping of other sounds would create perceivable rhythms. This was a problem when trying to create 'realistic' sound designs, but this propensity towards rhythmic repetition along with the opportunity to abstract sounds and layer them together using an octaval keyboard made the musicality of the soundscape (anticipated by Cage and the *musique concrète* movement) instantly available as a creative resource within the rehearsal room. At first, this process relied on the musicality and performance skills of the operator, but with the advent of sequencing, a sound-score could be written as a programmed sequence of sound cues (like a hi-tech piano roll).

Some continue to argue as Napier did, that sound design and composition should be kept as separate categories. Some, such as Richard K. Thomas (2001) are certain that musical composition now falls within the overall scope of theatre sound design. It should be remembered that a theatre score – whether made up of musical or non-musical sounds – is not music in the 'standalone' sense of concert or album music, which exists within and according to its own musical form. Theatre scores are structured by dramaturgical form and 'designed' to be heard in relation to the main object of attention (whatever that might be – the actors, the words, the set). They are usually an environment rather than an object.

Soundscape composition and *sound-scoring* were, in some ways, developments of the montaged tape 'skylines' used in the 1970s, but digital technology had enabled sounds to be played (either by human fingers on a keyboard, or by a computer 'sequencer') in far more intricate and tightly rehearsed relationships to live, onstage events and vocal cues. If one accepts that *musique concrète* or John Cage's framed noise are music, then the organization of any sound in relation to dramaturgy might be considered to be a form of musical underscoring. By inverse logic, the use of more traditional 'musical-sounding' cues composed according to, and structured by, dramaturgy rather than by musical form might be considered a form of sound design. Such is the argument, although this may have been heresy to Napier. I caused some controversy myself in winning the first World Stage Design medal to be awarded for sound design (in 2005) with a theatre score composed using musical morphology.

The Peter Sellars Introduction

I would guess that the most widely cited part of Kaye and LeBrecht's book is its *Introduction*, by the technically innovative theatre and opera director Peter Sellars. His *Introduction* sets out a manifesto which is oddly out of keeping with a 'how-to-do-it' textbook for beginners (albeit one that focuses far more on creativity than technical process).

Sellars offers a 'postmodern' ontological concept of sound as a link between cosmic environment and microcosmic self, which incorporates the 'spiritual', the phenomenological, the political and the technological. He calls this the 'total program of sound'.

2.7 Peter Sellars (1992) Extract from 'Introduction', in Deena Kaye and James Lebrecht *Sound and Music for Theatre* (New York: Back Stage Books)

We can shut our eyes, but we can still hear. We can shut our ears, but sound is still echoing inside our skulls. We exist in a universe of sound. In the beginning was the Word, and before the Word was written, it was spoken, and its sound keeps speaking in our minds and our hearts, and we can't stop listening.

There are many voices. Mostly we live inside a cacophony, a melange of whispers and shouts, of traffic congestion and bird song, appliance hum, exhaust fans, television, radio, alarm sirens, and angelic voices speaking softly in our inner ear.

In tandem with the related sense of smell, hearing is that sense that is most deeply associated with memory. Sound evokes place, not space. That is to say, sound is where we locate ourselves, not physically, but mentally and spiritually. Sound exists inside our heads. It is our greatest experience of intimacy, it transports us, it invades us. [...]

We are beyond the era of sound 'effects.' Sound is no longer an effect, an extra, a garni supplied from time to time to mask a scene change or ease a transition. We are beyond the era of door buzzers and thunderclaps. Or rather, door buzzers and thunderclaps are no longer isolated effects, but part of a total program of sound that speaks to theatre as ontology. Sound is the holistic process and program that binds our multifarious experience of the world. Sound is our own inner continuity track. It is also our primary outward gesture to the world, our first and best chance to communicate with others, to become part of a larger rhythm.

CONCLUSION

> Do not become a crank, and overload your productions with noises. After all, 'The play's the thing.' (Napier, 1936, p. 117)

Chapter 2 described an orthodox approach to sound design predicated on a traditionally literary repertoire within a standard production hierarchy. The writer's conceptual intention and dramaturgy remained the definitive 'thing' that calibrates the 'scope' of what sound design did, until this premise began to be challenged, towards the end of the millennium, by new company practices. The extracts have also shown how theatre, in its mixed environment of electroacoustic, vocal, musical sound and acoustic noises, was the art form best placed to make sense of and make artistic experiment with the technologically evolving soundscape. They also show how the *acoustemology* of theatre – its culturally reflexive sonic repertoire – continued to reference classical dramatic tradition while incorporating changing auditory times. We saw the development of montage, and the changing demands on the sound operator as a performer.

The chapter ended with Sellars describing sound not as 'that which is heard', but as an immersive concept, a 'holistic process and program that binds our multifarious experience of the world'. But let us not, as Sellars did in 1992, get ahead of ourselves. In the extract from the *Observer*'s review of the theatre year 2004 – 12 years after Sellars announced the end of the era of sound effects – Susannah Clapp shows the revolution still to be just around the corner. I think it provides a useful coda to the chapter.

The Year the London Stage Became Full of Noises

2004 has also been a year of imaginative technical expansion, a year in which the stage began to be full of noises. There have always been sounds in the theatre, but they've been thought of as effects: isolated illustrations of events

– thunder-rolls or the swoosh of breaking waves at the beginning of The Tempest, an occasional outburst of birdsong to signal spring.

The idea that there might be continuous thought and purpose behind this, rather than a boy in the wings with a whistle and a couple of coconut shells, has been slow to take hold. For most theatre audiences and critics, 'design' has meant a visual plan. But that's changing: in a few years, our concentration on looking rather than listening will seem Neanderthal.

Festen is a case in point. Jean Kalman's lighting – which allowed the ill-fated family to glow in old master colours at their last supper – was perfectly judged, as was Ian MacNeil's set, by turns bleak and sumptuous. But the truly startling ingredient was a soundtrack by Paul Arditti, which went well beyond the creation of 'atmosphere'.

No one would wish on the theatre what so often happens in the movies – sound used as an enhancer, a sort of auditory monosodium glutamate: see a gondola in Michael Radford's Merchant of Venice and you'll hear the ripple of strings. The noises Arditti wound through the action of Festen – the faint sound of dripping water, the faraway laughter of a child – were of a different order: informative as well as evocative. They cast a chill over the proceedings and also dropped hints to the secret at the heart of the family; they played against the dialogue without detracting from it.

Festen was the most striking sound pioneer. But it wasn't alone. At the (now consistently interesting) National, Matthew Warchus set Sam Shepard's Buried Child to a background of country music which caught the frontier desperation and awkward homeliness of the dramatist's idiom. And Simon McBurney, the rubber-faced Complicité actor (and The Vicar of Dibley's manic choirmaster) directed a revelatory Measure for Measure in which he banished the idea that the play was a romantic comedy.

He did it partly by drenching the scenes in drizzle and twilight and partly by producing the most threatening of double beds, which zoomed towards the heroine like a weapon, but, most of all, by using a soundtrack of beautiful, funereal strings. The play became a terrible ritual being performed to an unknown score.

Sound designers expanded the possibilities for the stage; actor-directors gave a new focus to productions in 2004. (Extract from the *Observer*, 26 December 2004)

Chapter 3

The Pre-History of Sound Design

INTRODUCTION

If the sonic dramaturgies of theatre reflect everyday auditory culture, then contemporary modern theatre exposes an anxious relationship with noise. Sound design typically shows how noise subsumes in its post-industrial permadrone; terrifies with its destructive overtones; annoys with its cultural unwantedness; unnerves us or nauseates us with its negative otherness. The early-modern theatre of Shakespeare, on the other hand, holds a mirror (or perhaps a sounding-board) up to the noisiness of everyday life, and seems unequivocally to celebrate it:

> *Hamlet* is a noisy play. It begins with disembodied voices in the darkness. It ends with the noise of ordnance off-stage. Between these two sonic events, non-vocalised sound is pervasive. Cockcrow announces the morning and hautboys the dumbshow. There are around a dozen heraldic flourishes involving trumpets, drums and ordnance. The final scene is especially rowdy, with trumpets and drums announcing the king, trumpets signalling the beginning of the duel, flourishes and ordnance when Hamlet scores a hit, the sounds of shots and marching soldiers off-stage as Fortinbras approaches, drums to accompany his entrance, and the ordnance that closes the play. An attentive study discloses such persistent references to the sonic realm that they can be regarded as thematic as well as theatrical devices. Apart from 'effects', instrumental and vocal music, this includes references to the voice and hearing, and vocalization which is purely sonic rather than lexical, such as the sound 'O'. (Johnson, 2005)

Chapter 2 looked at the inception of 'theatre sound design' as a professional role and a pedagogy. Chapter 3 takes a somewhat longer history, in order to look in more depth at those traditions which still resonate within the auditory cultures of theatre. It is a pre-history of theatre sound design because it predates the term, but also because it is a history that has yet to be written. This selection of extracts does not pretend to be that history, but merely to illustrate the ways in which the practices of the past shape those of the present.

The chapter looks at the sonic world of Shakespeare as a manifestation of early-modern aurality, then at melodrama, before turning to the 'picturesque of sound', the Meininger Players and theatrical 'rhubarb'. It then notes how melodrama and the hubbub of the elaborately-picturesque mise-en-scène fell silent at the command of the pen, as dramatists like Chekhov, Maeterlinck and Ibsen claimed as the author's sonic domain not just the words themselves but the spaces between them. It concludes then, where Chapter 2 began, at the beginning of the twentieth-century.

SOUND 'WITHIN THE WOODEN O'

In *The Acoustic World of Early Modern England – Attending to the O-Factor* (1999) Bruce R. Smith examines the relationship of the 'early modern subject' to the aural environment of Elizabethan England. Smith himself calls it an 'historical phenomenology'. It describes early-modern England as an oral/aural culture in which the 'subject' (of the realm and of the soundscape) is connected to and placed in the physical and cultural environment through sound. The suggestion is of a kind of aural eco-system of interdependency. The subject is involved in sound as a physical act (a performance), a sensory experience (something heard), an act of communication (a projection of psyche through the body into the world) and as a political act (an act done *because of, for* or *with* other people.) Each of these is portrayed as a circular relationship between self and environment, of corporeal production/ambient resonance/corporeal reception, a concept Smith calls the 'O' Factor, or simply *o*.

Aside from positing this intriguing thesis of a link between physiology, phenomenological perception and cultural history, the book also brings together information from diverse sources relating to early-modern theatre practice. Importantly, it attends both to non-vocal and vocal sound as part of a single auditory experience. In the first extract below Smith describes the range and manner of noisemaking in the public amphitheatres of Elizabethan London, which seem to retain the traditional aural exuberance of the pageant. In the second extract he considers the vocal and non-vocal components of Shakespearian performance as a consciously crafted, complete sonic programme. (Elsewhere in the book (pp. 229–39), he describes in detail the ways in which the contrasting pitch in men and boys voices was also dramaturgically orchestrated.)

3.1 Extract from Smith, B. R. (1999) *The Acoustic World of Early Modern England – Attending to the O-Factor* (London: University of Chicago Press), pp. 218–20, 242–5.

Customarily it was three trumpet blasts, filling all 231,028 cubic feet of the acoustic space, that signalled the start of performances at the Globe. Thomas Dekker seems wittily mindful of the difference between reading a play and hearing a play when he starts off the printed text of *Satiromastix*, acted at the Globe in 1601, with a kind of prologue "*Ad Lectorem*" ("To the Reader") in which he casts the ensuing list of printing mistakes as a "Comedy of Errors." What the reader sees on the page becomes an equivalent for what he or she would have heard in the theater: "In steed of the Trumpets sounding thrice, before the Play begin: it shall not be amisse (for him that will read) first to beholde this short Comedy of Errors, and where the greatest enter, to give them in stead of a hisse, a gentle correction" (Dekker 1953–61, 1: 306). Dekker's Epilogue to the same script also invokes the power of trumpets to '"set men together by the eares." The members of the audience who especially needed it, or so Dekker's Epilogue implies, were the standees whose proximity to the play is given a distinctly sexual turn: "Gentlemen, Gallants, and you my little Swaggerers that *fight lowe*: my tough hearts of Oake that *stand too't* so valliantly, and are *still within a yard* of your Capten: Now the Trumpets (that set men together by the eares) have left their Tantara-rag-boy, let's part friends." From the "Swaggerers" who are standing below him the speaker then transposes his speech upward to "the Gentle-folkes (that walke i'th Galleries)" (1953–61, 1: 385, emphasis added). If Dekker can be trusted, plays in London's public theaters began with the auditory focusing of trumpet calls. The plays that ensued were full, not just of human voices, but of sound effects.

Instruments for providing some of those effects are detailed in Henslowe's inventory of the Admiral's Men's goods, drawn up in 1598. As the company's costumes and props make up a palette for visual design, so their musical instruments and other sound-producing devices make up a "palette" for *aural* design. Included on Henslowe's list are four groupings of musical instruments: (1) "a trebel viall, a basse viall, a bandore, a sytteren," (2) "j sack-bute," (3) "iij tymbrells,"and (4) "iij trumpettes and a drum" Henslowe's diary for 1598–99 includes sizable payments (up to 40 shillings each, equal to the takings from 480 standees) for a sackbut, a bass viol, and "a drome when to go into the contry," as well as other unspecified "enstrumentes" (1907: 114–18; 1961: 101, 102, 122, 130). What some of the other instruments may have been are suggested by a speech in Dekker's *Old Fortunatus*, acted by the Admiral's Men the year after Henslowe had made his inventory. Shadow comes on while Andelocia is being charmed asleep by a lullaby. "*Musicke still*," reads the stage direction: "*Enter Shaddow.*" In describing what he hears, Shadow in effect reiterates Henslowe's first entry and adds one other instrument: "Musicke? O delicate warble [recorder or flute] ... O delicious strings [viols]: these heauenly wyre-drawers [cittern and bandore]" (Dekker 1953–61, 1: 138–41; Chan 1980: 31). The cittern and the bandore were both guitar-like instruments, the bandore providing the bass to the cittern's treble (Munrow 1976: 80–3). With the addition of a recorder or flute, the instruments grouped in Henslowe's first entry make up an ensemble that sixteenth and early seventeenth-century musicians knew as a "broken" consort. (It was "broken" because it was made up not of just one "family" of instruments, like a consort of recorders or viols, but of representatives from several different "families.") Morley's *First Book of Consort Lessons*, published the same year *Old Fortunatus* was performed, calls for just this ensemble of flute, treble viol, bass viol, cittern, and bandore, with the addition of a treble lute. Philip Rosseter's *Lessons for Consort* (1609) is scored for the same set of instruments. In the case of the Admiral's Men, the standard broken consort might have been supplemented by two other instruments in Henslowe's inventory: the trombone-like sackbut and one or more of the tambourine-like timbrels (Long 1961–71, 1 28–9, 34). In such ensembles it was the bowed and blown instruments that carried the tune, the plucked and tapped instruments that provided rhythm. A lutenist, if one was handy, might have offered virtuoso variations on the melody (Chan 1980: 33).

To a different category of sound entirely belong the three trumpets on Henslowe's list, along with the drum. Lacking valves, early modern trumpets were restricted to the equivalent of bugle calls. In the theater their main use was for flourishes, fanfares, and military signals (Long 1961–71, 1: 25). Other items in Henslowe's inventory are percussion instruments. An entry for "ij stepells, & j chyme of belles, & j beacon" has been interpreted by Michael Hattaway as sets of various kinds of bells: clock bells ('steeples"), hand bells ("a chime"), and a bell for ringing alarums ("a beacon") (1982: 32). David Munrow describes a chime as something more like a set of miniature cymbals: hung in a wood frame, the hemisphere-shaped chimes were struck with hammers, not rung by hand (1976: 34–5) Certain items inventoried by Henslowe among the company's props should be thought about not only as visual icons but as sound-making devices: "j longe sorde," "viij lances", "j copper targate, & xvij foyles," "iiij wooden targates, j greve armer," "j buckler," "j shelde, with iij lyones, and "j gylte speare" would have contributed their distinctive crashes, clinks, and thuds to sounds within the wooden O.

Guns do not figure in Henslowe's mentor but stage directions occasionally call for the firing of an unspecified form of "ordnance" or "piece" or, sometimes more precisely, of "chambers," small pieces of unmounted ordnance customarily used for firing salutes (OED, "chamber" 10). It was the stage direction *"Drum and Trumpet, Chambers discharged"* in Act One, scene four of *Henry VIII* that set the Globe on fire in 1613 (F1623: 1.4.50). Fireworks, like firearms, fail to make Henslowe's list, but exploding squibs were a standard aural event whenever devils armed on the scene from hell (Leggatt 1992: 67–70). Another stupendous sound effect, usually the aural sign of supernatural happenings, was thunder. Ben Jonson, using the prologue to *Everyman in His Humor* (1616 text) to justify his disdain for such gimcrackery divulges how thunder was made, by a bullet rolled about, presumably along a wooden timber (3: 303). From ethereal recorders to finely grained viols to blasting trumpets to booming artillery, the outdoor theaters of early modern London were full of sounds besides those made by human voices.

[...]

Sound in early modern theater is important not so much for what it is as for what it signifies. What audiences actually heard in the theater and what they imagined they heard may not always have been the same thing. In the printed text of Coriolanus, premiered at the Globe in 1608, there appears a stage direction that calls for one set of sounds while the accompanying speech describes another set. Act Five, scene four, is one of the play's several crowd scenes that are amplified by drums and trumpets:

MESSENGER 1
Why harke you.
Trumpets, Hoboyes, Drums beate, altogether
The Trumpets, Sack-buts, Psalteries, and Fifes, Tabors, and Symboles, and the showting
Romans Make the Sunne dance. Hearke you. *A shout within*.
(F16a3: 5.4.49–52)

What the audience in fact hears are trumpets, hautboys, and drums – loud enough
in themselves. What the Messenger *tells* them they are hearing is a much wider
range of instruments and a volume of sound that, figuratively at least, pushes
beyond the theater's walls to the limits of the cosmos. Pierre Iselin has called attention to the way in which music in early modern scripts is *always* framed by language
– and usually, Iselin argues, in an ironic way that keeps language firmly in control of
musical sounds (1995: 96–113). The moment in *Antony and Cleopatra* illustrates
Stephen Handel's point that sound is perceived at three distinct levels (1989:
181–82). In trumpets, hautboys, and drums the audience gathered in the Globe
would have heard, first of all, certain *physical* phenomena: a range of distinct
frequencies and intensities, particular patterns of attack and decay. At the same
time, they would have heard certain *perceptual* phenomena that are not so easy to
calibrate: "brightness" in the trumpet, "pointedness" in the hautboys, "dryness" in
the drums. The Messenger's speech invites the audience, finally, to hear certain
imaginative phenomena, to hear the sounds *as objects*. Most obviously those
objects are the ones named in the Messenger's speech: trumpets, sackbuts, harps,
fifes, drums, cymbals, a mob of people. Beyond that, there is the essence of these
individual objects: "trumpet-ness," "drum-ness", "mob-ness." By a process of
metonymy, the audience also hears the essence of all these objects taken together:
danger, anarchy chaos. What the sounds mean is the result of all three kinds of
phenomena – physical, perceptual, imaginative – impinging on the audience's
senses at the same time.

What the audience hears, in the last analysis, is not just physical properties of
sound, nor even psychological effects, but the acoustic equivalent of a visual scene
– an "aura," perhaps. Evidence from scripts written for the outdoor theaters from
1590 to 1610 invites us to distinguish several distinct "auras" or "aural scenes."
Brass instruments define what might be called "the royal scene" or, more broadly,
"the power scene": high in pitch, forceful in volume, quick in attack and decay,
cornets and trumpets produced sounds that were sharp, hard, and bright – properties that were assumed by the royal personages who made their entrances to
such sounds. A different sort of aura, "the hunt scene," was established by wind
horns. "*Winde hornes. Enter a Lord from hunting, with his traine*" (F1623: Ind1 S. D.
after 13): the broad, plangent bursts required in the Induction to *The Taming of the
Shrew* are also scripted to be heard in *Titus Andronicus* 2. 2., *A Midsummer Night's
Dream* 4.1, *The Tragedy of King Lear* 1.4, and *A Woman Killed With Kindness* (scene
3). "The combat scene" assaulted the audience's ears in bursts of brass, the
rumbling of drums, and the bellowing of gunfire. The explosion of firearms, let us
recall, ranks among the very loudest sounds anyone was likely to hear in an age
before internal combustion engines. Quick in attack and decay, running the gamut

from the trumpet's keening to the drum's riot of multiple pitches to the ordnance's chaos of noise, the sounds of the combat scene served to evoke pitched battles. The same ensemble of sounds might also be used in connection with sword fights. In both the 1604 quarto and the 1623 folio of *Hamlet* gunshots accompany the fencing match between Hamlet and Laertes. "The game scene" takes on aural shape in the tabor's low tap and the pipe's high whistle, as in the Morris dance performed in Munday's *John a Kent and John a Cumber*, probably acted by the Admiral's Men in 1589. If pipe and tabor accompanied jigs at the ends of plays, as Kemp's extratheatrical exploits suggest they did, then the game scene of folk festivity provided the sounds ringing in the audience's ears as they left the theater. Although each of these aural scenes has its visual counterpart – presence chamber, woods, battlefield, countryside – each is less a physical place than a kinaesthetic experience. The limits of vision in specifying that experience are indicated by the aura hautboys seem to have created. Technically, hautboys were members of the shawm family, double-reeded instruments whose loud, carrying sound made them a natural for town bands. A persistent distinction in early modern English between shawms in general and hautboys in particular may have turned on pitch or volume or both: "*haut-bois*" means "*high wood*." Taking the hint, most historians of musical instruments assume that hautboys were shawms in the alto (G_3 to D_5) and soprano (D_4 to A_5) ranges. Their shrill quality, sounding to some witnesses like skirling bagpipes, was proverbial (Munrow 1976: 40–1; Galpin 1965: 123; Long 1961–71, 1 20–1). The opening stage direction to *Henry VI, Part II* seems to capitalize on this assaultive quality: "*Flourish of Trumpets: Then Hoboyes*" heralds the entrance of King Henry and his court (F1623: S. D. before 1.1). Why both kinds of instruments? What hautboys could provide that early modern trumpets could not was melody. First the trumpets establish command over the sound field, then hautboys come into play as music for a stately passage over the stage. It must have been the example of shawms in town bands that cast hautboys as aural components of "the processional scene." The ceremonial movement of bodies in space helps to explain the conventional use of hautboys as accompaniments to dumb shows in entertainments at the universities, the Inns of Court, and the court of the realm, not to mention "The Murder of Gonzago" in the folio text of *Hamlet* (Naylor 1931: 169; F1623: 775). In *Antony and Cleopatra*, acted at the Globe in 1609, the direction "*Musicke of the Hoboyes is under the Stage*" underscores the pageant-like scene in which Hercules abandons Antony. Within that highly reverberant space the sound of the instruments must have been very loud indeed – and its totalizing sweep complete. "Musicke i'th'Ayre," proclaims one of the listening soldiers. The other locates it "Vnder the earth" (F1623: 867). It is tempting to describe such a moment as "the cosmic scene," even if Jonson locates that effect in thunder. Power, hunting, combat, game, processional, supernatural: in each of these distinctive fields of sound human voices find a dominant place, but they share the aural scene with artificially produced sounds. When it comes to human voices within the aura of the wooden O, auditors likewise hear an amalgam of physical phenomena (volume and pitch), perceptual phenomena (qualities Quintilian describes as "clear or husky, full or thin, smooth or harsh, narrow or diffuse, rigid or flexible, sharp or blunt"), and imaginative phenomena (the voice of a king, the voice of a maiden disguised as a page, the voice of an air spirit, the voice of an earth spirit). The object the audience hears in a human voice is character.

The Classical Acoustemology of Harmony and Chaos

> Shakespeare wrote for sound rather than for print. This shifting and precarious balance between sound and sight affects our 'reading' of *Hamlet* in two ways. Technically, in terms of the resources that Shakespeare draws upon, sound is used in very complex ways to communicate his themes. The pre-electric visual technology of the unroofed Elizabethan theatre placed a considerable burden on dialogue and music for communicating such details as lighting, setting, place and occasion. But this has a thematic resonance also. Shakespeare is writing for a society that is experiencing a transition, and therefore a tension, between two modes of knowing: visual and aural. (Johnson, 2005)

The pre-modern world was in a sense defined by sound, both because it was a world in which ideas primarily were communicated and held orally, but also because it was a world understood through sonic analogies and tropes. The classical drama of the Renaissance blossomed, in England, during a transition from this ancient oral/aural culture, to a modern world understood through reason and described in the visualist concepts and terminologies of what would become known as the Enlightenment. This period is called 'early modern' partly to indicate that modernism was not yet established, and that many of its concepts were still in early discussion, while more ancient, pre-modern precepts still dominated culturally.

The transition from an oral/aural – and therefore body-centred – culture of analogical understandings to a culture of intellectualism and transcribed ideas is manifest in the drama and theatres of Shakespeare's London and traced in the dialectic between the soniferousness of early-modern drama and its wordplay of ideas. The technê of theatre too, as it relocated from the resonant wooden Os of the sixteenth-century to the Patent playhouses of the seventeenth, reflects, in its history, a transition from a world discussed orally and understood culturally though aural *effect* to a more textual world, concerned increasingly with *cause*, in which being able to see was considered more important than being able to hear. The connection between aurality and orality is self-evident, but the notion of analogical aurality perhaps needs some glossing.

In the previous extract, Bruce R. Smith mentions a 'range of instruments and a volume of sound that, figuratively at least, pushes beyond the theater's walls to the limits of the cosmos'. In order to understand the sonic dramaturgy of Elizabethan theatre one must first understand the close relationship, in the early modern mind, between noise, music, the body and the way in which the cosmos was conceptualized. We must understand that sound was not merely what was heard, but an entire cosmic aural eco-system within which all structure, proportion and randomness was connected and interdependent. Consider this famous passage from *The Merchant of Venice*:

> There's not the smallest orb which though behold'st
> But in his motion like an angel sings,
> Still quiring to the young-ey'd cherubins;
> Such harmony is in immortal souls,
> But whilst this muddy vesture of decay
> Doth grossly close it in, we cannot hear it
>
> (Act V, Scene 1)

People believed that the music and noise one hears in everyday life were merely the audible manifestations of universal order and chaos, the oppositional poles within a single theoretical 'sonic' force which held the material universe together (its cosmic celestial spheres as well as its microcosmic human physiology). While this general idea had been reiterated by successive philosophers through the classical ancient Greek period, the middle ages and into the Renaissance, the concept is usually described as 'Pythagorean' after the ancient philosopher and mathematician Pythagoras who observed principles of harmony in operation in daily life (noticing the proportionate pitches of blacksmiths' hammers of different weights) and developed harmonic theory using vibrating tensile strings (indeed, the stringed instrument – the lyre of Apollo – came to symbolize sophisticated, cultured artistry, as opposed to the rasping wind instrument, which represented uncultured, rudely guttural and primeval expression of the followers of Dionysus). Pythagoras and his followers observed that similar harmonic intervals and proportions seemed to recur frequently in natural structures and phenomena, and they extrapolated that this harmonic proportionality was no coincidence, but responsible for celestial coherence and orbit – the famous 'music of the spheres'. This mathematical notion was developed by Plato and his followers and became intertwined with various classical creation, birth and death myths (for example the 'song of the sirens'). These resemble the sonic analogies of creation myths from other cultures; the concept of the music of the spheres is not dissimilar to the ancient Upanishad concept of *Nada Brahma* – 'the world is sound' – or the Hindu/Buddhist concept of *prana* – the universal vibration.

The alignment of the microcosm – the universe of the human body – to this macro-cosmic sonic force was an important principle in mediaeval physiology (just as it is in the Chinese notion of the *chi*). It is difficult for us to understand today, perhaps, how the early-modern subjects that made up Shakespeare's audiences understood this wider concept of sound to account for their internal health, emotional disposition, and the environmental 'health' of the whole universe. As David Lindley points out in *Shakespeare and Music* (2006) the public would bring to the theatre an ontologically aural understanding of a universe in which they were connected through sound to others and to the cosmos as a whole. In Boethius' sixth-century scholarly iteration of the long, Pythagorean tradition of aural theory, *musica instumentalis* – music which is heard – was merely the audible part of a universal sonic eco-system. The balance of dissonance and harmony evident in the soundscape was merely the audible manifestation of the balance of order and chaos in the universe (*musica mundana*, the macrocosm) and the human condition (*musica humana*, the corporeal microcosm).

Music and *sound* were more than auditory concepts. Within this theorem of sound, matter, fate, spirituality and health interconnected. Acoustic sound was its manifestation, a symptom of something bigger, but through it one could alter or affect natural processes. By intervening within *musica instrumentalis* – for example, by formally dancing, or playing harmonic music in the face of chaos or disharmony, it was possible to provide a cure for noisy cosmic or microcosmic imbalance (see Lindley, 2006, pp. 30–50 and *passim*). Attali (1985) suggests that music, in this pre-modern sense, was a form of sacrificial act of cosmic appeasement rather than an artistic or entertainment commodity.

Lindley cites examples of such dance/music 'moments' from *Much Ado about Nothing, As You Like It, A Midsummer Night's Dream, Romeo and Juliet* and several other plays, but notes that while the audiences would recognize the conventional moment, there are normally more complex ironies, subtexts and implications about them than the mere 'showing' of human and cosmic harmony. He does, however, cite, as a plain example, *Henry VIII* Act 4, Scene 2, line 79, where, 'to sad and solemn music' six 'personages clad in white robes' dance and hold a garland over the head of the sick and sleeping Queen as an 'angelic performance and simulation of celestial harmony' (Lindley, 2006, p. 135).

It would be wrong to suggest that *all* theatre music and sound were merely code for cosmic ontology, but this was certainly a discourse that Shakespeare's contemporary audiences would have picked up instinctively in a way that we might only academically understand.

Intra-Diegesis

Lindley points out that that music on the Elizabethan stage was played in full view – *intra-diegetic* in the modern theoretical terminology:

> Music has, of course, been a constituent part of theatrical representation since the Greeks, but it is vital to understand the fundamental differences between its operation in the Shakespearean theatre, and the purposes it serves in modern productions. For while the music for which Shakespeare calls does heighten atmosphere, or gives a particular emotional colouration to speech and action, it is always part of the world of the play itself heard and responded to by the characters on-stage, and not, as in later theatrical practice, or in film and television, an independent adjunct for the audience's ears only, acting as a commentary or metatext. It is true that the boys' companies provided additional music both before the play and between the acts, and audiences at the outdoor theatres

expected musical entertainment, including songs and dance, to be part of the fare they were offered. It is also undoubtedly the case that more music was heard than the stage directions in surviving texts indicate. Nonetheless, instrumental music – whatever symbolic weight it might carry – is almost always assumed to be audible to the characters on stage. (Lindley, 2006, p. 112)

Instrumental Symbolism and Irony

Sound functioned on several levels, including a *metatextual* level within the scene. Incidental use of particular sounds and instruments, or particular musical arrangements, all carried clear meanings in relation to the dramatic moment. Percussive sounds were associated with elemental chaos (storms, high seas, seismic unrest) and with war; brass with human intervention; stringed lyrical instruments with idyll, resolution or the sweet release of death, slow rhythms with mourning etc.

As we saw in the second Smith extract, the precise choice of instrument for an entrance *flourish*, or an *alarum*, is again something that modern audiences can only imagine intellectually, but which would have been culturally obvious to early-modern audiences. Instrumental symbolism had classical roots in ancient Greek theatre. The *aulos* reed-pipe represented Dionysian rudeness and the crafted, stringed lyre represented Apollonian serenity and order (see Loraux, 2002, and Connor, 2004). Lindley describes extended and more complex codifications in the various different reed, stringed and brass instruments of Elizabethan theatre, which he categorizes in terms of gender. He enters into particular detail about the codified, metatextual meanings of different types and contextual uses of trumpets and drums.

The audience's literacy in this (now) hidden meaning could be assumed. Lindley explains how early-modern dramatists played to it, employing symbolic counterpoint – often ironic – between music and dramatic moment. The use of, or reference to, soft, lyrical music at times of violence, for example, remains a familiar dramatic device. Much of the more complex Shakespearian irony though (for example, the use of the wrong type of trumpet or the wrong number of blasts for a given context) is unrecoverable in modern productions. Auditory culture and conventional theatre literacy have both moved on. Some formal conventions, however, persist:

> the muffled drums that slowly beat the dead march still resonate today. Explicitly called for at the end of *Coriolanus*, *Hamlet*, and *King Lear*, the measured, doleful sound aptly underscores the 'weight of this sad time' (and, more prosaically, ritualizes the practical business of carrying bodies off-stage). The same sound must have been deployed in other tragedies and histories where it is not specified in the texts, though 'dead marches are not employed by Shakespeare or his contemporaries when a character is sullied by crime.' (Lindley, 2006, p. 117)

So while some Shakespearian musical devices became separated, through time, from their codified meanings, they lived on and developed as stylistic conventions, as part of the musical morphology of melodrama. Melodrama, it is thought, in turn influenced Beethoven's *Fidelio*, and the subsequent development of opera, as well as the development of film music and other musical forms. Contemporary composers or sound designers can rely on an audience to read underscoring intended to communicate joy, sadness, anxiety, tension, the accelerated or decelerated passage of time and so on, partly because it has a competence or literacy in convention that emanates from early-modern theatre.

Rhetorical Silence

And what is this metaphor we call silence? Typically, silence is used to convey an abstinence or forbearance from speech/utterance. In other words, silence is the intentional or imposed state of muteness. Silence denotes an inaudible condition or moment of complete stillness. Silence is a threshold, the limit to language, the very realm Hamlet witnesses as he remarks in his parting words, 'the rest is silence.' (Miller, C. P, 2007 at http://csmt.uchicago.edu/glossary2004/ silence.htm, accessed 16.02.2009)

Pause in the flow of dialogue was very rare in classical drama, being confined usually to the panting in the formal breaks in stage fights or the non-verbal clamour of battles. Where there are pauses, they are rhetorical (for example the scripted pause in *Coriolanus* V:iii: Andrew Gurr notes (1980, p. 161) that this is one of only three such pauses in the entire Shakespeare canon).

In classical dramatic acoustemology, silence was alluded to metaphorically rather than produced on stage. Theatres of the time would not, in any case, have allowed for effectively sustained silence as part of theatre experience; pauses in the verbal or musical programme would have revealed the sounds of people talking and shelling nuts, and in the outdoor theatres, the local sounds of the city. The concept of silence was understood in terms of corporeal stillness, or, as Miller remarks above, as gestural figure in relation to speech.

Speech, that is, as opposed to voice. In the original folio version, Hamlet's last vocal sounds are not the familiar words 'The rest is silence'. The line is delivered and then the life-breath – signified in sound – departs his body with the scripted sounds O, o, o, o.

How trivial this looks on the page. But consider how that could have been played, how deeply disturbing would be the inarticulate despair and agony of a body from which 'life', in the form of the speaking mind, had departed – recall, this is the last utterance of a man who, it was widely believed, had in fact lost his reason. These final sounds he makes, apparently detachable 'afterthoughts' that some printers casually excised, could well have been one of the most horrifying moments in Hamlet's navigation of his liminal space. And it is irreducibly acoustic. (Johnson, 2005)[1]

Hamlet thus migrates into the silence of eternity by giving up his voice.

MUSIC 'IN PRODUCTION' AT THE BLACKFRIARS THEATRE

Production Music and Atmosphere

Lindley's analysis of sound as metatextual code does not mean that a trumpet blast did not also function as a way of focusing and calibrating (i.e. establishing an auditory expectation of dynamic range by showing the audience a known, loud sound) the auditory attention of the throng as Smith describes, or merely as a way of calling the audience back from the streets (and nearby taverns). Neither does it deny the visceral, 'carnival' pleasure of gut-shaking, spine-jangling loud sounds such as horn blasts, fireworks and cannons. It is worth noting that in the broad, horizontally panoramic soundscape of the open-air amphitheatres (see Smith, 1999, p. 217) there would also have been a practical need for a loud sound to redirect attention from one side of the stage, where one set of characters was exiting, to the other, where a new set was entering.

Jacob Isaacs' *Production and Stage-Management at the Blackfriars Theatre* (1933) looks to such pragmatic necessities of stage management to explain some formal conventions of late Elizabethan and Jacobean theatre. It is also, I believe, the first book to use the phrase 'atmospheric music' in relation to theatre. This is not something often discussed in relation to early-modern theatre, but Isaacs claims that this atmospheric function of what he terms 'in-production' music derived from the passing fashion of the masque. Isaacs notes the use of 'vilest out of tune music' in Marston's *Malcontent* at the Globe in 1603 to herald the entrance of the villains, a familiar feature of melodrama.

3.2   Extract from Isaacs, J. (1933) *Production and Stage-Management at the Blackfriars Theatre* (London, Oxford University Press), pp. 10–13, 24.

Music was one of the chief back-stage concerns. It occurred before the play, at the beginning, all through the play, and at the end of the play. I have never been able to

---

[1] For a contrary position, see Brown, J, R, 'Multiplicity of Meaning in the Last Moments of *Hamlet*,' *Connotations*, 2, 1, pp. 16–33 and, in response to letters, 2.3 pp. 275–86 (1992: Münster / New York: Waxmann Verlag).

understand the quarrel about Act-divisions. There always were divisions between the acts, however short they may have been. In texts of plays, scene divisions and markings are a literary matter. In the theatre a scene was a simple matter. When the stage is completely empty, a scene ends. When actors come on again, a new scene begins. This may be independent of a change of place. Whenever necessary, the prompter indicates that the stage is *cleare*, or when certain actors have to remain after the body of characters have departed, the prompter will mark, *Exeunt – Manet, X, Y, and Z.* Jonson's method, the French and classical method of marking a new scene where there is any alteration in the number of characters on the stage is another matter. Scene division is automatic on the stage, but act division is both a structural and artistic matter and a practical necessity. Plays were written in movements, and certainly acted in movements. One of the chief ways of marking such divisions was by means of inter-act music, marked on plots and in prompt books. The quarrel there too seems illusory. There was inter-act music in the private theatres as a regular practice; it was to be found, but not so regularly, on the public stage. It is also found in earlier festival performances where, whether at Court or at the Inns of Court, elaborate scenes or properties had to be shifted and the audience entertained. Anthony Munday's *Fidele and Fortunio, Two Italian Gentlemen*, 1585, has the clearest indication of such use of music at a special performance. The concluding direction of each act reads:

> The first Act being ended, the Consorte of Musique soundeth a pleasant Galliard.
> The second Act being ended, the Consorte soundeth again.
> The third Act being doone, the Consort sounds a sollemne Dump.
> The fourth Act being ended, the Consort soundeth a pleasant Allemaigne.

These music indications are not found in the original Italian from which the play is adapted. In Marston's *The Wonder of Women, or The Tragedy of Sophonisba*, a Blackfriars play, the concluding direction of Act I runs: 'The Ladies draw the curtains about Sophonisba, the rest accompanye Massinissa forth; the cornet and organs playing full music for the Act.' Here 'Act' means act interval. Act II begins: 'Whilst the music for the first Act sounds … enter … .' Careful variation of the instruments is observed: Act III opening: 'Organs mixt with recorders for this Act.' Act IV opening 'Organs, Viols, and Voices play for this Act.' Act V opening: 'A base lute and a treble violl play for the act.' I give these at length in order to distinguish between inter-act music, which may be long or short, as indicated in marginal prompt notes, and a fanfare of trumpets or flourish of cornets, which draws the audience from its gossiping or nut-cracking or from the theatre bar, that earliest of institutions.

There were five kinds of music used in the private theatre:

1. The overture concert, sometimes as much as an hour long.
2. The full inter-act music.
3. The preludes to acts, and the concluding flourish of the play.
4. Incidental music of a practical kind, trumpets, comets, drums, etc.
5. Atmospheric music, doleful dumps, 'horrid' music, 'infernal' music, 'soft' music.

In the public theatre (see the much-discussed opening of Marston's *Malcontent*) the private theatre concert was replaced by an *hors d'oeuvre*, 'your salad to your great feast' in the form of an Induction.

One of the most revealing directions for use of music and the employment of theatrical necessity in music and lighting for dramatic effect is found in the Induction to Marston's *What You Will,* a Paul's play. 'Before the Musicke sounds for the Acte: [i.e. the preliminary flourish, and not the overture) Enter Atticus, Doricus, and Phylomuse, they sit a good while on the Stage before the Candles are lighted, talking together, and on suddeine Doricus speakes'; later comes the direction: 'Enter Tier-man with lights.' In Marston's *Malcontent*, also played at the Globe, music is used at the beginning of Act I for atmospheric introduction: 'The vilest out of tune Musicke being heard. Enter Bilioso and Prepasso.' In the second act the lighting is helped under cover of the preliminary act music. 'Enter Mendoza with a sconce, to observe Ferneze's entrance, who whilest the Act is playing: Enter unbraced two pages before him with lights.' Dumb show is often performed with the act music as accompaniment.

[…]

My final concern is with the music as an element in production, and for this there is abundant evidence from plays of the highest dramatic quality in which the production is consciously and integrally linked up. When the Court Masque, by inevitable process of grafting, was made a part of theatrical production, it lost its expensive settings and bulky and elaborate movable properties, but it retained that which was most suitable and welcome in the private theatre – its music. Of masques merely as interpolated adornments there is little that need be said, but there is musical elaboration with masque as a basis. The utilisation of atmospheric music in Marston's *Wonder of Women* with its

> Infernal music plays softly while Erictho enters, and when she speaks ceaseth.
> Infernal music softly;

and

> A treble viol and a base lute play softly within the canopy,

is an important transitional stage. The transition from battle music to soft music to make an atmospheric point is frequently used, but in *The Malcontent's* last act, of which a portion has already been cited as spectacle, there is a mixture of masque and plot unravelling that is a show producer's piece.

[…]

Here [in the last act of the *Malcontent*] every device of tension is employed, and the mot exquisite control in production is necessary if the effect is not to be marred. In its effects of make and break in music, I have seen only one modern play-production which could give an idea of the subtlety attainable. Those who saw the Habima Players in their performance of *The Dybbuk* two years ago will remember the consummate rendering of tragedy in the wedding dance broken up by the intruding beggars who 'to infernall musick' claimed the bride for each change.

MUSIC AND MELODRAMA

Noises Off and Invisible Music

Of the 240 years of theatre sound practice between the Restoration and Mr. Jones the noisemaker at Drury Lane in 1904, whom we met in Chapter 2, we know surprisingly little. Italianate architectural framings that had been a fashionable import of the Jacobean court evolved into the archetypal proscenium arch, which restricted the audience's sightlines to one broad aspect and thus allowed the use of painted cloths and other scenic 'flattage' to give an illusion of visual perspective in an upstage 'scene'. The eventual retreat of the thrust apron stage to a position almost wholly upstage of the so-called fourth wall of the house curtain line had three important effects on the development of theatre sound convention.

The first of these was the necessary evolution of interlude music – or the *entr'acte* – to fill the time and mask the considerable manual and machine noise of scene changes. This tradition of scene-change music persists to this day, often purely as an aesthetic dramatic device to set a new mood or indicate the passage of time even when there is no physical scene change other than a change of lighting state.

The second effect was the creation of wing-space – the 'off' of *noises off*. In practical terms this was a place to hide sound effects machinery (wind machines, thunder sheets and the like) from the audience's sightlines. The sound that these machines produced would seem to emanate from the 'scene', wherever one happened to be sitting in the auditorium. 'In the round' or on thrust apron stages, sound effects had either to be manufactured in view of at least some of the audience, or housed either behind or in a sub- or rear-stage room, which did not make for convincing illusion or parity of effect throughout the auditorium. We can hazard a guess that noises-off remained somewhat crude: symbolic interventions rather than components of an illusionistic scenography. We can partly deduce this from the sensation caused by de Loutherbourg's *Eidophusikon* (an early, small-scale precursor to the Diorama and other nineteenth-century automated proto-cinematographic shows, described in Hardcastle's *Wine and Walnuts* (1823) pp. 281–304). The full potential of proscenium framing to create controllable, picturesque collusions of lighting, sound and moving scenery was clearly still untapped in 1781. Indeed, Hardcastle suggests, as late as 1823, in *Wine and Walnuts* that the 'ingenious machinists of the scene room' set their wits to work on applying such effects on the 'regular stage' (pp. 281–304). Given the technology employed in early seventeenth-century masque and semi-opera, one might perhaps have expected scenic art to have evolved further than this. But the expense of the masque and 'Restoration spectacular' had proved unsustainable, and London had, instead, turned to Italian opera, leaving spoken theatre as very much the poor relation in terms of production budget. One must also remember that it wasn't until 1763 that Garrick finally removed audience seats from the stage at Drury Lane.

Musicians now had to cover scene changes when the curtain was down as well as provide interpolated music and underscoring when the curtain was up, and they were relocated from the position Lindley describes in the midst of the drama to the sub-stage orchestra pit which opened onto the auditorium. A corollary effect of this, and the third major effect of the retreat behind the proscenium arch, was that the music found a new liminal space, now so familiar from film soundtracks, from which it seems to frame the scene and underscore the drama. It effectively became disembodied or invisible, unless one chose to look down into the pit. As one watched the drama, it was almost as if the music existed in one's head – like the *phonomnesis* or the *auditory imagination* discussed on p. 215.

A new auditory space became available, which somehow bridged the oppositional divide between audience and stage, and which 'belonged' to both. While sounds emanating from the wings palpably belonged specifically to the scene, the music (and non-musical sound) which emanated from this apparently liminal, framing space seemed to underscore the audience's emotional response as much as it underscored the production's performative intent. In later years, loudspeakers positioned on the proscenium arch also found this 'in-between' space, and for the sound designer, the decision of whether to locate a sound or music effect here, rather than on stage or, latterly, around the rear of the auditorium, became critical.

Musical Commentary

By the peak of melodrama, this liminal musical underscoring had become intrinsic to the dramaturgy. According to David Mayer, the conductors of pit orchestras were in effect the authorial partners of the playwrights. While original scores were composed, it became more common practice to adapt pre-existing music to create bespoke underscores. In their 'cut up' style these prefigured, in musical form, the soundscape 'montages' of the twentieth-century, as well as the filmic convention of using cultural associations of pop music to lend an additional dimension to the aural commentary. In some cases, musical anachronism itself makes a point. A historical melodrama underscored with a contemporary pop song suggests timeless relevance. This was, to an extent, an established convention. For example, Ophelia's songs in Hamlet:

> Shakespeare is using popular music in ways that have become increasingly common in recent film: to evoke shared memories, but in ways that suggest the disruption of the order they represented. Like such late twentieth-century films as The Big Chill, they would thus carry associations for the audience that would be essential in their contribution to meaning and affect, including proclaiming the full extent of Ophelia's derangement. Indeed, the associations of these familiar popular songs would be of primary rather than secondary importance. Had

Shakespeare written or commissioned new songs which made no reference to pre-existing materials, it would have been necessary to compose lyrics which explicitly spoke of derangement. (Johnson, 2005)

The audience's cultural familiarity with the music therefore becomes a kind of participatory dramaturgy, while the cadences and rhythms of the music still do their work of underscoring emotional vectors in the liminal space between performance and reception.

As Mayer points out, melodrama often gets a bad press. It is often taken to represent theatricality at its crassest: the kind that now seems ludicrous when we view early silent film made in a melodramatic style (and, indeed, as Mayer describes screened with orchestral scores tailored from ready-made parts, – at least in the big cities. In the regions the orchestras were often replaced by the archetypal solo pianist). Nevertheless, much of the syntax and convention of musical underscoring – both cinematic and theatrical – that is used today (with and without irony) derive from melodrama, and early melodrama influenced Beethoven and others in developing operatic form.

3.3 Abridged extract from Mayer, D. (1980) 'The Music of Melodrama', in D. Bradby, L. James and B. Sharratt (eds), *Performance and Politics in Popular Drama* (Cambridge: Cambridge University Press)

The purpose of this paper is to demonstrate and reinforce observations I have made on earlier occasions [Mayer, D. (1976) 'Nineteenth Century Theatre Music', *Theatre Notebook*, 30, 3, pp. 115–22] that nineteenth-century popular entertainment continues and elaborates the eighteenth-century practice of combining in various forms drama and music, and further, that when, on the continent and thereafter in England, Ibsen, Henry Arthur Jones, Pinero; Wilde, Granville-Barker, to name but a few pioneering playwrights, introduced the so-called New Drama, one of the sharpest breaks they made with established theatrical custom was to end the practice of accompanying dramatic action with music. Serious drama, call it melodrama or tragedy, was suddenly music free. Hedda Gabler's short bursts of piano-playing and subsequent suicide, Paula Tanqueray's death, the Reverend Michael Feversham's admissions of sin and hypocrisy happen against offstage silence, not above and in addition to the woodwinds, strings, and brasses of a thirty-piece pit-orchestra. We in the twentieth-century have inherited a comparatively new practice, not a long-established tradition, and, mistakenly, we have taken the older tradition to be some peculiar manifestation of the Victorian stage. I am increasingly convinced that our failure to take into account the extent to which drama was staged, and staged by choice, with full orchestral accompaniment derives from a misreading of testimony given before committees of Parliament and statements in the press by partisans of minor theatres who, before the Licensing Act of 1843, were attempting to curtail the monopoly of the patent houses and who fastened on the obligation under the 'burletta' licence to provide music as a point to press their attack. Contrary to these partisan statements, the minors as well as the patent theatres employed and enjoyed accompaniment from full pit-orchestras rather than infrequent and unwished for chords struck from untuned pianos.

[…]

If the music of melodrama as well as melodrama itself has had a bad press, it may be because melodramatic music, just as melodramatic incidents, characters, and dialogue, could be readily assembled from ready-made parts, even as mosaics are fashioned from ready-cut chips of coloured tile.

[…]

Melodrama's dependence upon musical accompaniment and the degree of collaboration between playwright Sims and composer Sprake are both illustrated through the prompt-script and score to Sims's and Henry Pettitt's Adelphi success London Day By Day (1889).

[…]

The score to London Day By Day, depending upon whether or not one counts repeats, is comprised of some thirty-five to forty-five musical pieces. Some are of no more than a few brief moments' duration. Others, the cues and segue pieces, intended to connect scene-ends, scene changes, and beginnings of new scenes with emotionally evocative melodies, are several minutes in length. Each of these pieces is numbered in sequence, although some numbers in the sequence have no music by them, merely the injunction to repeat a numbered theme introduced earlier in the score.

[…]

As we note the almost continual presence of music in this particular episode of revelation, domestic quarrelling, attempted blackmail, murder and flight, it will be well to recall that Sims's dramas were repeatedly commended and as often attacked by London critics for their almost excessive stage realism. Sims could be described by Augustin Filon as the author of 'a kind of popular humour together with a touch of Zolaism', and by H. G. Hibbert as 'Zola diluted at Aldgate Pump'. Although musical accompaniment is conspicuously unrealistic and not in the least Zolaesque, both the above critics and all others, whether praising or attacking Sims's work, exempt music from their observations. My inference is that the presence of music was an almost unassailably strong convention, to be taken for granted, even when, as in London Day By Day, it was scored for first and second violins, flute, clarinet, cornet, trombone, bassoon, oboe, horns, and drums. On tour such luxurious instrumentation might dwindle; when funds ran low it was certain to. But music was, nonetheless, an essential ingredient of the play. In an autobiographical novel, Jerome K. Jerome recalls of his tour with a fit-up company an orchestra reduced to a cornet and violin and how in small towns 'a piano, hired in the town, represented the orchestra. We couldn't get a piano on one occasion, so the proprietor of the hall lent us his harmonium.'

The size of the Victorian theatre orchestra may have been inconsistent – strings, woodwinds, brasses, and percussion in houses prosperous enough to afford as full an orchestra as managers considered necessary, but other houses making do with a single cornet and fiddle or a wheezy harmonium when the luck ran out. But the need for music never varied, for it was music that helped to focus attention on the stage. Music vividly and explicitly described aurally the visible action of scenes, identified characters for audiences through recognisable themes, and coaxed an extra measure of emotional acquiescence from rapt spectators. Whilst there was melodrama, invariably there was music.'

Coda to Mayer on Melodrama: A Dramatic Musician

In 1878 the Victorian author Charles Reade wrote a long letter to the editor of *The Era* to lament the death in poverty of Edwin Ellis. Ellis was a composer of theatre music and a band leader. The main thrust of Reade's letter is to complain about the injustice of artists such as Reade dying in poverty, with their contribution to theatre unnoticed, having received less than half the salary of a 'third class' actor. In making his case Reade suggests how mid-Victorian theatre music interacted with the other elements of the stage, and indeed with the audience.

The short extracts are taken from Charles Reade, *Readiana: Comments on Current Events*, London, 1881, pp. 28–31, reprinted from *The Era*, probably Sat. 26 October or Sat. 2 November, 1878. This was kindly brought to my attention by David Mayer.

> TO THE EDITOR OF *THE ERA*.
> Sir, – There died the other day [20 October, 1878] in London a musician, who used to compose, or set, good music to orchestral instruments, and play it in the Theatre with spirit and taste, and to watch the stage with one eye and the orchestra with another, and so accompany with vigilant delicacy a mixed scene of action and dialogue; to do which the music must be full when the actor works in silence, but subdued promptly as often as the actor speaks. Thus it enhances the action without drowning a spoken line.
> [...]
> I suppose two million people have seen Shaun the Post escape from his prison by mounting the ivied tower, and have panted at the view. Of those two million how many are aware that they saw with the ear as well as the eye, and that much of their emotion was caused by a mighty melody, such as effeminate Italy never produced – and never will till she breeds more men and less monks – being played all the time on the great principle of climax, swelling higher and higher, as the hero of the scene mounted and surmounted? Not six in the two million spectators, I believe. Mr. Ellis has lifted scenes and situations for me and other writers scores of times, and his share of the effect never been publicly noticed. When he had a powerful action or impassioned dialogue to illustrate he did not habitually run to the poor resource of a 'hurry' or a nonsense 'tremolo,' but loved to find an appropriate melody, or a rational sequence of chords, or a motived strain, that raised the scene or enforced the dialogue.

THE PICTURESQUE OF SOUND

The sounds which accompanied the wondrous picture, struck the astonished ear of the spectator as no less preternatural; for, to add a more awful character to peals of thunder, and the accompaniments of all the hollow machinery that hurled balls and stones with indescribable rumbling and noise, an expert assistant swept his thumb over the surface of the tambourine, which produced a variety of groans, that struck the imagination as issuing from infernal spirits.

Such was De Loutherbourg's Eidophusikon; and would that it were in being now, when the love of the fine arts has spread in so vast a degree! (Hardcastle, 1823, p. 303)

The Alsatian scenic artist de Loutherbourg, whose stage cloths were deemed to be so fine that pantomimes and music were written specially for them (see Nagler, 1959, pp. 398–402) and whose *Eidophusikon* caused a sensation in the London art scene between 1781 and 1821, was responsible (according to Hardcastle, 1823, p. 296) for introducing a new artform – *the picturesque of sound*.

He intended the Eidophusikon as fine art – as a moving, living picture. Although its contemporary proponents included Reynolds and Gainsborough, its lasting impact was less in the visual arts than in the succession of automated panorama shows, such as the *Diorama* and *Myriorama*, through which cinematography was conceived. De Loutherbourg was brought to London by Garrick as a scenic artist, and the Eidophusikon was that thing that designers attempt from time to time – scenography as art; an actor-less theatre. Its small proscenium aperture – little more than six feet wide and four feet tall – was made to look like a land-scape painting, hanging on a wall, but in fact it framed a stage space, eight feet deep. Within it, de Loutherbourg created a succession of atmospheric 'moving pictures' of London vistas and dramatic storm and maritime scenes, culminating in a fiery vision of hell. The moving scenery, although composed with an artist's eye without the need to accommodate the presence of actors, recreated in miniature the kinds of stage technologies employed since the early seventeenth-century, just as the use of a large bass drum for various percussive effects and simulations, a silk-clothed wind machine and rain effects employing wooden resonant chambers and dried peas, drew on traditional stage technologies. The innovation was in the synchronized use of coloured, directional and even moving lighting, and, particularly, in the integrated automation of all the effects. This automation facilitated the powerful synaesthetic effect of scenographic synchronicity which was further developed in Daguerre's Diorama in Paris (1822) and London (1823).

Not for the last time, the technê of theatre was influenced by developments in the art of moving pictures, or what would come to be known as cinematography. The popular success of the Eidophusikon as a sideshow at the end of the eighteenth-century pointed the way into the nineteenth and the audiovisually orchestrated spectacular mise-en-scène. In their themes, these were to go beyond the traditional, ancient repertoire of natural and preternatural phenomena, and become concerned with the purveying of exotica.

The early-to-mid nineteenth-century saw a general fashion for exotic collecting that drew crowds to the Great Exhibition, the Plaster Cast Courts at the Victoria and Albert Museum and the Reptile House at London Zoo. Lavishly dressed theatrical epics such as Byron's *Sardanapalus* (1822) or Charles Kean's 1850s Shakespeare revivals at the Princess Theatre drew audiences with increasingly spectacular stagings that packed the scene with exotic opulence and detail, and with performances seemingly heightened by the theatrical energy of the environment (see Kershaw, 2007, pp. 257–99 for an interesting theory of 'energy' and 'vitality' within the theatre environment, with reference to Kean). With its use of coloured gas lighting (from 1817) and then, lime light (1826), this was must-see theatricality on a spectacular scale, the *Cirque Du Soleil* of its day. And like *Cirque du Soleil* it demanded spectacular sound on an epic scale.

Among those on whom Kean's lavish and electrifyingly theatrical productions made a deep impression was the young travelling aristocrat who would later become Georg II, Duke of Saxe-Meiningen. The theatre company that he would go on to form, the Meininger Players, toured Europe from 1874 to 1890, and, in production terms, became highly influential in the development of modernist theatre with scenes seemingly populated by casts of hundreds, if not thousands.

THE DUKE OF RHUBARB

The Meininger Players are significant in theatre history for several reasons, but are particularly known for their spectacular sound. They combined the audiovisual synchronicity of the automated panorama show with dramaturgical innovation, dispensing with the use of the pit, and using diegetic music and sound to effect melodramatic underscoring from within the world of the play. In 1904, Vincent wrote that the Meininger Players brought stage sound 'to a high degree of perfection' (see Chapter 2). Their legacy resonates in many twentieth-century sound effect conventions and generic sound practices: the epic 'crowd' scene; the use of sound in gothic drama and horror; the elaborate sonic narratives of plays like Ridley's *Ghost Train* (1923), BBC radio sound effects and cinematic Foley sound.

Georg II, considered by some to be the prototype of the twentieth-century *director*, is supposed to have personally overseen all creative departments of his ensemble much like the actor-manager – although Georg directed from the auditorium, not the stage.

Or did he? Meiningen seems to have had the director's knack of taking the credit for the work of his team. It is now recognized that it was more probably Ludwig Chronegk's stagecraft and eye for detail that achieved Meiningen's theatrical concertos of sound, light and costume.

> In 1866 he [Chronegk] joined the Meiningers, with whom he acted until 1870, when he became 'regisseur'. Two years later he was appointed stage-director, and from that time dates the fame of both company and director. Chronegk, whose eye for stage-realism was far in advance of his time, realized that the puppet-like manoeuvres of the supernumeraries were neither natural nor graceful, and he took each individual in hand and converted him or her into an independent force. He reanimated the various individuals of the mobs, caused them to act as human beings, and in so doing revolutionized German stage-methods. This course antagonized the conservative element, and in consequence Chronegk was denounced by members of his profession, and more particularly by a short-sighted press. He persisted, however, and lived to see his methods endorsed and imitated. (Singer and Mels, 2008)

Chronegk developed or assembled the stage effects machines and techniques that became archetypes of scenic theatricality through until the 1950s and beyond.

> A slight mist or fog, used, for example, in the night scenes of *Julius Caesar* or for the smoke of the poisoned candles in *Bluthochzeit*, was produced by drawing a piece of mottled, grayish glass in front of a lamp. Sunrise or sunset could be effected with different colored glass. The strange appearances in Act I of *Julius Caesar* and the impressive moving clouds were merely a shadow play of colored glass turning in front of a light and reflected on the backdrop. This extravagantly admired illusion was emphasized by the sound of pouring rain. (Koller, 1984, p. 101)

When editing *Star Wars* in 1976, George Lucas found that relatively crude, small-scale visual-effects could be rendered utterly believable by giving them epically scaled, organically 'real' sounds and setting them in a huge orchestral setting. Chronegk's illusions worked on just this principle: the power of carefully orchestrated speech, music, vocal and non-vocal sound bound together scenic elements in one vast scenic illusion. The Meininger worked within the controlled proscenium frame, making full use of hidden wing-space, painted scenery and designed costume all lit, in the dark, by new lighting technology. 'Who can forget,' wrote a contemporary critic, 'the realistic crowds, the bier scene with its sad tolling of the bell in *Der Prinz von Homburg*, the storm with its flying clouds in *Tell*, the rain shower in *Das Kathchen von Heilbronn*, the noise in *Wallensteins Lager*, the burning of Paris in *Bluthochzeit*, the uprising of the populace in *Fiesko*?' ('Das Gastspiel der Meininger', Kickerilai (Vienna), Sept. 30, 1875).

Anne Marie Koller describes some of the techniques:

To simulate thunder, a sound he found difficult to reproduce accurately, he suspended a large drum topped by several billiard balls high above the stage; when the drum was struck, the rolling balls produced a dull sound of thunder, which grew louder as the strokes were stronger. Rain was imitated by rolling dry peas in a sieve.

The conventional means of imitating the crackle of gunfire, by using a wooden roller or by scraping a light board with a nail in it over a barrel organ, did not produce the sharp, irregular rattle of a weapon precisely enough to please the duke. For this, he attached small fireworks to the back of set pieces. The sound of bells or drums was familiar on the Meininger stage. (Koller, 1984, p. 103)

Such techniques recall those used in the Eidophusikon some hundred years before (described in detail by Hardcastle, 1823, pp. 281ff). Indeed, tightened drumskins, silk, heavy balls, resonant chambers, grain, dried pulses – similar makeshift technologies have probably been used in theatre sound production for as long as theatre has been made. It is in the context of their application in relation to the overall dramaturgy and technê of theatre that innovation lies. The Meininger accomplished what Hardcastle had wanted when he saw the Eidophusikon, the application of *the picturesque of sound* on the regular stage.

'Especially effective,' one critic judged the sounds of the bells on the Alpine cattle. 'In such things they are successful in making the sound come from the right side and from the right distance. The effects are so appropriate and inexpensive that no stage director should overlook them. Only everything must be done carefully and handled skilfully; otherwise, it would be better to keep quite away from such attempts and show the public by writing on a piece of canvas what each item should represent ...' (Koller, 1984, p. 101)

Meiningen, who had a penchant for ghost stories, revived Grillparzer's gothic tale *Die Ahnfrau* (The Ancestress) in 1878. This surprised people at the time, but the genre is an obvious vehicle to showcase technical artistry and theatrical genius.[2] Meiningen's production featured sound and music effects that would later typify the horror film genre.

the creaking of the weathervane, the howling of the wind, the flickering of the fire, the whining and wailing, the moaning and groaning in innumerable places, the squeaking of the doors at the entrance and exit of the Ahnfrau, and the strange and melancholy sound at her appearance. (Koller, 1984, p. 101)

Indeed, the drama was now enacted within what might now be called a cinematographic frame – within a moving, and sounding, picture. Where

---

[2] One thinks of a similar spate of gothic adaptations and revivals in the late 1980s and early 1990s, which relied heavily on the skilful use of sound and music (for example, Jon Pope's productions for the Glasgow Citizens' Theatre and the Shadow Syndicate or Jonathan Holloway's for Red Shift).

scripted musical occurrences allowed (such as the choruses in Schiller's *Wallenstems Lager* and *Die Rauber*, the fool's songs in *Twelfth Night* and the Bohemian shepherd's music in *The Winter's Tale*), costumed actor-musicians provided musical underscoring 'in character', visibly within the picture. Meiningen knew that for his stage magic to work to its best effect, he needed to create an overall, self-contained believability and cohesive integrity in the mise-en-scène.

Crowd Scenes

Meiningen had experienced Kean's epic Shakespeare crowd scenes in the 1850s, and seems to have become obsessed with the orchestration of the dynamics and panoramic dispersion of crowd noise. Each voice had its own part, working sometimes in unison, sometimes in counterpoint to one another. The solo speaking voice emerged from and spoke among them. There were, apparently, experiments with composite nonsense words such as *rhabarber* (from which the anglicized approximation 'rhubarb' is thought to have derived), but this all too easily gravitated towards rhythmic chanting.

> The Duke wanted the rhythm of the crowd noises to be varied, so he did not write out spoken parts for each group as Kean had done. Instead, about 30 people stood, sat, or lay backstage, each with a different newspaper or book, and read aloud. One would read, for example, 'Emperor William, who is now in his 85th year, has not undertaken to accompany Bismarck'; another, 'In addition to the earth a whole mass of comet families or isolated comets revolve around the sun'; still another, 'But Jacob spoke to his mother, Rebecca, "Esau is a hairy man"'; and so forth. Meanwhile, others chattered, laughed, joked – and the audience heard the rising excitement of an approaching mob in Paris or Genoa. The stage director modulated the sound by the wave of a hand. (Koller, 1984, p.137)

Georg would invent new processions or assemblies simply to get a crowd into the production. The cast was bolstered by the offstage extras (and it was all hands to the deck, with carpenters, hairdressers, scene painters – anyone available – pressed into action). In 1876 the *Berliner Chronik* commented:

> The handling of the crowd is almost brought to perfection here. When Casca strikes the blow to Caesar, a single, heart-shattering cry runs through the mass of people gathered around the Curia. There follows a deathly silence; the murderers, the senators, the folk, stand a moment as if bewitched and frozen before the body of the mighty Caesar; then a storm breaks out, the movement of which one has to see, the roaring of which one has to hear, to realize how powerful, how high and how deep, the effect of dramatic art can go. In the scene following that in the Forum, one great and surprising moment excels the earlier one: as Antony is raised on the shoulders of the crowd and there, in the midst of the wildest movement, reads Caesar's will; as the enraged citizens grasp the bier with the corpse and others with torches mill about; and finally, as Cinna the poet, in the wildest turmoil, is murdered – as these scenes follow one on the other, a person could

believe he was actually present at the beginning of a revolution. (Frenzel, Karl (1876) *Berliner Chronik*, Deutsche Rundschau, 3 151–5)

The believability of such scenes impressed Stanislavski, who attended several of Meininger's productions. But, as the twentieth-century broke, the 'deathly silence' was perhaps more the sign of things to come.

THE DRAMATURGY OF PAUSE, QUIETNESS AND SILENCE

One of the most important passages in modern drama is not a line of spoken dialogue. It runs as follows:

> They all sit thoughtfully. It is quiet. Only the mumbling of FIERS is heard. Suddenly a distant sound is heard as if from the sky, the sound of a breaking string, which dies away sadly. (Stage direction from Chekhov's *The Cherry Orchard*, Act II)

Sometimes, we are not sure whether we heard something correctly and listen harder. The harder one has to listen and the less certain one is that one has heard correctly, the more intense things become. In a new era when believability mattered, theatre sound became perceptually calibrated, or 'normalized', to the level of the unamplified human voice. Musicals aside, theatre sound design became one of the quietest of sonic arts and one of the most intense. There are few other artforms where one has the oddly sublime experience of being part of a crowd straining to hear parts of the programme. Mishearing, ambiguity and uncertainty are parts of theatre's subjective aural aesthetic.

As the twentieth-century dawned, the era when the most terrifying noise was to be man-made rather than natural, theatre fell silent. Or rather, silence, almost tangible, descended on the stage. Silence occupied the stage like a pall of heavy gas. As Mayer says, in the so-called 'New Drama' of Maeterlinck, Ibsen, Chekhov etc., great and tragic reckonings would be underscored not by tumultuous orchestral music, but by silence from pit and from wings. Noises-off and other sounds receded into the distance or into uncertain space and time, perhaps real, perhaps imagined. Silence became a theatre material: flowing from the writer's pen and occupying the stage with an opaque presence. Dramatists wrote with pauses and in passages of dramatic time described by stage directions rather than words.

Pause

Without the false floor of melodramatic underscoring, verbal pauses revealed unheard depths:

> The famous pauses in [the Moscow Art Theatre's] productions of Chekhov, [Osip Mandelstam] said, "are nothing other than a holiday of pure tactile sensation.

Everything grows quiet, and only a silent tactile sensation remains." This is exactly right: what happens in a Chekhov silence is that the tactile world, the visible world (which the talk is aimed unconsciously at keeping at bay), this history-in objects, quietly encroaches on the human, like the creeping vegetation in Sartre's Bouville. Suddenly you can hear the ticking of objects and the ceaseless flow of future into past: the world is no longer covered by conversation. (States, 1985, p. 74)

As we saw in the last chapter, in classical drama, verbal pauses were rare and tended either to be rhetorical devices or necessitated by action (during a sword fight for example). Silence was a figurative allusion, often to death (the ideal of silence as a respite from noise was a later idea). The pauses in the new drama of Maeterlinck and Chekhov, in particular, are not necessarily rhetorical rests between words, but show people lost for words, or simply not speaking.

They are gaps in conversation; one might interpret them as fault lines or crises in cultural discourse; if they hint at death, in relation to the classical tradition, it is through showing its inevitability in the flow of time over the mundane. According to Bert States, Chekhov's silence derives from his affinity with the world of objects.

Ibsen's pauses, on the other hand, owe more to rhetorical tradition. His silence derives from the world of ideas and 'bristles with attentiveness and expectation, with thinking' (States, 1985, p. 74). According to States, Chekhov's silence begat Beckett's, and Ibsen's begat Pinter's. Certainly Pinter's pauses, scored in 'words' made of dashes and dots, exist on a plane with the verbal morphology; but they are also like holes in the ice, revealing dark and terrifying sub-verbal depths and undercurrents.

Ibsen seems more consciously engaged with melodrama and with the scoring and underscoring of human emotional vectors. He uses the pause to create dramatic suspense or unease as part of a rhythmic and melodic narrative of human action. Chekhov, on the other hand, uses his silence to disconcert; his pauses are windows of local social awkwardness or dysfunction that reveal strange or symbolic sounds in the distance (a faint sound from the sky that might be a bird or a breaking string; the fire-alarm in the Three Sisters; axes falling in the cherry orchard.) These hint at cosmic disharmonies in a classical way, but they are never unequivocally natural or supernatural according to the traditional repertoire of elemental noise-symbols or ghostly sonic apparitions: there is a modern suggestion of psychological imagining or mishearing in their symbolism.

Take the breaking string. One might say the notion of harmony itself, both in a musical and mathematical sense, but also as a Platonic trope; of balance and ideal proportion; of idealism itself perhaps, began with Pythagoras' measurements of proportional harmonics in taut strings. The music of the spheres; the golden section; the Vitruvian man, *musica mundana* and *musica humana*; Bach; Mozart even, the aesthetics of the Enlightenment; what more potent sign could there be for a moment of epochal transition than the sound of a string breaking?

Did Chekhov intend this? We do not know. As a dramatist, he was certainly a man of the theatre; he knew its traditions and understood its phenomenology. Igor Drevelaev writes more on this effect in the next chapter. Stanislavski (1968, pp. 81–122) describes the writer as a composer, a musician, someone fascinated by noise in the material world and by the physical processes of theatre production.

> he often expressed his thought not in speeches but in pauses ... Since he was incapable of disjoining man from Nature, from the world of sounds and the things that surround him, he put his confidence not only in our actors but in all those who contribute collectively to our art.[3] (Stanislavski, 1968, 82)

The breaking string effect happens in one of his famous pauses and emblemises the 'ceaseless flow of past into future' contained in their silence, which is never a sonic void but a spatiotemporal field of ticking and creakings which play on the conscious perception so ambiguously that they might seem to be tactile sensations. It is within this bed of ambiguity that he plants his sound effects, on the cusp between audibility, touch and imagination.

The Cusp of Hearing

The text of *The Cherry Orchard* indicates that the breaking string should sound like an owl or a heron – and that it should be done so quietly so as to appear as though it were 'some way off' or 'from the sky'. This is an allusion to a classical sign of cosmic disquiet, but Chekhov also seems to be prescribing something half-way between sound and the imagination; an auditory figment of the kind sometimes experienced (along with a heightened awareness of residual tinnitus in the hearing) when subjected to silence in a state of heightened attention. In the essay 'The Theatre of Sound' which frames this volume, I describe *phonomnesis*, or imagined sound, and explain how it occupies the same auditory space, in our consciousness, as perceived sound. I explain that in cases of synaesthesia or schizophrenia, or when we hallucinate through tiredness, we hear things 'out there' which normally we would only think 'in here'. These sounds appear every bit as real as perceived sounds. In a way, they are as real: all sound is merely thought, and any sound which one appears to hear 'out there' is in only a psychoacoustic projection. CAT scans show that most of the same areas of the brain 'light up' when one hears a sound in the imagination or memory as when one hears sound sensorially.

---

[3] That said, Chekhov would frequently lose his temper at Stanislavski, whose quest for scenic believability led him to fill the stage with what Chekhov regarded as extraneous singing birds and barking dogs; so too would he rage at the stage crew's inability to realize the alarm sound in Act III of *The Three Sisters* just as he imagined it, not as a realistic sound, but as a quasi-musical dreamlike ambiguity. This led him to direct the production of the effect himself, with apparently disastrous consequences (Stanislavski, 1968, pp. 111, 117).

Sonic hallucination was a known convention of theatre sound, deriving partly from the gothic tradition and before that from the tradition of supernatural sound (which we will consider further in the next chapter). Thirty-three years before *The Cherry Orchard*, Henry Irving had constructed elaborate sound effects so the audience could 'hear' Mathias' confused aural and psychological states in the melodrama *The Bells* (1871; see Irving, 1951, pp. 188–211). The Old Vic 'effectsman' Frank Napier, who had to perform the breaking string sound effect in the first London production interpreted it within a gothic melodramatic tradition, calling it 'spooky'. He used a musical saw – an instrument associated with music hall magic and mesmerism acts.

This melodramatic tradition, and the earlier mediaeval tradition of stage magic and spook that we consider in Chapter 4 are not, however, subtle. Chekhov is clear about the breaking string: 'it is quiet'; and its ambiguities are partly as a result of its quietness. The scripted sound recalls earlier traditions, but it was not Chekhov's intention that the sound should appear either unequivocally supernatural or unequivocally psychological. Only Mathias can hear the bells, only the febrile Hamlet can hear the ghost in Gertrude's bedroom (and the audience in each case), but, in *The Cherry Orchard*, the sound of the weird breaking string is unequivocally there in the world of the play; it is heard and discussed by several people so it is clearly not imagined by a deranged individual psyche. And yet, in coming from the sky, neither is it an explicable phenomenon. It is ambiguous and odd, but its main dramaturgical function is to foreground the silence which allows it to be heard (or misheard).

Silence

In his treatise on *Silence* a few years earlier (in *The Treasure of the Humble*, 1897, pp. 1–22) the symbolist playwright Maurice Maeterlinck, whose own dramatic explorations of silence and sound as a parallel text to the verbal had influenced both Ibsen and Chekhov, contrasts the morbid silence of the individual with the supernatural power of the 'multiplied' silence of a group or crowd:

> there is a passive silence, which is the shadow of sleep, of death or nonexistence. It is the silence of lethargy, and is even less to be dreaded than speech, so long as it slumbers; but beware lest a sudden incident awake it, for then would its brother, the great active silence, at once rear himself upon his throne. Be on your guard. Two souls would draw near each other: the barriers would fall asunder, the gates fly open, and the life of every day be replaced by a life of deepest earnest, wherein all are defenceless; a life in which laughter dares not show itself, in which there is no obeying, in which nothing can evermore be forgotten ...
> And it is because we all of us know of this sombre power and its perilous manifestations, that we stand in so deep a dread of silence. We can bear, when need must be, the silence of ourselves, that of isolation: but the silence of many – silence

multiplied – and above all the silence of a crowd – these are supernatural burdens, whose inexplicable weight brings dread to the mightiest soul. We spend a goodly portion of our lives in seeking places where silence is not.

Except, it seems, in the theatre. Whereas in the mid nineteenth-century, every theatrical moment had been filled with noise, sound and music, with scarcely a panting beat between verbal salvo or musical set-piece, the dawn of the twentieth-century saw dramatists actively seeking settings for their dramas where silence *was*.

Prolonged Silence

The play *Justice* (1910) by John Galsworthy has a scene consisting of nothing more than the following direction:

FALDER's cell, a whitewashed space thirteen feet broad by seven deep, and nine feet high, with a rounded ceiling. The floor is of shiny blackened bricks. The barred window of opaque glass, with a ventilator, is high up in the middle of the end wall. In the middle of the opposite end wall is the narrow door. In a corner are the mattress and bedding rolled up [*two blankets, two sheets, and a coverlet*]. Above them is a quarter-circular wooden shelf, on which is a Bible and several little devotional books, piled in a symmetrical pyramid; there are also a black hair brush, tooth-brush, and a bit of soap. In another corner is the wooden frame of a bed, standing on end. There is a dark ventilator under the window, and another over the door. FALDER's work [*a shirt to which he is putting buttonholes*] is hung to a nail on the wall over a small wooden table, on which the novel '*Lorna Doone*' lies open. Low down in the corner by the door is a thick glass screen, about a foot square, covering the gas-jet let into the wall. There is also a wooden stool, and a pair of shoes beneath it. Three bright round tins are set under the window.

In fast-failing daylight, FALDER, in his stockings, is seen standing motionless, with his head inclined towards the door, listening. He moves a little closer to the door, his stockinged feet making no noise. He stops at the door. He is trying harder and harder to hear something, any little thing that is going on outside. He springs suddenly upright – as if at a sound – and remains perfectly motionless. Then, with a heavy sigh, he moves to his work, and stands looking at it, with his head down; he does a stitch or two, having the air of a man so lost in sadness that each stitch is, as it were, a coming to life. Then turning abruptly, he begins pacing the cell, moving his head, like an animal pacing its cage. He stops again at the door, listens, and, placing the palms of his hands against it with his fingers spread out, leans his forehead against the iron. Turning from it, presently, he moves slowly back towards the window, tracing his way with his finger along the top line of the distemper that runs round the wall. He stops under the window, and, picking up the lid of one of the tins, peers into it. It has grown very nearly dark. Suddenly the lid falls out of his hand with a clatter – the only sound that has broken the silence – and he stands staring intently at the wall where the stuff of the shirt is hanging rather white in the darkness – he seems to be seeing somebody or something there. There is a sharp tap and click; the cell light behind the glass screen has been turned up. The cell is brightly lighted. FALDER is seen gasping for breath.

> A sound from far away, as of distant, dull beating on thick metal, is suddenly
> audible. FALDER shrinks back, not able to bear this sudden clamour. But the sound
> grows, as though some great tumbrel were rolling towards the cell. And gradually
> it seems to hypnotise him. He begins creeping inch by inch nearer to the door. The
> banging sound, travelling from cell to cell, draws closer and closer; FALDER's hands
> are seen moving as if his spirit had already joined in this beating, and the sound
> swells till it seems to have entered the very cell. He suddenly raises his clenched
> fists. Panting violently, he flings himself at his door, and beats on it. (Galsworthy,
> J, *Justice*, 1910, Act III, Scene 3, http://www.online-literature.com/john-galsworthy/
> justice/6 accessed March 2008)

Again, the absence of speech seems to focus attention on material circumstances. The panting, the thickness of the door, the hard coldness of the metal
– these things are more eloquently manifest in acoustically revealing verbal
silence than they would be in descriptive dialogue.

There is sudden silence, which seems absolute, there is the silence of a
pause in which the word begins to show, and then there is the noise-forest of
prolonged silence. Gradually the ears grow accustomed to the auditory
'dark'. Stillness is revealed not to be still at all, but crawling with small ticks
and hums. Even in the quietest theatres, silence has a sound perhaps best
described as something between tinnitus and the imagination. Like the
human body, theatre is a noisy organism, and theatre silence is the sound of
that noisy organism holding itself still; like John Cage's in the anechoic
chamber, its body whirs, throbs and hums at a systems level even when
silenced; things seem to be crawling around its skin. Theatre buildings are
sonically alive in their managed airflows; in their thermodynamically
expanding and contracting materials; in their permeability to outside noise
and in the living bodies which they contain. A potent presence lurks in this
organic architecture of noise, which may be referenced or exploited
dramaturgically. This exploitation of the density of auditorium silence is
already there in proto-modernist plays such as Maeterlinck's *L'Intruse* (1890),
and by the time of Beckett's *Waiting for Godot* (1959), verbal sparseness has
become a hallmark of modernism.

AURAL DRAMATURGY AND SYMBOLISM

Blindness is a recurrent state in Maeterlinck's work; sound becomes the
primary link between the psyche and the external world. The intricate use of
sound effects places the audient in the empathetic position of having to read
significance in mundane sounds. The inevitability of impending death in
L'Intruse [The Intruder] is conveyed almost entirely through the continuing
sounds of the mundane, pitiless in their indifference to human tragedy.

The italicized directions of *silence* knowingly submit the auditorium to the
forest of its own noise. The dialogue talks about the sound of a clock ticking
symbolically throughout. During the course of the scene the clock chimes

and there is a crescendo of offstage noise, and then, finally 'there is a deathly silence' which can only mean that the clock has also stopped.

The ticking is a symbol of time passing, but it is also a cipher for silence. It is a way of telling the audience that the world of the play is silent without allowing the whole theatre actually to become silent, which would risk shifting the focus of the audience's attention from the stage to their own circumstances in the auditorium. Maeterlinck reserves that utter silence – that 'supernatural burden' of crowd silence, as he would later describe it (see above), for the moment of death itself.

Since one tends only to be aware of small sounds such as ticking, creaking, dripping and so on, when there is an absence of talk, company and movement, small stage sounds 'tell', by implication, of local silence. This is true of Chekhov's famous sound effects and is why I believe they should be performed very quietly, on the cusp of audibility. If one can hear a clock ticking, or a distant sound so faint that we are not sure whether it is a breaking string or a bird, then, by implication, one must be in a very quiet environment. Small sounds impose an empathetic state on the audience by association: one only becomes aware of clocks ticking when one is alone in a room, waiting perhaps, or unable to sleep.

3.4   Excerpt from *L'Intruse* by Maeterlinck (1890)
        (http://www.theatrehistory.com/plays/intruder.html)

THE GRANDFATHER: Is it light outside?

THE FATHER: Lighter than here.

THE UNCLE: For my part, I would as soon talk in the dark.

THE FATHER: So would I. *[Silence.]*

THE GRANDFATHER: It seems to me the clock makes a great deal of noise ...

THE ELDEST DAUGHTER: That is because we are not talking any more, grandfather.

THE GRANDFATHER: But why are you all silent?

THE UNCLE: What do you want us to talk about? – You are really very peculiar tonight.

THE GRANDFATHER: It is very dark in this room?

THE UNCLE: There is not much light. *[Silence.]*

THE GRANDFATHER: I do not feel well, Ursula; open the window a little.

THE FATHER: Yes, child; open the window a little. I begin to feel the want of air myself.
    [The girl opens the window.]

THE UNCLE: I really believe we have stayed shut up too long.

THE GRANDFATHER: Is the window open?

THE DAUGHTER: Yes, grandfather; it is wide open.

THE GRANDFATHER: One would not have thought it was open; there is not a sound outside.

THE DAUGHTER: No, grandfather; there is not the slightest sound.

THE FATHER: The silence is extraordinary!

THE DAUGHTER: One could hear an angel tread!

THE UNCLE: That is why I do not like the country.

THE GRANDFATHER: I wish I could hear some sound. What o'clock is it, Ursula?

THE DAUGHTER: It will soon be midnight, grandfather.

[Here THE UNCLE begins to pace up and down the room.]

THE GRANDFATHER: Who is that walking round us like that?

THE UNCLE: Only I! Only I! Do not be frightened! I want to walk about a little. *[Silence.]*
– But I am going to sit down again; – I cannot see where I am going. *[Silence.]*

THE GRANDFATHER: I wish I were out of this place!

THE DAUGHTER: Where would you like to go, grandfather?

THE GRANDFATHER: I do not know where – into another room, no matter where! No
matter where!

THE FATHER: Where could we go?

THE UNCLE: It is too late to go anywhere else. [Silence. They are sitting, motionless,
round the table.]

THE GRANDFATHER: What is that I hear, Ursula?

THE DAUGHTER: Nothing, grandfather; it is the leaves falling. – Yes, it is the leaves
falling on the terrace.

THE GRANDFATHER: Go and shut the window, Ursula.

THE DAUGHTER: Yes, grandfather.

[She shuts the window, comes back, and sits down.]

THE GRANDFATHER: I am cold. *[Silence. THE THREE SISTERS kiss each other.]* What is that
I hear now?

THE FATHER: It is the three sisters kissing each other.

THE UNCLE: It seems to me they are very pale this evening. *[Silence.]*

THE GRANDFATHER: What is that I hear now, Ursula?

THE DAUGHTER: Nothing, grandfather; it is the clasping of my hands.

[Silence.]

THE GRANDFATHER: And that? …

THE DAUGHTER: I do not know, grandfather … perhaps my sisters are trembling a little?
…

THE GRANDFATHER: I am afraid, too, my children.

[Here a ray of moonlight penetrates through a corner of the stained glass, and
throws strange gleams here and there in the room. A clock strikes midnight; at the
last stroke there is a very vague sound, as of someone rising in haste.]

THE GRANDFATHER: *[shuddering with peculiar horror]* Who is that who got up?

THE UNCLE: No one got up!

THE FATHER: I did not get up!

THE THREE DAUGHTERS: Nor I! – Nor I! – Nor I!

THE GRANDFATHER: Someone got up from the table!

THE UNCLE: Light the lamp! …

[Cries of terror are suddenly heard from the child's room, on the right; these cries
continue, with gradations of horror, until the end of the scene.]

THE FATHER: Listen to the child!

THE UNCLE: He has never cried before!

THE FATHER: Let us go and see him!

THE UNCLE: The light! The light!

[At this moment, quick and heavy steps are heard in the room on the left. – Then a deathly silence. They listen in mute terror, until the door of the room opens slowly, the light from it cast into the room where they are sitting, and the Sister of Mercy appears on the threshold, in her black garments, and bows as she makes the sign of the cross, to announce the death of his wife. They understand, and, after a moment of hesitation and fright, silently enter the chamber of death, while THE UNCLE politely steps aside on the threshold to let the three girls pass. The blind man, left alone, gets up, agitated, and feels his way round the table in the darkness.]

THE GRANDFATHER: Where are you going? – Where are you going? – The girls have left me all alone!

CONCLUSION

In a tour through the pre-history of twentieth-century sound design conventions, this chapter visited the rich acoustemology of Elizabethan England, where everything has a symbolic place in a universal aural eco-system; we then moved on to the invisible, extra-diegetic musical commentary of melodrama and the picturesque of sound and thence to Meiningen's obsessive pursuit of believability, and the sonic dramaturgy of new dramatists writing with pause, silence and dynamics as well as with dialogue.

The twentieth-century would be a noisy one, but it would also be the one which resounded in the silences left by its industrialized warfare and genocides. We should leave this chapter to reverberate in the sparse acoustemology that characterized modernist drama. In Samuel Becket's *Waiting for Godot*, the stage direction *silence* repeats like a negative leitmotif (for example, see *Waiting for Godot*, Beckett, pp. 59: 64–5). The sound designer has no business in this play. The play itself *is* designed sound. Its words seem to be carved, in relief, from a block of noisily opaque ...

[silence]

.

Chapter

4 *Alternative Takes*

Chapter 3 looked at sound in relation to dramatic tradition and theatre convention. This chapter steps back from the immediate field of practice to suggest some alternative ways of thinking about sound in relation to theatre. It offers some examples of other ways of thinking about the organization of sound and noise in relation to dramaturgy. The first two are from outside the field; the second two are the theories of practitioners.

First, it takes an anthropologist's view of the role of sound in relation to 'theatrical' ritual practices. It then looks at the relationship between sound and stage magic. Then the contemporary Moscow-based director and composer Igor Drevalev reprises themes of pause and silence, covered in the last chapter, from his perspective within Russian theatrical tradition. Finally, the electroacoustic composer and performer Scott Gibbons of Socìetas Raffaello Sanzio makes a statement about the relationship between sound and theatre in the form of 27 questions.

SOUND AND RITUAL PRACTICES

In the Platonic tradition theatre – indeed any art – is definitively *not accidental*. (Aleatory theatre is deliberate; that is, it deliberately uses random processes, so the dramaturgy is not accidental.) Any words, images, gestures or sounds included within a theatre performance are assumed by its audience to be deliberate and deliberately significant within the overall production. Accidental phenomena which the audience sees or hears in the theatre (an usher dropping a bundle of programmes; an illuminated Exit sign; bar staff loudly preparing for the interval outside in the crush bar; an ambulance passing[1]) are assumed not to be part of the meaning of the production. Although these sounds are part of the overall acoustemology of 'going to the theatre', the audience, ushers, actors, production team and even the theatre architects conspire to prevent sonic accidents or circumstantial intrusions

---

[1] [The one I love is that harbinger of death in grand opera – the sound of a curtain being drawn across a rail. This comes from the ushers preparing the exit doors for the end of the show, and it sings, as it were, right across the top of the music. – Series Ed.]

from happening once the performance has begun. A community of people, some paid to be there, others paying, converge on a special place for a given period of time for a variety of social and professional reasons, but the centre-piece of the event, the performance, is a time when convention governs and accidents (or unconventional behaviour) are banished.

Conventions change according to culture: heckling from the side of the stage by gallants was, for a time, tolerated by social convention in Shakespearian theatre,[2] but eventually banned, whereas Shakespeare's company, in their bid to be artistic leaders, were apt to mock the noisier theatres – pre-eminently the Red Bull in Clerkenwell. Nut-cracking by the hoi-polloi during the performance – despite the plea for silence often contained in prologue speeches – was a perennial annoyance (see Lawrence, 1935), much as mobile phone rings and rustling sweet wrappers are today. There is a dialectic tension between these conventional annoyances and tolerations within the room as a cultural place, and the dramaturgically organized sounds of the stage.

In the following extract, the social anthropologist Anthony Jackson discusses sound in relation to 'theatrical' ritual practices other than theatre *per se*.

4.1   Anthony Jackson (1968) 'Sound and Ritual' Reprinted from *Man*, New Series, Volume 3, No. 2. (June) pp. 293–9

A recent article in *Man* posed the question of the relationship between percussion and ritual (Needham, 1967). In this article I attempt to place that relationship in a wider framework by discussing the meaning and use of sounds in human society generally. It is obvious that such an undertaking must inevitably oversimplify the multifarious uses of sound in society if it is to be encompassed within the space of a short article. Consequently, what I have to say admits a number of exceptions to the generalisations to be drawn.

An initial approach to the topic of sound and society would be roughly to classify the types of noises heard by man. These fall into two distinct categories: natural sounds and man-made ones. In the first category may be placed those sounds caused by natural phenomena, animals included; while in the second category are all human-produced sounds. One outstanding difference between the two cate-gories is that the former contains no music, only noises (Lévi-Strauss 1964: 27). This does not imply that all man-made noises are musical of course, but it denies bird-song, for example, any 'consciously contrived beauty of form' (*Oxford English*

---

[2] [It was also there in the Restoration pit – Sir Charles Sedley's wit was reputed to be so quick that he could, from the audience, complete a rhyming couplet in a tragedy before the actor did so, but usually with a word that was highly inappropriate. – Series Ed.]

Dictionary), this being merely an instinctively patterned signal. Man does make music and its significance lies in the fact that it is a socially ordered and patterned sound. Although man's greatest achievement, speech, is the commonest human noise, I shall have little to say about it. Besides being used for speaking, the voice is also employed for chanting and singing; it is not a mere signalling device amongst many others.

Such a broad division as outlined above only provides a background to the central problem: *which sounds are significant to society*? More particularly, we need to enquire into which sounds are important in ritual. It is obvious that the chance noises of the natural world cannot, because of their unpredictability, be of much value in the ritual itself, which is not to say that they are without significance; they may be 'commanded' to appear in the ritual. Numerous such imitations are recorded: thunder (Frazer 1922: 60–83), the sound of wild animals (Turnbull 1965: 310), etc. These sounds would then fall into the human noise category.

For the purpose of this discussion only human noises are considered and these may be categorised in four ways (see Figure 4.1)[3]:

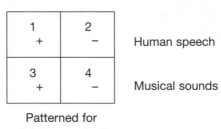

Figure 4.1   Categorization of human noises

This classification gives the following sub-divisions: 1) human-like speech; 2) non-human-like speech; 3) musical sounds; 4) non-musical sounds. Each and any such sound may be produced by the human voice or by instruments.

Cell 1 contains the language as spoken and understood by the society in question; it may also include sounds made by instruments that 'speak' – drums, whistles, etc. By contrast, cell 2 refers to non-human speech, or the 'voice of the gods and spirits' that is not used for ordinary social communication. Such sounds may be made by disguising the voice (as in the case of shamans and spirit mediums), or by the use of foreign or archaic speech, or the use of instruments such as the bullroarer or trumpet. Cell 3 includes musical sounds made either by singing (the voice as a

---

[3] From the point of view of ritual imitation, non-human sounds could be similarly classified:

   Animal sounds: 1) patterned instinctive signals: bird-song; 2) discontinuous sounds: cries and roars.
   Natural phenomena: 3) rhythmical sounds: waves and wind; 4) non-patterned sounds: thunder, earth tremors.

musical instrument) or by playing instruments. The essential point is that these sounds are ordered by convention and serve to express and convey emotion. Cell 4 contains noises arising either from workaday activities or from deliberate din-making; even unpremeditated human sounds like sneezing, yawning, hiccupping, etc., might be included. These sounds are not patterned like music, although they may be used as signals.

This classification has been drawn up to point to a distinction between ordered patterns of sound which tend to be rhythmical and those which are unordered and discontinuous. A fourfold grouping is admittedly a coarse sieve but further refinement at this stage would complicate the argument unnecessarily. There is also an additional factor to be considered with regard to the diagram, that of silence.

Having considered the types of sound available, the question arises why certain sounds are picked out and deliberately used in ritual? Obviously, accidental noises are of no significance to the rite itself but may gather importance should they be prohibited. In other words ritual may ban as well as enjoin certain sounds. With regard to silence, Lévi-Strauss (1964: 306–7, 333–6) points out that it receives meaning only by contrast with noise. In fact, the type of noise against which silence is being contrasted may be significant, and each cell in the diagram may thus be considered to have a corresponding silence. Certain ritual occasions demand silence, others demand noise. While this is a commonplace, it is generally passed over in favour of paying attention to what is being said or done. Little analysis has been made on how and when certain sounds as such are made use of in the course of a ritual, this including the prohibition of particular noises. Apart from the common fact that many peoples regard sound *qua* sound as having magic-like qualities, we do not know very much about how people rank different types of sound in ritual, either positively or negatively.

There are, however, some examples of the contrast noise/silence and Douglas (1954: 12) has a relevant passage about the prohibitions of noise among the Lele. Here noises associated with the day, for example women pounding grain, are forbidden at night, while drumming is a night-time activity since dancing does not take place during the day. At times of important religious ceremonies, or on rest days, workaday activities which make drum-like noises (pounding grain or working in the forest) are absolutely forbidden. It is believed that such sounds would bring the village into dangerous connexion with the forest and would annoy the forest spirits. As might be anticipated, the rule concerning drumming is reversed on rest days (i.e. dance days) and drums may be beaten in daylight. Another contrast is that dance drums must not be beaten during periods of mourning.

Similar examples are to be found elsewhere in the world. In Australia, the Warramunga prescribe noise before death and silence afterwards; in South America, a Bororo rite concerning the ancestors requires silence first, then noise (Lévi-Strauss 1964: 334). These examples illustrate that there are special attitudes towards noise and towards ritual silence.

Having dealt with the absence of noise in ritual I now turn to examine the use of sound in the light of the schema put forward. The first two cells (on speech) I propose to gloss over because they are already well treated. The importance of the spoken word in ritual may be taken for granted in this discussion, which is more concerned with the role of percussion and ritual.

Taking non-musical sounds first, involuntary noises such as sneezing and yawning may be dismissed despite the fascinating associations held to exist between these sounds and the other world (Wagner 1954: 43). What is relevant to the choice of sounds in ritual can only be socially produced noise. Two good examples of noise-making are provided by Lévi-Strauss (1964: 292–5, 306–7, 3 33–6; 1966: 250, 349–51, 354, 360–3), viz. the charivari and the *vacarne*, the former relating to the noises made at unpopular weddings, the latter to the din made at eclipses. Lévi-Strauss ingeniously links these two phenomena since, he argues, they are both expressions of the threat of disorder, one social, the other cosmic (See also Douglas 1966: 94 sqq.). Other examples may be taken from Christian ritual, where perhaps they might not have been expected. At one time it was quite customary to let off fire-crackers and other explosions at midnight on Easter Saturday (Frazer 1922: 345), a custom still surviving in Sweden. Another example is the silencing of church bells before Easter Sunday and the replacing of their sound by the noise of 'instruments of darkness' which clatter and bang (Lévi-Strauss 1966: 348–52).[4] Such clappers were also used in China to mark the beginning of the period of cold food, when fires were extinguished.

These examples must suffice to show two points: a) the use of percussion and explosions as din-makers – what Eliade (1964: 75) calls the anti-demonic magic of noise as opposed to musical magic; b) the use of noise as a marker in Freedman's sense (1967: 17) and as mentioned by Needham (1967: 612). Thus noise or unpatterned sounds reflect uncontrolled situations or transitional states or threats to the patterned social order.

Before examining the central category of musical or patterned and rhythmical sound, I wish to return to the general theme of sound and ritual and to look first at the ritual aspect. The purpose is to seek correspondences between the overall structure of ritual and the particular use of structured or patterned sound. This faintly resembles Lévi-Strauss's analogy between myth and music except that this time it is more nearly a homology.

Ritual provides a frame and a *marked off* time or place that alerts a special kind of expectancy (Douglas 1966: 63). Of all physical stimuli sound is an ideal marker, it is pervasive and far-reaching yet capable of infinite variation. By contrast sight is more limited and less variable, less able to denote subtle changes in the ritual. It may be just coincidence that many rites are conducted at night or in dim light, although this could be merely to enhance the relative importance and sensitivity of the ear. A noteworthy fact is that a deaf ritual specialist is an anomaly whereas a blind one is common enough.

---

[4] Lévi-Strauss discusses 'les instruments des ténèbres' and cites van Gennep and Frazer. He quotes the following:

> Then Clappers ceasse, and belles are set againe at libertée,
> And herewithall the hungrie times of fasting ended bee.

If rites have a marked off time, it means that they are to be specially placed in chronological time and hence there must be indicators to denote the beginning and end of the rite besides the sequential order of events. The use of silence and of noise as markers has been mentioned; music obviously can be employed for continuity and there are other devices such as bells and drums which may be used to mark off intervals within the ceremony itself (de Nebesky-Wojkowitz 1956: 399). Again, different types of sound may be used to betoken or symbolise different ritual occasions (Yalman 1964: II 5–50).

On the other hand rites may be regarded from a different viewpoint and be seen as ordering time itself (Leach 1961: 132–6). The *rites de passage* demarcate stages in the life-cycle and, as Leach remarks, are connected with time and changes in the status of a moral person. Transition rites are peculiar in that they contain internally a number of distinct changes: those of separation, the marginal state, aggregation and, finally, the return to secular time. Other rites, one might hazard, do not involve so many switch-overs in mood and theme. Thus there is a need for many markers in transition rites. But because of the importance and also the danger of marginal states (Douglas 1966: 94–113) it is possible that noise takes on additional significance to the participators: it may be prohibited (Lévi-Strauss 1964: 334–5) or prescribed (Van Gennep 1960: 77, 106, 151, 156, *passim*).

If it is true that transition rites are characterised within by distinct changes, then percussive noises might well be the most appropriate markers, for not only can they produce an implied note of warning but they can easily break up a patterned sequence. This use of percussion is far more effective than using any other musical instrument, apart from the bullroarer and trumpet (which have, it was noted in cell 2, other functions as well). The main characteristic of percussion instruments is that they are monotonic, which renders them unsuitable, alone, for melodic use but which makes them admirable for producing rhythm. Now a change of rhythm is far more significant than a change of melody in denoting change of mood, besides being more easily detectable. Hence a change of tempo can very effectively mark a transition within ritual, especially towards a climax.

Rhythmical sounds are predominantly man-made and are readily identifiable with social order, whereas din or arrhythmical noise is more typical of a breaking of man-made order; thus Lévi-Strauss's examples of charivari and *vacarne* reflect a breakdown of order. As Douglas (1966: 94) says, 'ritual recognises the potency of disorder' for 'disorder spoils the pattern' yet 'its potential for patterning is indefinite'. Therefore breaks in the patterns of events may be reflected in disordered, arrhythmical sounds while a taking up of a rhythmical beat again reasserts human control over events – but this is speculation.

[...]

It is noticeable that percussion, especially the drum, plays a large role in ritual. In Africa one finds that drums are often regarded as sacred and that there are also many drum cults. Such cults are often associated with transition rituals, those of the Lovedu (Krige and Krige 1954: 66–8) for example; with accession rites among the Ashanti (Busia 1954: 202) and the Ankole (Oberg 1940: 150–61); and with kingship generally. In Rwanda (d'Hertefelt 1965: 421–2) drums are believed to function as mediating symbols between the king and the source of his power. To the shaman of course the drum is of prime importance – it is his 'horse' (Eliade1964: 173).

Why should the drum be accorded so much power and significance? Is it chance that singles out this instrument for the purpose of communicating with the gods, spirits and ancestors? While it is true that in some regions, notably the Americas, the drum is often replaced by the rattle (which could be regarded as a drum beaten from within), this difference is unimportant for they are both percussive instruments. The clue to the importance of the drum must lie in the capacity of rhythmic sound makers (for clapping is equally effective) for producing a feeling of contact with the other world. The reverence for the drum cannot rest on mere convention and it is obviously not the thing in itself that is important but the drum as played, i.e. its sound. Drum sounds are rhythmical and provide the beat for singing and dancing which may lead to trances, ecstasies and thereby to 'communication' with the other world. The potent factor is the rhythm and the question is why this should produce psychological effects at all? The answer seems to be that external rhythmic stimulation affects the natural brain rhythms, thus giving rise, in certain cases, to abnormal psychological states. Since the brain is a common denominator to all mankind,[5] it follows that what is true at the neurophysiological level must be universally true, irrespective of society or the individual. This point has been recently made by Sturtevant (1968) in his reply to Needharn, and he gives a lucid summary of Neher's (1962) findings on the influence of drumming and the incidence of unusual behaviour.[6]

The fact that music and/or rhythmic stimulation is world wide stems, not from chance factors, but from the very fact that basically we have little choice – we live in society and we all have brains that may be influenced. Which is not to say we have no choice, for we can avoid other men and, fortunately for us all, the brain can grow immune to repeated stimuli *if we wish it to*. In other words, whether or not we allow ourselves to be influenced by rhythm is a matter of choice. Yet it seems that men want to have such stimulation. That certain rhythms are pleasing perhaps means no more than to say that there are correspondences between external and internal rhythms. By setting up such harmonies between social and natural pulsations, men experience euphoria, hallucinations, etc., which are forms of dissociation that may also be produced chemically by alcohol and drugs, the two most widely used means of enlarging the consciousness. Thus the decision to use certain types of sound is an empirical one in that it can give desired effects.

---

[5] The human brain is similar in structure and size to that of other primates, so that there is here a ready-made test situation. It is generally agreed that the chimpanzee comes nearest to man as regards behaviour and the astonishing thing is that chimpanzees living freely and undisturbed in the forest like to drum and dance! Details of a chimpanzee festival of dancing and drumming is reported by Reynolds (1965), and by Reynolds and Reynolds (1965).

[6] Professor Sturtevant's letter came to my attention after this article was written and when I had made the identical point. As he sums up the matter so admirably it would be supererogatory to list the argument again.

If one looks at the other side of the coin, noise/silence, another physiological limit is reached, for it appears that we need a certain amount of sensory stimulation to remain sane. A familiar example is Arctic hysteria, the result of silence and isolation.[7] Thus in everyday life we live in a world of natural and human noise, somewhere between the extremes of utter silence and sharply imposed rhythmical stimulation, the natural and social co-ordinates of our existence.

If ritual is seen as a striving towards contact with suprahuman powers, a transcendence of everyday reality, then it is not surprising that men will employ such means as will give them this feeling of surpassing normality. It so happens that rhythmic sound is one such means and hence stems its employment in ritual; this also accounts for the superiority of this form of sound over all others. A corollary of the use of rhythm in ritual is the occurrence of dancing as well, for this too is a direct result of brain stimulation. Certain rates of rhythm compel dancing or physical movement (see Walter 1961: 86–103 for a description of this 'forced' behaviour which underlies ordinary social dancing). The use of alcohol on such occasions simply heightens the sensitivity of the brain to rhythmic stimulation,[8] as was noted by Durkheim (1961: 258).

To summarise, I have endeavoured to show that the sounds chosen for ritual purposes are patterned in order to achieve certain ends.[9] Both speech and musical sounds are socially patterned and hence can vary from society to society; but basically they can be used to produce similar psychological states because, in part, these derive from a common neurophysiological base – the structure of the brain. Such sounds are invested with symbolic significance for these reasons and often special attitudes are adopted towards them. Broadly speaking, cells 1 and 3 in the diagram stand for social order as expressed in ritual, while the other cells denote a break or a transitional phase in social ordering. I have also considered the opposition sound/silence, both as regards ritual and as regards its physiological consequences.

It will have been observed that percussion and transition occupy a key place in the relationship between sound and ritual, a point particularly stressed by Needham.

---

[7] Even partial deprivation like deafness produces personality disturbances (Landis and Bolles 1950: 61–71). Experimental reduction of all external stimuli to a very low level produces hallucinations and other nervous disorders (Vernon et al. 1961).

[8] It can hardly be a coincidence that in our own society we are witnessing the present vogue of beat rhythms, drug-taking and other psychedelic (mind-widening) phenomena. They are all a craving for a certain type of brain stimulation. It would make a good sociological enquiry if one investigated the rituals involved in these performances!

[9] Rhythm may be used for indoctrination and conversion, for example Revivalist hymn singing (see Brown 1963: 223–43, 294–307). By contrast Western monotheism on the whole avails itself of music which avoids a strong beat, with the consequence that the music tends to be otherworldly and not conducive to dancing. In the West, dancing has been relegated to the secular province of life – a difference that sharply marks off Western ritual from much of the rest of the world's ritual activities. The theological reasons for this divorce of music and dancing are basically sound.

It is hoped that the above discussion has, by widening the frame of reference, indicated possible lines for future research in the field of ritual.[10]

MAGIC THROUGH SOUND: ILLUSION, RECEPTION AND AGREED PRETENCE

Illusion

In the last chapter we saw how theatre practice did not become concerned with theatrical believability until the end of the nineteenth-century. This is not say, however, that the *trompe-l'œil* (or *trompe l'oreille*?) did not feature before this in otherwise non-naturalistic productions.

There is pleasure in the well-turned perceptual trick. In Ros King's *Life and Works of Richard Edwards*, we read the following description of a 1566 production of Edward's *Palamon and Arcyte* at Corpus Christi College, Oxford performed for Elizabeth I:

> Theseus with Hippolyta, Emily and ladies now enter, hunting a hart. Windsor lets us know that the hunt was represented in the play by off-stage sound effects achieved with a real pack of hunting dogs, and no doubt horns, outside in the quad. This created pandemonium inside the hall. His first draft says, 'the ladies in the windows cried out "Now!" and hallowed', though 'ladies' is changed to 'boys' in the second draft. Both concur that the Queen exclaimed, 'O excellent, those boys are ready to leap out at the window to follow the hounds' (Windsor, fol. ii8v). The first draft, with intermittent legibility, then goes on to compare Edwards's achievement in the verisimilitude of the setting for this scene with that of three of the most famous ancient Greek artists: the sculptors Praxiteles and Polycletus and the painter Apelles. This is the highest compliment that could be paid in the context of classical and Renaissance theory on art as mimesis. Windsor is insisting that the hunting effect was not real life – as the audience response seemed to assume – but true art, imitating the very essence of life. (King, 2001, p. 81)

Or, one might say, this was a trick – a form of conjuring or magic. Magic may have 'low' cultural associations (with mountebanks and street performers, music halls or end-of-the pier shows), but there is also magic involved in the

---

[10] In the analysis of ritual the role of music is often undervalued. It could well be the case that music is an essential component, not only in establishing social relationships which is one of the functions of ritual but also in setting the pattern of ritual incantations. Music can only be understood polythetically (i.e. step by step) unlike verbal statements which may be grasped monothetically. It is the sharing of inner time, Bergson's 'durée', which the musical process creates, thus giving rise to communication that may account for the chanting and intoning of words in ritual. Incantation places words in a musical context and makes them sounds to share with others, not simply words to be intellectually understood. From this point of view repetition in ritual may be likened to a musical encore. The social relationship aspect of music outlined above is discussed by Schutz (1964: 159–78).

concept of *mimesis* and in the notion of theatre itself. Jackson suggests in the last chapter that, through social ritual, people often seek 'contact with suprahuman powers, a transcendence of everyday reality', and that 'men will employ such means as will give them this feeling of surpassing normality'. It is curious, then, that the words 'magic' or 'thrill' do not feature in any of the lists of the functional scope of theatre sound given in Chapter 2. What of the cavernous artificial reverberation which transforms Widow Twanky's laundry into Abanazar's cave? What of the visceral shock of stage-pyrotechnics that misdirects attention from the mundane? What of echoey disembodied voices manifesting from the ether, even the opera-singing decapitated head in Birtwistle's *Sir Gawain and the Green Knight*? From the ghost's voice in Hamlet to the string breaking in *The Cherry Orchard*, seemingly from the sky, sonic illusion and magic have been part of theatre's definition.

Horror and Spook

We saw earlier how the Meininger relished gothic tales of the supernatural for their sonic opportunity. In a darkened room, sound can be chilling: the whistling of wind in the nooks and crannies of buildings or in wild woods, the creaking of floorboards in empty buildings, or in the half imagined voices or sounds of the night. Such sounds have their musical equivalents in the melodramatic instrumental repertoire: low tremolo strings, tympani glissandi, soft cymbal rolls, musical effects such as the flexi-tone, the vibraslap, the musical-saw, and, later on, the Theremin and synthesisers, which create other-worldly or supernatural tones.

And then there is vocal horror: the distorted voice of the possessed child in the *Exorcist*, the rasp of Darth Vadar's voice or the sickly cadence of Peter Lorre's child-killer in Fritz Lang's *M* (1931), Lang's first sound film and one through which many sonic and melodramatic horror devices found their way from the theatre to the screen (most famously, the sound of the killer's chilling whistling). Such demonic voices are also part of theatre's magical tradition:

> The androgynous, the idiot savant, the 'half-breed', the freak which appears half animal (the Elephant Man), are all exhibits in the chamber of mythic anxieties and horrors. Of all of these, perhaps the most horrific is the undead dead. They exist as various archetypes which haunt our musings on mortality: from the zombie created by voodoo to the monster created by science. In the twentieth century it also takes the form of the prosthetic human being (as in Pynchon's novel *V*) or the android which continues to function even when totally dismembered, as in Ridley Scott's *Alien*.
>
> Above all it is the 'ordinary' human being who is somewhere between the living and the dead who fills us with horror, and of these, none more so than the one who continues to utter in death. Given the pallid inadequacy of the printed playtext, it is important to take a moment to try to capture the ghastly intensity, the embodied immediacy of this experience ... The sounding dead is a particularly disturbing

embodiment of the liminal. It dismantles one of the most obdurate of all phenomenological certainties: the distinction between life and death, the literal vitality of
vocalisation and the profound silence of the grave. (Johnson, 2005)

In the following extract we can see how such examples are an ancient
theatrical tradition.

4.2   Extract from Philip Butterworth (2005) *Magic and the Early English Stage*
(Cambridge: Cambridge University Press, pp. 98–100, 102–4)

The conscious working of the reality–illusion relationship is not only central to the
conventions by which theatre exists, but also to the creation of magic through
conjuring, legerdemain or sleight of hand, ventriloquy and other forms of overt
deception or pretence. The perpetrators of magic feats or tricks frequently rely on
diversion and deception as a means of confusing the visual sense of the audience.
It is the ability to visualise that is most frequently diverted or disorientated when acts
of magic are created. However, the reality–illusion relationship may also be affected
by the use of sound.

In the *Origo mundi* of the *Cornish Ordinalia* a stage direction requires the following action: '*Et fodiet et terra clamat et iterum fodiet et clamat terra.*' [And he shall dig,
and the earth cries: and again he shall dig, and the earth cries.] The significance of
the action within the biblical narrative is that God has expelled Adam and Eve from
Paradise and Adam now attempts to dig the earth so that he 'may raise corn'.
However, he declares that 'The earth will not let me break it.' The inherent ambiguity in the stage direction is intriguing. Clearly, it may not be possible to say how the
requirement expressed in the stage direction was originally achieved, but it is possible to consider some implications and their potential influence upon the nature of the
inherent theatrical statement.

Firstly, how does the earth cry? Presumably, the sound of the crying earth is
intended to communicate just that to the audience. The audience needs to know
that it is the earth that cries. What does this sound like? Who knows what the crying
earth would sound like? Clearly, whatever sound was produced to indicate that the
'earth cries' would have needed to appeal to the imagination of the audience in
order to contextualise and give significance to the sound. The possibilities
surrounding the nature of this sound and its production invite interesting questions
about the character of and implicit conventions in its communication to the audience. It might be presumed that the sound is a 'live' one and produced by someone and/or something. If it is made to occur through the latter, what kind of object
or instrument might be used? Is the creator of the sound, whether person and/or
instrument, seen by the audience? Is it important that the audience be able to
recognise that the 'cries' actually come from the earth at the point where the
digging is carried out by Adam? Answers to this question inevitably lead towards

concerns about the nature of reality, illusion, deception and agreed pretence in the communicated statement.

If it is that the sound is intended to come from, or seem to come from, the point at which the earth is dug, the pretence may lead to use of illusion, although this is not inevitable. What are the means of its creation? A person may be positioned out of sight beneath the 'earth' in some sort of cavity in order to produce the sound *in situ*. Alternatively, a person who is in view of the audience may make, or cause to make, the sound 'as if' it comes from the ground. A further possibility exists in the sound being regarded as that which 'represents' the sound of the earth crying, in which case, the terms of reference by which the significance of the sound is communicated would need to be established. In such an instance the audience does not primarily appreciate the sound for its supposed verisimilitude but for its meaning.

Of itself, the stage direction in the *Origo mundi* does not divulge sufficient information to determine how the 'earth cries', but two other stage directions in the *Resurrexio Domini* of the *Cornish Ordinalia* offer the following information in respect of the attempted burial of Pilate:

> *et tunc proicietur extra terram*
> [and then he shall be thrown out of the earth]
> *et tunc ponent eum in terra et proicietur iterato sursum*
> [and then they shall put him in the ground,
> and he shall be thrown up again]

The implication here is that the 'earth' possesses sufficient depth to enable the ejection of Pilate. This might be achieved by a depression of some kind in the natural earth or within some built-up staging. If the information contained in the text may be trusted to indicate accurate action, then the instruction given by the Carcerator or Gaoler to Garcon, the Servant, to 'take the head, By the feet I will let him down, Within the earth' suggests that Pilate ends up on his back. In this position Pilate is unlikely to throw himself out of the earth. It is more likely that others cause his ejection. Perhaps the most obvious method might consist of Pilate being tossed in a strong earth-coloured cloth. This kind of action would seem to meet the intention behind the requirement expressed in the stage direction, although it presupposes sufficient space and depth in which to stage manage the action. Given the need for such space it is possible that the creation of sound to signify that the 'earth cries' in the stage direction in the *Origo mundi* may take place in and from the same space. The 'earth' may well be a designated *locus* within the performance space. Further support for this possibility may be found in the stage direction in the *Passio Domini* of the *Cornish Ordinalia* that requires an earthquake to occur. Where better could such an earthquake take place than in a *locus* designated as 'the earth'? Indeed, the same means suggested for the ejection of Pilate may be adopted for the visual effect of the earthquake.

Accompanying sound would presumably also take place at this point. Such treatment is recorded in the late fifteenth- or early- sixteenth-century Passion play in Provençal:

E a fa la
finta de fa terra-
tremol qual que,
ce hon fa
an tellas, lo que hon
faça core las tela[s]
a cobri lo trovat.
[And to perform the trick of the earthquake one covers the stage with pieces of cloth and
shake[s] them.]

In this instance, the sound of the earthquake is provided by rolling stone balls on a
wooden framework below the stage platform that is supplemented by firing cannons
10 or 12 times 'promptly'.

Since no one knows what the crying earth in the *Origo mundi* would have
sounded like, nor indeed knows what the actual sound would be, it seems that the
help needed by the audience to contextualise the sound would have been strongly
influenced by its location. If the sound comes from the 'earth' where Adam digs,
then identification of the source of the sound, in relation to the delivered text and its
timing, may carry meaning over and above that of its nature. The theatrical option as
to whether creation of the sound be hidden or seen by the audience is not immediately clear. However, communication of sound may be imprecise or indistinct if its
creation is not witnessed by the audience.
[...]

[On Disembodied Heads That Speak and Birds of Metal That Sing]

In George Peele's *The Old Wives Tale* (c. 1590) two stage directions embrace the
following:

Heere she offers to dip her Pitcher in, and a head speakes in the Well.
Head. Gently dip, but not too deepe,
For feare you make the golden birde to weepe,
Faire maiden white and red,
Stroke me smoothe, and combe my head,
And thou shalt haue some cockell bread,
Zant. What is this, faire maiden white & red,
Combe me smooth, and stroke my head:
And thou shalt haue some cockell bread,
Cockell callest thou it boy, faith ile giue you
cockell bread.
Shee breakes hir Pitcher vppon his heade, then it thunders and lightens, and Huanebango
rises vp: Huanebango is deafe and cannot heare.

The 'heade' appears to be a physical entity rather than just a disembodied voice, for
the breaking of 'hir Pitcher vppon his heade' is a requirement stipulated by the stage
direction on behalf of the communicated statement to the audience. The stage
direction tells us that the 'head speakes', but how does it do this?

In Greene and Middleton's *Friar Bacon and Friar Bungay* (1591) both text and
stage directions require the use of a 'brasen head' created by Friar Bacon in order

to 'tell out strange and vncoth Aphorismes', The relevant stage directions are as follows:

> Enter Frier Bacon drawing the courtaines with a white sticke, a booke in his hand, and a lampe lighted by him, and the brasen head and miles, whith weapons by him.
> the Head speakes.
> Heere the Head speakes and a lightning flasheth forth, and a hand appeares that breaketh down the Head with a hammer.

The stage directions signify that the 'brasen head' is a portable property and Miles' words in the text may indicate the eventual resting place of it when he says, 'now sir I will set me downe by a post, and make it as good as a watch-man to wake me if I chaunce to slumber', If the 'post' is a real one, then it is possible that the head is placed on top of it. If, on the other hand, the post is one of the pillars that supports part of the upper structure of the theatre, then the head may be simply hooked on to it and the curtain from behind which the hand appears may be positioned immediately behind the pillar.

Stage directions in *Alphonsus King of Aragon* (1599) by Robert Greene make the following requirements:

> Let there be a brazen Head set in the middle of the place behind the iv.i Stage, out of the which, cast flames of fire, drums rumble within, Enter two Priests.
> Cast flames of fire forth of the brazen Head.
> Speake out of the brazen Head.

In this case the text informs us that the 'brazen Head' is a representation of 'Mahomet', before which the two Priests and King Belinus kneel in order to focus their dialogue with 'Mahomet'. The positioning of the 'brazen Head', as determined by the stage direction, is precisely located as 'the place behind the iv.i Stage' (forestage). Thomas Dekker, in his *If this be not a good play, the Devil is in it*, includes a 'golden Head' called Glitterbacke, which both 'ascends' and 'descends'. Glitterbacke is involved in considerable dialogue with Shackle-soule and Scumbroath. At the end of the scene a stage direction instructs that the golden head 'Goes downe'. 'Ascending' and 'descending' are therefore presumed to be carried our through or on a trap

Positioning of the respective heads in each of the above examples appears to be important. The 'well of life', 'a post', 'iv.i Stage' and a presumed trap are all locations at which heads are sited. Such fixed sites for the heads might lend themselves to the technique of constructing brazen heads of the kind offered by William Bourne in his *Inuentions or Denises* (1578):

> And as the brasen head, that seeme for to speake, might bee made by such wheele work, to go either by plummets or by springs, and might haue time giuen vnto it, that at so many houres end, then the wheeles and other engines should bee set to worke: and the voyce that they did heare may goe with bellowes in some truncke or trunckes of brasse or other mettall, with stoppes to alter the sound, may bee made to seeme to speake some words, according vnto the fancie of the inuenter, so that the simple people will maruell at it.

The mechanical intricacies suggested in Bourne's account may appear too complex or inflexible for the kind of theatrical use cited above, in that timing of the sequence is determined by 'plummets or by springs'. However, the fact that the conveyance of sound 'in some truncke or trunckes of brasse or other mettall, with stoppes to alter the sound, may bee made to seeme to speake some words, according vnto the fancie of the inuenter', seems to be most appropriate in respect of manipulation of the 'head' to produce spoken words. Whether the heads stipulated in the above stage directions possess moveable jaws is unclear, for within their respective contexts such articulation is not necessary – the heads simply speak as icons. Bourne develops his repertoire of established and potential techniques with regard to sound production through artificial birds:

> and also to make birds of mettall to sing very sweetly, and good musicke, it may bee done with wheeles, to goe at any houre or time appoynted by plummets, an then to haue pipes of tinne or other fine metall to go with bellowes, & the pipes to haue stops, and to go with a barrell or orher such like deuise, and may bee made to play or sing what note that the inuenter shall thinke good when he dooth make it: and also there may bee diuers helpes to make it seeme pleasant vnto the eares of the hearers, by letting the sound or wind of the pipes to passe through or into water for that will make a quauering as birds do. &c.

The technique of passing sound through pipes in water to 'make quauering as birds do' is one of the ones employed today among the range of 'bird calls and decoys' produced by the 'Acme Whistle Company'.

THE DRAMATURGY OF SILENCE

Chapter 3 considered silence in relation to theatre history (in particular, in relation to stage naturalism and symbolism).

In this extract from his 2007 address to the Prague Scenofest, the Russian composer and director Igor Drevalev examines silence within a far broader and more eclectic sweep. Drevalev speaks as a contemporary practitioner within the Russian theatre tradition. The presentation was written to be spoken and heard in relation to practical demonstrations using a group of performers. I have kept it in its original form as a set of speaker's notes.

4.3   Extract from an address by Igor Drevalev to the 2007 Prague Scenofest

---

There are a lot of types and forms of theatre. And there are many genres within theatre. They are all united by the one phenomenon: Real theatre creates other reality.

Whether it is a tragedy or a comedy, a show or a farce, street, ethnic or religious theatre.

Theatre creates other reality. Sometimes it is just entertainment, sometimes it is a try to understand what a man is in this world, sometimes it is a contact with God. This reality may be like our everyday life and may differ from it.

But this is the other reality into which a spectator gets.

The great dramatist said: 'All the world's a stage'. This is a beautiful and wise metaphor, but it is a metaphor. 'All the world is all the world'.

Ancient philosophers could say: 'All the world is a sound'.

We can say that for centuries sound did not reveal itself entirely. Mostly it was a speculative category as musical instruments were quite simple and limited in timbre and diapason etc.

But potential power of sound was known always. Many myths about creation say that the universe was created with the sound.

In the esoteric doctrines of ancient Egypt sound was the first to disturb the eternal silence and so it was the reason for everything created in the world preceding light, air and fire.

In Hinduism the sound Aum brought cosmos to genesis. It contains the essence of the Universe.

The sound of Krishna's flute was a reason for the world creation.

Biblical God spoke with Israel by voice.

Gods in many traditions have an ability to give voice to natural elements: water, wind and animals or enable them to play musical instruments. Goddess-mothers were drawn with lyres in their hands as a sign of world creation.

In other words, working on a sound score for a performance we do not just illustrate the events of the performance. In certain sense we create the cosmos, the universe in which our characters will live and die, love and hate, enjoy and suffer.

We know what sound is. But what is silence?

May be, it is just the absence of sound?

In music there are pauses. Is it silence? As a rule, it is not.

It is an interrupted sound.

Moreover there is no absolute silence if you are a normal and healthy person. Even if you are placed into an absolutely isolated from sounds room, you will hear the sound of your blood.

In psychological sense silence is not a form of sound or its absence. But silence exists as an opposition to sound. It is not a physical quantity, it is a philosophical quantity. I will explain it by the following example.

This is a tragic story. It is told by an old man. He was 9 at that time. The story took place during World War II. The police ordered people to leave their houses. When people gathered they were brought to the country. They did not realize where they were being taken, they yelled and cried and tried to calm down their children.

They went out of the town, came to the bridge and on it. From there they saw an embankment, a ditch and machine-guns on the other river side.
They understood everything. They realized that it was the end.

And suddenly silence fell, – the old man said. In one second silence came. Thousands of people all together got silent as one.

That was silence. That was opposition to the sound. That was death.

In other words, in the performance there are three types of silence.

Silence as kind of sound. That is like we do not hear sounds at the moment but we suggest that it exists.

Silence as an interrupted sound. For example, in pauses within a sound or a musical score. This belongs to the category of time and time manipulation in the performance.

And *silence as an opposition to sound*.

Thus, we defined that sometimes the absence of sound is not silence as the absence of lights is not darkness.

Can we hear silence? Yes. We can hear silence by its accent between sounds or after a sound.

But it is very important to understand that if an actor on the stage was talking and stopped, it is not silence. He just stopped talking. This is a pause. It belongs to the definition of time, which is of great importance, for example, in Chekhov's plays. But if an actor was talking and stopped, and we suddenly realized that something important has happened, for example, the hero died. Then silence starts to sound and influence spectators not less but even more emotionally and psychologically than sound or tragic music …

So, before talking about scenographic aspects of sound in theatre we must realize the two most important philosophic principles as a basis for creating a sound score for a performance.

First one. A performance creation is a creation of the other reality, the other cosmos, the other universe. And the sound score determines the style and unity of the performance, its atmosphere and sometimes even genre.

And the second one: One should be very attentive with the correlation of sound and silence in the performance taking into consideration what I have just said. Very often the correlation of sound and silence is like the correlation of life and death. This is very important not only for serious performances but also for humorous and laughable ones …

And to my mind, a performance becomes a real performance if it is more than the sum of all its components. There must be something else.

And there are, to my mind, three basic types of sound usage in a performance. Indeed there are more than three, but we will not talk about them in detail as it is under the limit of our topic.

So.

The first type is an illustration. It is the most simple in intellectual sense type though it requires taste and care. We illustrate an action, i.e. when the scene is laughable we use cheerful music or sound score. When we have a love scene, for example, we use lyric music or sounds that characterize the complicated inner world of the characters etc.

The second type is a counterpoint. It is also often used and makes spectators suffer with the characters.

When the scene is dramatic or tragic we use cheerful music or funny sound core. It produces the effect of bitter irony about imperfection of our life which is very close and clear for every person. This is laughter through tears and vice versa.

And finally, the third type. I would call it as estrangement or 'keeping out'. It is as if you watch the action from bird's-eye view or just on the side. From some distance.

This type is philosophic. It allows unifying very heterogeneous scenes – sad, cheerful, dramatic, lyric, – watch them and comprehend. It allows seeing the entire situation and finding its sense and meaning. And spectators who felt sorry for one hero and hated another suddenly keep out and see the great and mysterious river of life that brings bad and good heroes into eternity. A music fragment of 'The black monk' is of such type ...

To my mind, the entire history of theatre may be divided into three periods. I do not talk about national, ethnic or religious theatre. I talk about classic theatre.

The first period comprises the time from the great plays of ancient Greece to Shakespeare. That was theatre of word that performed the function of scenography and action besides general meaning and artistic functions.

The second period starts from Shakespearian times. Those are the 16th to 17th centuries. That was theatre where besides words action was brought to the fore-front. As a rule, it was connected with outer actions – battles, fights, murders etc. In this theatre, as in previous, bad and good characters act but their direct physical confrontation is inescapable.

The third period starts with Anton Pavlovich Chekhov's plays. He hid all actions inside. Action in his plays takes place in pauses.

Besides, Chekhov does not create bad or good characters.

And all his characters seem not to hear each other.

Due to the fact that action is deep inside, author stage directions-metaphors get special meaning. They are accurate, laconic and hard to carry out ...

Chekhov perhaps was the first to use stage direction as a metaphor. The most famous example is 'a sound of a broken string' from 'Cherry Orchard'. I saw many performances after this play, staged by very good directors with thoughtful sound and music score. But I can not say that at least one of them had good sound.

We understand what sound should mean.

As though somebody from the heaven, maybe God, sends us a sign saying that life on Earth is over, that everything on Earth is over and irreversible. Here is the great wisdom and great sorrow. We understand it. But this is like Paganini's or Mozart's notes. Just notes that are very hard to play to become pure music ...

Maybe, Chekhov could genially predict that someday theatre will have new sound abilities, and his metaphor will be possible to embody ...

Chekhov wanted simplicity. But simplicity is the most complicated.

This is how they tried to get the needed sound in Moscow Art Theatre about 100 years ago in 1904 in the first staging of 'The Cherry Orchard'.

They searched for the sound with the help of long strings of different thickness and metal hanging backstage from the top, from the gallery under gridiron to the floor, to the stage floor and a thick tousled rope that was drawn out, and it whipped the strings with various strength. Every blow was accompanied by a double-bass accord and a blow of vertically set two-handed saw. Chekhov said that this sound lacked sad key and it had to be taken by voice. 'Wrong, wrong', – he repeated, –

'more mournful, sad and soft'. They tried to add human voice. But they failed, and Chekhov was dissatisfied.

'This is so simple, it is all written there', – he said ...

There are certain archetypes of perception.

Sergey Prokofiev once searched for a timbre reproducing the sound of wind instruments used by crusaders. He said: 'I do not need the timbre of real tubes from the 13th century.

I need a timbre that would correspond to our view about the sound of these tubes.' He mixed up the sounds of various instruments achieving the necessary effect.

It is because there are archetypes of perception. And in spectators' conscious that, 'other' world must differ from the one we are used to.

Under the archetypes of perception I mean the birth of spectators' stable associations as a reaction on a certain sound, timbre, mode or rhythmic construction. This is connected with the place and time of action, with the atmosphere of the performance and other aspects of sound scenography ...

The archetypes of sounds perception are quite stable. This is due to a man's perception of the world in general and concrete national cultural tradition in particular. The same, for example, happens with the language.

Pay attention to the fact that almost in any language words that determine basic meanings, like the sun, bread, death, God and etc., do not change for centuries. Words that do not have such deep meanings die out, and new words appear instead of them.

But in contradistinction to the language, sound is more abstract and we may consider that certain archetypes of perception are distinctive for all people or at least the majority of them. It is because in some global sense we have one history and one culture.

More unique archetypes surely differ or even contradict each other ...

But if sounds or their imitation are perceived by spectators, if they are associated subconsciously with something, then they influence the spectators' psyche in the context of the performance or above it.

Ancient thinkers and sound designers' from various parts of the world belonging to various religious doctrines and philosophical schools for centuries tried to find and systemize associative relations and influence of sound on a man.

For example, sufistic wise men of Medieval India found the following systematization.

As in some other traditions all sounds by their default meaning, or as we today would say by the archetypes of perception, are divided into five groups: earth sounds, water sounds, fire sounds, air sounds and ether sounds.

Earth sound is unclear and monotonous, it bears shiver, activity and movements in a body, its form is like a half moon, its colour is yellow. All string instruments both with metal and venous strings as well as percussion instruments such as drums, cymbals and etc. represent earth sound.

Water sound is deep, its form is snake-like, its colour is green, and it is best heard in sea roar. Sounds of running water, highland streams, sound of rain knocking, sound of flowing water – they all have soft and living influence and a tendency to awaken imagination, dreams, affection and emotions.

Fire sound is very high, its form is screwed, its colour is red. It may be heard in thunder blow and in volcano eruption, in crackling of a fire. All these sounds have a tendency to scare.

Air sound is vibrating, its form is a zigzag, and its colour is blue. Its voice is heard during a thunderstorm, when the wind is blowing, and in morning breeze whisper. Its influence is destructive, wiping and piercing. Air sound finds its expression in all wind instruments, made of wood, copper or bamboo.

It has a tendency to burn fire in hearts. Air sound surpasses all other sounds as it is alive, and in every its aspect it causes ecstasy.

Ether sound is in itself, it has all forms and colours. It is a basis for all sounds. It is a shade, a semi-tone that does not stop. Its instrument is a human body as it reveals only with the help of a body.

Though it is all-penetrating it is not heard. It reveals to a person when he purifies his body from material qualities. A body may become an instrument when the internal space opens, when all its cavities and veins are free. Then the sound that exists in cosmos manifests itself. Ecstasy, insight, peace, fearlessness, excitement, joy and revelation are the results of this sound. This sound raises only those who opens themselves with the help of spiritual techniques known by mystics ...

We do not need to use either this or any other classification. While creating a sound score for a performance we may use our own sound system. It is significant to remember this to get full emotional and meaningful influence on spectators ...

I would like to say that creating and using new electronic sounds we must remember that their novelty in spectators; perception is short, and tomorrow they may seem old. But they may use archetypes of spectators' perception in a new way.

If a man does not want to see anything, he will close his eyes. But it will take much effort to hear nothing.

In ancient times thinkers of East and West realized what powerful influence on a man's soul may not only sounds but sound combinations have. That is what we understand under the notion of mode.

For example, philosopher Plato considered the most elevated, manly and morally perfect Dorian mode. You can imagine it visually as a scale from the note mi. This mode, by the way, was very popular in ancient Jewish music.

Phrygian (scale from re) was considered exciting and suitable for war whereas Lydian (scale from do, the one we know as a major scale) was considered to be womanish, tender, relaxing and so unsuitable to the up-bringing of a free person.

In the ideal state Plato allowed only two modes: Dorian in peace and Phrygian in the time of war ...

It is important for us composing a sound score for a performance, i.e. a specific virtual world, to remember that we create our own harmonic system.

This system influences spectators. In some sense, the influence of sound combinations on a man may be compared to the Chinese acupuncture. The correct placement of needles in concrete points of a human body makes a necessary effect.

Of course, our perception changes. But quite slowly. For example, the most unpleasant for a man is a baby's cry. It is used in sound weapon …

You know that the acting ensemble and the atmosphere of the performance were the support that helped to create Moscow Art Theatre. They made it the best theatre of the world in some period of time.

Stanislavski created sound score very extremely seriously and detailed.

'Behind the stage orioles and cuckoos cry, zhaleykas play, trees are fallen, disharmonic hums, billiards balls roll, then some long and scaring sound blows up as though something heavy falls down to the strings, hums and roars,' – a critic wrote about the premiere of 'The Cherry Orchard'. The last 'something heavy falls down to the strings' was as you guess a try to make the effect of a broken string we have already mentioned.

In creation of the sound score all actors and workers took part. Today it seems funny.

The actors twittered in birds' voices, Stanislavski himself was searching for a sound of frog croaking with a comb кэym in his hands.

'Do not forget about mosquitoes,' – Stanislavski wrote in his director's plan.

'Silence, then birds are crying, mosquitoes overcoming, a new flock flew.'

Chekhov did not like it, he argued with Stanislavski.

'May I kill at least 2 mosquitoes?' – Stanislavski asked Chekhov, being upset. 'You may', – Chekhov answered, – 'but in the other play my hero will say: What an amazing place – no mosquitoes at all.' And I will write a new play, and it will start with how wonderfully silent! No birds, no dogs, no cuckoos, no owl, no nightingale, no watches, no bells and no cricket …'

THE RELATIONSHIP BETWEEN SOUND AND THEATRE

Scott Gibbons is an electroacoustic composer whose best known theatre sound works have been for the Socìetas Raffaello Sanzio (which include *Genesi: From the Museum of Sleep, Tragedia Endogonidia*). He characterizes his work as a two-fold exploration, into the possibilities of natural acoustic sound on the one hand, and those of audio technology on the other … often focusing around frequencies that are at the outermost limits of human hearing, and embracing quietness as a central element. He wrote the following 'statement' specifically for this volume.

4.4   Scott Gibbons: Statement on the Relationship Between Sound and
        Theatre

What sounds are in this space?
Are they few in number, or many?
Are there any missing, or any in excess?
Are there some that may be imperceptible?
Can they be individually identified?
What is the nature of each?
Malevolent, benevolent, indifferent?
Masculine, feminine?
Is it an object, character, or scenographic device?
Does it move, or is it fixed?
Is it static or dynamic?
What can be known about its depth, its mass, its height, its texture, its consistency?
Does it invoke other sensory perceptions; is it invoked by other senses?
What is its trajectory, its age, its expiry?
Does it belong here?
Is it interesting, evocative, emotive?
Can one have a direct experience of it, or is awareness about it only inferred?
What is its relationship with me?
Is it in fact in this space, or is its presence elsewhere being made known through
some invasive process?
What is its relationship with other objects-characters-scenographies-sensations?
Does it belong to another, emanate from, or is it the cause of (...)?
Could it be understood as 'sound', 'noise', 'music', 'voice', or 'speech'?
Does it assist, complicate, elucidate, hide, inform or provoke?
Does it also perceive me/you/them/us; and if so, does this engage it?
Is it sentient?

How would it answer these questions?
How would another person answer these questions?

5

Five Sound Designers in Their Own Words

The previous chapter collected extracts together from outside the traditional scope of theatre sound pedagogy. Chapter 5 rejoins the history of theatre practice and brings it up to date through the words of sound designers reflecting on their own creative practices, processes and theories. I am aware that these are all male voices. Many of the most innovative of the new generation of theatre sound designers are women, and in some future volume or edition of this one, I hope to be able to rectify this omission.

We start with Napier, from whom we have already heard in Chapters 2 and 3.

NAPIER BEYOND REALISM

Resident at the Old Vic, during the late 1920s and 1930s, Frank Napier designed and performed the sound on some of the first London productions of key twentieth-century modernist texts such as *The Cherry Orchard*, and also on the classical repertoire. This was at a time when traditional prop-based techniques were still dominant, but used alongside emergent technologies of recorded or electrically produced sound. We have access to his insights thanks to the popularization of amateur theatre in the years between the wars, which led to a number of books on professional technique aimed at the amateur market. In this excerpt he shares, with his amateur readership, his insights from working on the cutting edge of European modernism.

5.1 Extract from Napier, F (1936) *Noises Off* (London, Muller), p. 106

In certain kinds of production realism is deliberately avoided in the setting, lighting, acting, and so on. These various branches of dramatic art are treated in some unusual manner suitable to the play that is being produced. Plays about machinery as handled in the Russian theatre afford an obvious example of this point. In these the actors are, so to speak, mechanized in speech, movement, costume, and make-up. The setting also abounds in geometrical shapes suggesting machinery. Some plays can be produced with the accent on the fantastic or the grotesque. Others, poetic plays, are sometimes handled in the manner of modern ballet and all the movements and gestures become almost those of a formal dance. One hesitates to describe these kinds of treatment as 'formalization' or 'conventionalization' or 'stylization' or any of the other 'izations' or 'isms'; the precise meanings of which are so hard to determine (I have chosen the first for want of a better), but, whatever they are called, it is clear that the off-stage effects must undergo the same kind of treatment as the rest of the play, otherwise there will be no artistic unity.

It will doubtless be asked, How can a noise off be made in the manner of modern ballet? Visions rise in the mind of artistic youths armed with drumsticks doing arabesques from bass drum to thunder-sheet. But what I mean is this, that in the dance, natural movement is 'tidied up' and arranged to form a pattern, so noises off can be 'tidied up' and arranged to form a pattern of sound which approximates to music. Indeed, music is frequently substituted outright for such effects as battles and storms.

In tidying up movement to form in dance, the choreographer has to deal with questions of time and space, but in tidying up noise, the only factor is time. Therefore formalized sound effects automatically become rhythmical.

Let us consider some examples. In 'Le Viol de Lucrece', by André Obey, the crowd-shouts in the last scene are formalized, and the same treatment is used in Thornton Wilder's translation. Unfortunately I have not seen either version performed, but I am told that in the French production of Michel St. Denis with Le Compagnie des Quinze the crowd was brought on to the stage and employed there more or less continuously in making groupings and poses indicative of sorrow with vocal utterance to match. The vocal utterance was closely comparable to keening, which is simply formal lamentation.

The translation suggests that the crowd should be kept off-stage and used as sound only. The situation in the play is this. Junius Brutus, friend to Lucrece's husband, Collatine, is making a long funeral oration over the body of Lucrece. To this the crowd react not with continuous sound but with single utterances on definite cues. Each member of the crowd cries, 'Ha!', tuned to the emotion proper to each moment, so that the total effect of the crowd sound is that of chords punctuating the speech of Brutus, the soloist. It must, I think, be tremendously exciting in performance.

Another example of the same kind of effect, this time on-stage, is afforded by the formal 'laughter in court' in the one-act play, 'Murder Trial', by Sidney Box. In this instance, whenever the judge makes a joke, all the characters (except the prisoner) laugh in unison, 'Ha! Ha! Ha! Ha!', four times on descending notes. The effect, by its very artificiality, is very amusing.

In these three examples it is the fact that the effects are rhythmical, either in themselves or in relation to their context, that gives them their formality. In searching for an example of a formalized noise off other than a crowd or battle effect I remember that in a certain production of Flecker's 'Hassan' that I saw some years ago, the

Procession of Protracted Death was presented in this way. A portion of the cyclo-rama was lit with red, and upon it was cast the shadow of Masruh, the executioner, moving up and down as though in the act of thrashing. The principal sounds that could be heard were the cries of the tortured, the crack of the whip, and a heavy crash of chains on the stage. These sounds were arranged in order, timed with the swing of the shadow, and repeated in a constantly recurring phrase – "Brump! Crack! Scream! Brump! Crack! Scream!" and so on. Pure rhythm.

As it happens the effect was not a success. Though logical, it was done, as I remember, in too heavy-handed a manner. There was no suggestion of the subtleties of torture, which are foreshadowed in the speeches of the Kaliph in the Divan scene. However, that does not alter the fact that it is rhythm that formalizes a sound effect.

Therefore, for any given effect, a rhythm must be found, which does not destroy the recognizable character of the effect. Fortunately this is not difficult, since most sounds are intrinsically rhythmical or can be repeated in a suitable tempo.

PAUL ARDITTI ON THEATRE SOUND DESIGN IN THE DIGITAL AGE

Arditti was one of a number of professional sound designers (others included Mic Pool, Chris Shutt, Paul Groothuis and Steve Brown) working in the subsidized British repertory theatres of the late 1980s at a time when digital technology whetted an appetite for the more creative use of sound in theatre. As a member of the National Theatre sound department under Peter Hall, he had access to emergent digital technology that was too expensive for most commercial producers or regional reps at the time. The National also gave him the opportunity to collaborate with composers such as Harrison Birtwistle. When Peter Hall left the National to form his own eponymous company, Arditti went with him and worked on a succession of productions which used innovatory sound systems and concepts. Arditti was one of the first to fully exploit digital samplers (designed ostensibly for use on rap music) for the playback of sound effects, often in partnership with composers and musicians, who could be made to trigger sounds from a variety of musical interfaces (including keyboards, drums, marimbas and adapted lutes).

Arditti has worked collaboratively in devised productions with directors such as Simon McBurney, and occasionally on musicals (such as *Billy Elliot*, with his long term collaborator Stephen Daldry, for which Arditti won a Tony award in 2009) but is better known as a sound designer for plays. As Head of Sound at the Royal Court from 1993 to 2002, Arditti was able to encourage consideration of sound in the development of new writing. He was the first sound designer to win two Olivier Awards, one for a musical, one for a play.

5.2   Interview With Paul Arditti, Conducted at the Almeida Theatre, 15 January 2007 For This Volume

Ross Brown (RB): *Is it fair to say that the sound department of the National Theatre in the late 1980s was seminal in the emergence of theatre sound design as one of the key dramaturgies of the digital age?*

Paul Arditti (PA): One of the big things that I remember from my time at the National was a chap called Nic Jones, a very good sound designer who doesn't do theatre anymore, but I remember going into this little studio at the National, he was sitting there with a Yamaha SPX reverb, which was one of the early generation of fairly affordable digital reverb units, which had a little freeze button on it which allowed you to record a second or so of audio. He was using that to create a complicated montage of an electronic pinball machine he was making out of individual plinks, plonks, clicks and whacks he'd recorded off a CD. He was recording them by hitting this freeze button to trigger playback in the manner of a little sampler onto a four-track tape recorder and building up this thing in a combined digital/analogue way and I thought, My God! This guy's spending so much time doing this and to such a degree of detail, rather than just taking a sound effect of somebody playing pinball, he actually was building it musically, rhythmically, in the manner of the music of that time, which was bands like *The Art of Noise* [producer Trevor Horn's electronic ensemble], who'd started to use early samplers. But he [Jones] was controlling every single sound, every individual percussive element and that set me thinking.

The same guy also set me thinking by playing thunder from a MIDI [*musical instrument digital interface*] keyboard through a sampler in the Olivier Theatre and every time he hit the keyboard a tremendous three dimensional sound came out. All the lights on the mixing desk flashed together in a way that I'd never seen before, as the sampler simultaneously output different 'lines' of thunder from eight different channels at once. The way that they randomly flickered around seemed to be incredibly organic. At that time, sound playback was usually linear: recorded in 1 or 2 or 4 or 16 tracks, and played back sequentially; suddenly you have this thing – a sampler – that almost made up its own mind about which tracks it played where and how it distributed a natural sound around the auditorium.

RB: *So he was triggering this from a MIDI keyboard?*

PA: Yes, at that time there was no other kind of electronic control, it was a MIDI keyboard plugged into a sampler, with a single thunder sample loaded off a floppy disk. The low notes would play a rumble and the top notes would play a brilliant crack and it was all routed randomly out and you just got a very natural sound. You could play up to 16 or however many voices the thing had. Enough to make it sound brilliant. Which is an idea I immediately stole and used on Peter Hall's *Late Shakespeares* season.

RB: *Did the operator have to perform this exactly the same each night?*

PA: Well the other thing that really appealed to me as somebody that came from a musical way of thinking, was that you could alter the way the sound effects sounded at a given performance, in the same way as an actor might change his delivery of a line. This particular show I was watching Anthony Hopkins playing Lear, and as he would shout "Blow winds!" or whatever, thunder would crack appropriately, it wasn't just a sound effect that came in on cue, but a living, musical response to what was going on onstage.

The other thing was that it was instantaneous and mechanically silent; there was no clicking or short gap with hiss before the sound effect started. We were using 7½*ips* [inches per second] tape cartridges at the National at that time, rather than reel to reel (because it was instant start and with DBX noise reduction was pretty free from hiss) ... even then, it was a question of press a button and wait a short gap and then the sound effect would come. Whereas the sampler was absolutely instantaneous and adjustable in the moment, so you played a low rumble with your left hand and then you whacked the keyboard as hard as you could with your right hand and you created a piercing crack ... it was like conducting a little orchestra. It was velocity sensitive, it was pitch sensitive and it was actor sensitive. What it suddenly did was make the sound operator a musician, which opened up a huge book of exciting chapters (and also, some union issues to be honest).

There were very few sound operators who were interested in operating that kind of show because it required a creative input and required taking a risk. I loved it but I wasn't a very good sound operator. And then, pretty soon, sequencers came along. I bought my first Macintosh computer in 1990 with the Vision sequencer, which enabled me to record performances off a keyboard into the computer and then play them back, which meant that I suddenly had a tool which was giving me unparalleled control over sound effects, but was also a tool which musicians understood. I was doing sound effects on a piano keyboard, using tempos, key changes, all sorts of things that every musician can understand.

Musicians began to realize that they were part of this as well. I came across a composer called Steven Edwards who worked initially as an assistant to Harrison Birtwistle on the *Late Shakespeares* that Peter Hall was directing. Harrison Birtwistle wrote some music – dots on paper; we employed some musicians to play it, sort of conventional theatre music. My job was to put microphones on the musicians and make them sound good, put a bit of reverb on, that's fine.

But Steven Edwards was also thinking about his own projects, and he and I started working with samplers to do music in the theatre without using musicians playing conventional instruments.

Meanwhile, Harrison Birtwistle, who had been working in IRCAM in Paris for some years, producing strange tones and drones from sound waves, came to us with a big fat 24 track tape and said 'can you copy tracks 3 and 7 because these are the ones that I want to use as drones on this show?'. We duly did this, realizing at the same time that if we used a looping sampler we could actually do the same thing that he'd taken years to produce, very very quickly, but taking musical instruments, the weather, elements – not electronic synthy sounds, but real, organic sound – as our starting point. We started to do things that we now take for granted: loop them; pitch change them; edit them; morph them in various different ways. We discovered that we could do that very quickly in a sampler, which then gave us a basis to start using samplers in the theatre as musical instruments at the same time as using them as sound effects machines. Which meant that there was a wonderful period during the late 80s and most of the 90s where musicians and sound designers were quite happily working together, mixing up each other's worlds, and doing musical sound effects, music made from sound effects, and this coincided with Steven Edwards and I doing a lot of work with Peter Hall and Peter Hall having a very open mind about it at this time.

So, we would chop up oceans into individual waves and play these individual waves, triggered all separately through different speakers to create a totally controllable and, we felt, very interesting seascape. Whereas before we might have just played a series of 1 or 2 different seas through the speakers. And also, what Steven Edwards brought to this process was the musicianship. So, whereas I would start off from a basis of sound effects, he'd start off from a basis of pitch and rhythm. He always preferred for a musician to be the ultimate controller at the end of the day, rather than a technician.

RB: *So, were sequencers and computerized show control not just a return, in effect, to pre-recorded tapes?*

PA: Only to the extent of allowing us to make a show repeatable. What we discovered was the performance aspect was fine for one show and one particular operator, but the needs of the industry are that a show usually needs to be passed on to more than one person. And the infrastructure is not as it is with music, to have properly trained deputies, so quite often the people you're dealing with are not necessarily highly trained. You could look at sound in the same way as a piece of scenery sometimes in a show, in that however beautiful, complex, three-dimensional and artistically achieved it is, you want it to be the same every night, so that the actors who are probably not doing the same thing every night, have a structure they can work within, where they feel secure.

These days, the musical is one of the few forms of theatre where the sound operator remains genuinely creative. The sound operator, for instance on *Billy Elliot*, has a massive mixing desk with all the microphones from all the actors and all the microphones from all the musicians as well as the sound effects, and blends them live every night. And takes account of different actors on stage and different musicians playing in the pit on a night-by-night and a second-by-second basis, and that is a performance.

In a straight play then I think it's a like a piece of scenery that needs to stay the same.

Ultimate reliability is the technician's Holy Grail. It's one of the things we always struggled for in the early years of digital technology, because for a while it was fabulous, but it wasn't designed for use in the theatre and it used to fall over quite a lot of the time. Everyone who's had a crashed computer can know how stressful that can be, and if it's in the middle of a show then that's tough. So we put a lot of time and energy into developing systems that are completely reliable and are exactly the same every night. I don't see that as a limitation of my creative freedom because I'm selfishly leaving on the press night and once I leave it I want the show to stay the same, unless it requires a deliberate change.

There is a range of operator control required, from mixing a big musical, to operating a straight play with a single or few sound effects in it (and everywhere in between). I think different types of plays need different degrees of intervention by the operator and different degrees of performability.

RB: *Simon McBurney (of the collaborative devising company Complicite) famously never finishes a show; it carries on evolving and is rarely the same night after night.*

PA: Yeah. You need to have all your wits about you when you work with him because everything changes all the time. But that's not to say that when you've rehearsed something in the afternoon it shouldn't happen in the evening. I was working for Complicite in a technologically intermediate time. It was all digital, but some of it was played back on mini disc and CD and some of it was sampler-based stuff. It was quite hard work to keep up because it took quite a lot of programming. Nowadays the programming is very quick on computers and so one can keep up with the changes that you're coming up with as well as the changes that Simon's coming up with. But also you can rely on something that you've done five minutes before a show actually happening as you've programmed it, as opposed to relying on the memory of an operator and a scribbled note in a script. What you do get very good at with McBurney is squeezing an awful lot of work into a very short time, and again, technology has made that a lot easier.

RB: *A couple of years ago you designed the sound for a production of the Dogme film Festen, and the reviews — notably Susannah Clapp's and Michael Billington's,[1] raved about the sound design with unprecedented hyperbole.*

PA: There's a design award given out by the Evening Standard every year and the sound, lighting and set of *Festen* jointly won the 2005 design award. I think that is more important than any of those reviews, in acknowledging Jean Kalman and Ian [McNeil] and myself as a creative team. This creative team came up with a design in which each element was very sympathetic to the other elements. The sound was very very simple in that show, very simple elements, most of it not very loud, very subtle, very clear, simple images — of a girl crying, some water dripping, a high

---

[1] It's the sounds one remembers most. The clink of a spoon on a wine glass. The laughter of a child. The gush of running water. All these reverberate through *Festen*, the Dogme film famously made into a play and running at the Lyric Shaftesbury in London. And, at the year's end, I find Paul Arditti's remarkable soundscape still echoes in my brain and unlocks memories of an event that signifies a major shift in the development of modern theatre: the rebirth of tragedy (*The Guardian*, 22 December 2004).

pitched sound which sounded like a tinnitus headache – it wasn't an expansive soundtrack, it was quite small. The lighting – very bright side lights, almost exclusively. The set – black, invisible set, the blackest fabric we could get with each of the side flats honed to a point so that light didn't reflect off the edges of them; black carpet and then a beautiful wooden table that just glided down from downstage to upstage, and a bed that rose up through the floor in darkness; almost just two elements really. A lot of work went into that simplicity.

I think that if sound design is going anywhere, it's in the direction of saying 'I am a grown up member of the creative team, I have a design history behind me, I have form, I have imagination, I know when I'm wanted, I know when I'm not wanted' – which I think is really important – and 'I demand to be recognized as important an element as the set and the lighting.'

And also, 'I'll understand when I'm left out – and that's as much a design decision as putting something in. I think that's the way its going. It's a human thing; it's not a technical thing.'

HANS PETER KUHN ON THEATRE AND SONIC ART

Kuhn cannot simply be described as a theatre sound designer, although his influence in the field has been significant. Perhaps he is better described as a theatrical sound artist. He has made sound environments and music for theatre in collaboration with Luc Bondy, Claus Peymann and, since the late 1970s, with Robert Wilson, among many others. He describes himself as one of the most 'prominent representatives of an all-embracing art with site-specific concepts'. His light and sound installations 'meld elements of theatre and performance with an intensive spatial sound-research and a concentrated play with auditory phenomena'. He has also worked extensively in dance theatre and ballet, with dancers like Laurie Booth, Suzushi Hanayagi, Junko Wada and Sasha Waltz, and received the 1990 Bessie Award for the music to Dana Reitz's *Suspect Terrain*.

In the foreword to Kuhn's book *Licht und Klang*, Bernd Shultz writes:

Like most contemporary sound artists, Hans Peter Kuhn equates sound and noise; with wilful indifference, he takes what he needs from the rich acoustic material provided by the sounds of everyday life. He also explores the juxtaposition of sound and silence pioneered by John Cage. Hans Peter Kuhn can be considered a precursor of some aspects of pop culture – techno and the latest digital-sound-processing styles – because of the way in which he electronically manipulates the surfaces of sound materials, gives them dynamics and rhythm, chops them up and recomposes them, and because of the easy confidence with which he uses the most advanced digital technology, samplers and computers.

The ways in which Hans Peter Kuhn makes use of acoustic material – from the human voice to ephemeral everyday sounds – are much richer and more varied than is the case with many other artists working at the intersection of music and the plastic arts. Sometimes his sound compositions are almost theatrical: he often uses a large number of loudspeakers and they come to 'play' an almost individu-alized 'role'. Sometimes he transforms the acoustic *objets trouvés* or jetsam of everyday life in such a way that the surface of the sounds is 'enlarged', as if under a microscope. This procedure engenders an entirely abstract realm of sound, which forecloses any specific associations. Sometimes nothing but matter itself seems to speak: a tone so deep that it is inaudible to the human ear causes an object to vibrate and can thus be 'seen'; or programmed impulses in a field of loudspeakers generate a rhythmic structure of electronic sounds that extends over space.

Not unlike Robert Wilson, Hans Peter Kuhn has developed a 'durative' aesthetics that is based on the simultaneous perception of both light and sound. Light creates a sense of presence and duration in space. Sequences of different sounds and noises create a sense of change. Sound thereby fulfils several func-tions: it creates a space that supplements or extends the space that is experienced visually, and it makes the viewer discover and enter an imaginary realm of imag-ined action. (Shultz in Kuhn 2000: 11–12)

5.3   Interview With Hans Peter Kuhn, Conducted in February 2007 For This
          Volume

Ross Brown (RB): *Your theatre works with Robert Wilson and your two installations for Artangel in London in the early 90s (HG and Five Floors) were very influential to theatre sound designers/composers and sound students in the UK who were trying to break away from the literary tradition of British theatre and move sound 'beyond the era of sound effects' (to use Peter Sellars' phrase.) Your work seemed to epitomize sound as part of a collaborative dramaturgy (rather than an afterthought) and suggested that sound designers could be creative theatre artists. Were you aware of the impact you had, and does theatre still hold any attraction for you as a sonic artist?*

Hans Peter Kuhn (HPK): Actually, no. I had no idea of the impact this had on the British theatre (sound) scene. I did much theatre work from the 70s to the 90s and started doing complex soundworks there in the mid-70s, when there was only sound as sound effects (the door bell rings, when the visitor comes) or as music to cover the noise of the scene change or as dramatic music (the hero dies – a largo comes in). Many things have changed since then and I am aware that I was some sort of influence to the German and American theatre scene, but besides a few touring plays I never really produced in Britain.

To answer the second part of your question, I have to admit that the fire is pretty much down. I still do every now and then a little theatre work, but it is mainly very off-off-off Broadway and not happening in the big scene anymore. I am not so inter-ested anymore. The point is that in theatre you always work in teams, which is OK, of course, and sound is never the first player. You always have to compromise and honestly I was tired of that. And I feel much better now, doing my purely own work, where I am solely responsible, but where I am also the main figure, which is nice too.

RB: *I think your influence in Britain was actually largely through the Artangel installations, funnily enough, rather than your theatre work (although there was something about HG that was deeply theatrical).*

HPK: Right, *HG* was quite theatrical, but *HG* was also a collaboration with Bob Wilson, whose visuals are very dramatic. And it is funny enough, although my solo work never had these strong dramatic images, that when I started with making installations in the early 80s, I was told by the art scene that my work was too theatrical/not enough 'art'. But that changed since the young people now are mixing all media.

RB: *Your work has never struck me as purely sonic (like music) but to be about making poetic, synaesthetic juxtapositions between sounds and images, or objects, or actions. There is this new word I've come across: sonification – associating sounds to actions, like beeps/unlocking your car, or camera shutter sound/taking a picture with a mobile phone. You seem to do this, but in a far more poetic way. Is this right, and is this something that still interests you?*

HPK: This is exactly what I am thinking of, only – to be very honest – exactly not in the way the industry does, as you mention it with the beeps when opening a car and so on. I am just now in Japan, this is a place with a very high amount of noise-making daily life objects, very often totally without any sense. The oil burner beeps when the tank is empty – as if you wouldn't realise that since it turns off at that moment as well! The rice cooker plays a German Christmas song when the cooking process is finished, but you still have to wait five minutes before you open it so the rice gets steamed. Total nonsense. I am waiting for the first guy to show up on TV who can whistle all the different melodies the trains have to announce the next station. And all these sounds are purely electronic garbage.

Anyhow, to come back to the point: I think that our perception is not working in separate sections, rather in a concert of all senses. You do not hear music alone, at the same time you see the orchestra (or the bookshelf with the loudspeakers), you smell the perfume of your neighbour (or the food smell from the kitchen), you feel the temperature and humidity of the space; you can even tell (with closed eyes) how big the space is you are in. The excitement before the concert starts or the quietness at night at home alone, listening to your favourite record – all these informations come to you at the same time while you are listening to the music. And they influence you, they influence the music. It is different music under different conditions. The same is true, of course, for all visuals. The famous film that gets two different sound scores is with the first sound score a comedy and with the second a tragedy. So I try to make pieces that deal with this phenomenon. I set up a visual image and combine it with an aural image, but they are separate and disconnected, the visual has its own 'story' as the aural has another one. So you experience a world that has two parallel simultaneous realities. And I guess that is what makes them what you call poetic. It is very hard to speak of one's own work as being poetic, other people can do, still I am happy if it appears as that. But of course I like the work to be some sort of deep and meaningful, but without a direct message. I hope that people change their mood or their speed when being in my spaces but I don't want to tell them how to behave. I want everybody to develop their own story (or none, which is OK too), not to listen to my story. And that maybe makes the work some sort of mysterious but it also gives a meaning.

Another point is that I try to set a visual statement, something people can rest their eyes on, so they are visually busy and that calms them down and they have time to listen. There is a famous story of a physicist and Nobel Prize winner, sorry I forgot his name. He was asked by an interviewer how he got his idea, how the process was when he realized his big achievement. The physicist answered: I was standing at a bus stop, waiting for the bus. When the bus came and stopped, the door opened and I put my foot on the first step ... I suddenly understood how everything goes together, everything was clear to me at that moment. The interviewer replied: But please, your work is written down in three big books and alone the formulas in it are not understandable to most people, and you say you got this all in the split second of putting your foot on the step? Well, said the physicist, we usually think of time as a linear thing – a line that connects the yesterday with the today and continues into the tomorrow. But it is possible to think that there is not only this one timeline. There might be more timelines available and they might have another direction to ours. And see, he said, when I was standing there at the bus stop, one of these other timelines, maybe one that is perpendicular to ours, crossed my timeline and I had an indefinite amount of time to travel on this other timeline, before my own timeline continued.

I love this story, because it explains exactly how I feel about my works. I establish a visual space that exists at the crossing point of two timelines and when you get there, you can stop your visual life for a short moment, but then you have a huge amount of time to listen.

RB: *You have said that you found the compromise of working in theatre frustrating, but I'd be interested in knowing a little more about the ways in which you collaborate with directors – or auteurs like Wilson. To what extent were you a partner in a collaborative creative process of devising?*

HPK: Well, I will have to make some statements at this point I guess. First I have to say that I worked indeed for 25 years in theatre and mostly in the big houses of (continental) Europe and the United States, so I had my share and I took it for quite a while. Second there are – or at least there were – two types of directors/theatre artists (in German we have the word *Theatermacher* – 'theatre maker' which is quite nice). One is the traditional mise-en-scène, the head of the play who usually has a literature background. For these people theatre is text. All other things are decoration for the text. So for these directors the very first person to speak to and to deal with is the dramaturg, next are the actors and that's about it. All other people are, let's call it 'not so important' – nice to have them here but actually not really necessary. Of course they would never say so aloud, but you can tell when you work with them. I had the joy to work with a number of this kind of people and still I was lucky because they were the best in the gang, I got all the stars. Nevertheless their interest in music, or worse in sound, was close to zero. You can imagine that the ambition level does not get really very high under these circumstances.

But then there are these other guys, they are not many and the most famous ones are Americans, that are among others Robert Wilson, Liz LeCompte of The Wooster Group, Robert LePage (Canadian, sorry), Robert Ashley. Of course you do not have to like all of these people's work, but their attitude against sound/music/light/video and other media in theatre is totally opposite. And I was lucky to have had the chance to work with Bob Wilson for 20 years and more than 30 productions. He allowed me to develop a totally separate sound world to his images, and since his skills are visual rather, I was very free in what I did, and maybe only because he was happy that there was somebody who took care of that part. Nevertheless I was able to make my own decisions and create my own work – as a part of a bigger production. Of course he was still the director and had a say in what was done or used and what not, but this is not the problem. I usually was participating in all rehearsals from the first day on.

I had my equipment around me, in the beginning it was three or four tape recorders, later came samplers and then hard disk recording systems. There was a mixer and some loudspeakers – of course not the full set, which was only on stage and in the auditorium. I pre-produced in the rehearsal studio and finished the work in the sound studio and in the final stage rehearsals. While Wilson was working with the actors on a scene I was preparing some sounds and played them immediately, so that the scene had a sound score from the very first minute. The result was of course that the sound/music became an integral part of the piece, it was not an addition. It was a bit like in an opera. And of course when the scene got changed I had to probably change my score as well, but my score also made Bob sometimes change the scene to fit. I had my sound library with me (in the beginning on ¼″ tape, then on audiocassette, then on DAT, then on CD and last on a hard drive – from very big to very small) and if we needed something I did not have, I went out to make recordings for it.

Now as I mentioned I did all this for 20 years and it was fun, but there comes a point, where even longstanding collaborations don't pull off anymore. And for me it was a point where I could not really come up with new ideas anymore, I felt empty. At the same time I had already had quite a lot of success with my own installations I have to admit, although I believe that I am modest, but it is different if the newspapers write about a piece and you do not get mentioned at all, or sometimes your work gets named with another person, or on the other hand you are the person they write about simply because it is your piece and nobody else is involved. So the decision was very easy. Since then I did a few smaller theatre productions, actually the biggest was with The Wooster Group, but mainly I left the 'dramatic' theatre. I am still making music for dancers, that is something I really like to do and will also continue doing.

But there is another point: even in a more or less perfect collaboration it is still so, that your ideas have to work together with everything else. It starts with the text. You have to deal with the text and spoken text is of course an acoustic event that competes with sound and music or rather vice versa. So if your head is full of nice sound ideas you have to cut down because you simply can't do all of that, nobody would hear the actors anymore. Of course you can give them microphones to make them louder, but then you turn up the music level and the game starts again, no chance. This can be interesting of course to create a sound score that deals with this situation and I did these things for many years. But as I said there is a point where you want to do the real thing.

Another opponent in theatre is the set. The set designers have beautiful ideas for a wonderful set. Good. Then you come and say: well, if we want to hear the sound in a good quality the loudspeakers have to hang somehow visually in the image. I totally understand that they hate this idea, since I hate loudspeakers too (visually!! – and I am happy that there are new technologies coming up that allow people to get rid of the big black boxes). So what do you do? OK, some parts of the set get made of gauze and you place the speaker behind it. Or you only have a stereo system at the portal. Two huge arrays of black boxes and a cluster in the centre in front of an Italian gold portal from 1865. Super!

Another thing – you want sound coming from all over the place. OK, many theatres today have surround speakers installed. I am afraid it is a bit my fault. I started hanging speakers in auditoriums in the 70s and it was almost sacrilege to do this. And I have to admit it did not look very nice, too. But usually the auditorium is dark during the performance, so I did not care so much. Maybe I just got lazy. But when I do my installations I have none of these problems and I can think about the work rather then about how to hide some loudspeakers. Is that good enough a reason?

RB: *You say that sound is never the first player in theatre. Do you think this is because of the tradition of literary dramaturgy or a preference for the visual?*

HPK: I do not expect sound to be the number one in theatre, but I do expect that it gets a real player. It is a fact that the actors are the first and most prominent parts of a production, that is clear, and it is no problem for me to be in the background, but still I want to be respected and acknowledged in my work and that is missing in the dramatic theatre, or at least it was for the time I worked in it.

RB: *Could this change? Should it?*

HP: I do not think it should change; there is the opera where music is the main part, which is all right. But as the modern opera singers get better trained as speakers these days, so they don't sound so dumb anymore when they speak, the theatre people should also open themselves to the other media. But in a way they are doing this already. The productions of today look a lot different from the ones 10 or 20 years ago. Nevertheless it's too late for me; I am not really interested anymore, sorry.

RB: *So what are your professional ambitions now? What do you want to be doing in five or ten years' time?*

HPK: Oops! At the moment I hope to continue with what I am doing for another while, I am still full of ideas and don't really urge for anything else. I am changing all the time anyhow; I am always looking into other areas and combine them with my concepts and by this of course my work changes and also the materials I work with change. In the last three or four years, for example, steel and marble became very important to me and I use these materials more and more, so I got a bit sculptural, who knows where this will end. Still I think that I will stay with sound and light as the main figures on my stage. Whenever people ask me, why do you do these things, what is your motive? I always answer that it is very simple, I simply love hearing. I like to hear. I appreciate the big sensation of listening and hearing. Fortunately nature and health allowed that both of my ears are in very good shape (a little bit age-reduced of course) and I can still enjoy listening to the world. It's fun!

JOHN COLLINS ON DEVISING SOUND WITH THE WOOSTER GROUP AND ERS

John Collins began his sound design career on Target Margin Theater's production of *Titus Andronicus*. He then designed and operated sound for the playwright and director Richard Foreman, among others. In late 1991, Collins founded Elevator Repair Service Theater (ERS) and directed its first production, *Mr. Antipyrine, Fire Extinguisher*. Collins has directed or co-directed every ERS show since, while continuing to work as a sound and lighting designer for other companies and directors. The company's work has been seen all over New York as well as in some of Europe's biggest festivals. The company's recent work, *No Great Society*, recently completed a run at New York Theatre Workshop. *Gatz*, ERS' marathon presentation of the entire text of *The Great Gatsby*, won many accolades on tour in the United States and Europe. Also in 2008, ERS premiered a new piece at New York Theatre Workshop based on William Faulkner's *The Sound and the Fury*. After 1993, John left his job with Richard Foreman and went to work as resident sound designer for The Wooster Group. He has received two Bessie Awards for his design work with The Wooster Group and two Drama Desk Award nominations. While becoming freelance in 2003, he continues to consult for The Wooster Group on sound and periodically tours with the company.

5.4   Interview with John Collins Conducted in February 2007 For This Volume

---

Ross Brown (RB): *Peter Sellars — an erstwhile collaborator with The Wooster Group — wrote in an Introduction to a theatre sound textbook that we are 'beyond the age of sound effects' and described a 'total program of sound which speaks to theatre as ontology'. Sellars talks about sound as 'place' and talks about connections between the sounds of the inner-self and the outer whole. He celebrates the condition of living in cacophony. This all seems to point to a theatre that has gone way beyond being the 'client' of sound design, has become 'aural' at its heart. My first question is: do you buy any of this?*

John Collins (JC) My answer: yes. OK – I'll give you more than that. I haven't seen Sellars' Introduction, but I agree with your assessment generally. If we are to take 'sound effects' to mean a system of adding sounds to performance in a decorative or superficial way, then yes, I think, when I'm feeling hopeful, that theatre and performance (however we may define or distinguish them) are tending to incorporate sound into the fabric of what is performed in a much more meaningful way, although there is still quite a lot of 'sound effects' work going on out there.

Design, in the theatre world in general, is becoming more sophisticated but still largely operating according to a very old (and deadly) paradigm. Designers have meetings, make drawings and visit rehearsals occasionally but are not the sort of primary creators that playwrights, actors and (sometimes) directors are. So their work gets added on or separately imagined and hence can't truly be a foundational part of the work.

RB: *If one was to try to map the history of the emergence of aural dramaturgy (or sound-led theatre, as some people prefer to call it) The Wooster Group (TWG) would certainly feature. In TWG's work, sound is not some separate, parallel commentary or soundtrack, but seems to be embodied by the performance – a vital component of each performed gesture. I'm interested in the processes that TWG use by which sounds are associated with physical actions, themes, gestures.*

JC: I guess in some ways I am responsible for making this 'sonification' a bigger part of The Wooster Group's aesthetic but I didn't invent it. In two shows of theirs that I saw from the audience before working for them, I was very moved by the way the sounds I heard seemed to be caused by the movement of the actors and, in some cases, the set; and, I was moved by the way the sounds seemed to move the actors.

In Frank Dell's *The Temptation of St. Antony* there was a constant bed of music that swelled and dropped with the movements of a huge wall that rose up on hydraulic rams and featured doors swinging open and slamming with actors strapped to them. When the doors flew open sound came through them. There was an amazing orchestra of live buzzers, sirens, canned music and the sound of tape being rewound and fast-forwarded. Above all, the sounds seemed to be emanating *from* the set. Then, on top of that, the actors were, for the most part, speaking into microphones. This had the effect of putting all the sounds I was hearing on the same plane and underscoring the suggestion that everything I was hearing was part of a deeply integrated organic whole. (Incidentally, it also turned the sound of an un-miked actor into a strange and novel sound.)

When I returned to see *Brace-Up*, their next piece, I immediately recognized the sound of the voices over the speakers and felt like I was back in that world. The show was quite different but achieved the same unity of what I saw and what I heard. In particular, I picked up on some wonderfully comical re-associations of some sounds with some actions – a creaking sound matching perfectly one actor forcibly turning another's head, a glass-breaking sound whenever one actor held a shot glass and jerked her hand toward the floor. These details woke something up in me and I became obsessed, for a while, with creating these comic equations in my own work.

When I came to work for The Wooster Group in 1993, this re-association of sounds was what I wanted to see and make happen. My work on *The Hairy Ape*, starting in about 1994 or 1995, was my first opportunity to bring this kind of sound re-association to the work myself. And I went a little crazy with it. A new, more powerful sampler keyboard helped, as did my piano training. I was soon adding a sound to just about everything I saw move on stage, borrowing samples and some ideas from my Wooster predecessors (one of whom I now worked alongside) and my work with ERS.

It's important to understand that sound, at ERS and at The Wooster Group, is not a technical discipline. It is insofar as it often, though not exclusively, requires some kind of technology to execute; however, in my experience I was always a performer at The Wooster Group first and a technician second. I came up with my ideas in rehearsal, in real time, and I invented a design to *perform* alongside the actors. I added sounds to bottles being thrown and caught, for example, and so had to be completely present as the one actor let go of the bottle and the other caught it. I added footsteps to actors walking and so had to be completely present in every step they took, literally.

So when it came time to perform the shows for audiences, I had no script, just body-memory. I was performing, always performing, and never simply executing a set of cues. Some shows, *To You, The Birdie*, for example, didn't even have cues that I could have written down if I had needed to. They simply had sets of rules – for example, when something falls into that space between the stage platform and the long table upstage of it, it has to splash or otherwise indicate the presence of water in that hidden trough; or, when that chair moves, even a little or by accident, it makes the sound of a running car.

For those shows that I helped The Wooster Group make, I was in the room for all the rehearsals and I had to keep myself (and the director) entertained. I would often get specific instructions from Liz LeCompte and sometimes from stage directions in whatever play we were mounting; my motivation, though, was to participate, to make myself a part of the performance – that's 'make *myself*'a part of the perform-ance, not just my sounds. The ideas I added often depended on my volition in the moment they happened.

Many come to the field of sound design from a musical or compositional back-ground. I came to it with a still burning desire to act on stage.

RB: *To what extent did sound figure in early conceptual discussions with TWG?*

JC: See my previous answer. The significance of any early conceptual discussions pales in comparison to the impact of the work that happens in the long rehearsal periods where everyone is present – designers, actors and director. The concepts, such as they are, are born out of the intensive, day-after-day creative problem solv-ing that demands the participation of the entire creative team.

The director has a very strong and constant presence but she's rarely a dictator.

She needs, desperately I'd say, for the room to be exploding with other people's ideas, other people's need to perform. She wields a mighty veto stamp and when she knows what she wants she can be maddeningly specific. But above all, understanding how to carve out your own space – as a designer or as an actor – is the key to thriving within and surviving The Wooster Group. In general, whenever anyone waits to be told what to do over there – in terms of design or performance or that murky area in-between – they find themselves left out of the fun, and, ultimately, the show that gets made.

So I guess I'd say that there, for any practical purposes, I was hardly ever aware of 'early conceptual discussions' at least not where my work was concerned.

RB: *How did the devising process work? When was sound introduced?*

JC: Sound is there from the very beginning (as is lighting, as is an evolving physical set). The process of devising each show was radically different and the only way to give an answer to that is to describe in detail the way each show was devised. Rather than do that, I'll just say that the ideas that are pursued in the creation of those shows come from Liz's interests in media, in illusion, in literature and language, in theatre itself and in the company's own traditions. Those ideas meet with the obsessions and interests of whoever happens to be in the room at the time the piece is made. The Wooster Group's work represents a thoroughly wrought theatrical vocabulary that is fiercely working to deny any sense of boundary between live actors, recorded images, broadcast images and recorded and live sounds.

RB: *Since 1991 you have run your own company (Elevator Repair Service Theater). Whilst I think many sound or lighting designers or theatre composers think they would make good directors I can't think of many that have actually gone ahead and done it (Heiner Goebbels perhaps). What's it like being in charge?*

JC: When I design in my own work it's for one of two reasons: I have a strong idea or I have failed to recruit someone else to do it for me. A few of my pieces have actually emerged entirely from a design concept (or challenge) and I have given myself the designer job in those cases. For *Room Tone* (2002–4), I wanted to create a piece of theatre in the kind of reality bending low-light I'd seen in several of James Turrell's light/sculpture installations. So we begin the entire piece by experimenting with light – no text, no dialogue, just light (though text followed shortly after).

Often I have brought in designers after some work has already occurred on a piece. But even then, those designers are forced to work with elements of a theatre or rehearsal space that have already worked their way into the fabric of the piece. And I've been lucky to work with some great designers who see this as clearly as I do and have been able to expand on those already present ideas in ways I hadn't imagined. A few examples:

Lighting designer Clay Shirky, after visiting a few rehearsals of one piece, began building a design based on our rehearsal lighting (wide, broad floodlights).

Sound designer Michael Kraskin placed a microphone outside on the sidewalk at Performance Space 122 and would occasionally bring up the sound of the noisy sidewalk (already leaking through the wall) into the speakers in the room. When buses would idle noisily outside the theatre, what had been an annoying distraction came to be perceived as a subtle sound effect deeply embedded in the fabric of the show. With a little work, he made virtually everything the audience heard (whether it was one of Michael's or something we had no control over) add to the presence of the piece.

Set designer Louisa Thompson built a richly detailed office setting based on the locations of some doors in a garage where we had been rehearsing and the environs of the upstairs of The Wooster Group's Performing Garage where, it so happened, I had been rehearsing on the sly for an ERS piece.

RC: *Describe a moment from one of your sound designs that you are particularly proud of and which you would best like to summarize your work.*

JC: The badminton game at the beginning of *To You, the Birdie* is my favourite and proudest bit of sound design. It actually lasts about four minutes and consists of two actors, Scott Shepherd and Ari Fliakos, furiously batting a badminton birdie back and forth across the stage with rackets and trying to keep it in the air as long as they can. There's nothing scripted, it's just a game. I play it with them using a set of rules: there were three different sounds for birdie-hitting-racket (and I tried not to use the same one more than two or three times in a row), a sound for the birdie hitting the floor, a buzz to indicate the end of a point, applause for good moves, the sound of the birdie going off the back of the stage (a splash) and the sound of the birdie being tossed in the air (a tweeting bird, I know, I should be ashamed).

I had to keep up with Scott and Ari and successfully anticipate their very unpredictable actions so that the sounds I made could be perfectly associated with them. It took keeping 10 fingers on the keyboard and both eyes on the stage at all times. I controlled volume by velocity of key-strikes on my sampler keyboard. Occasionally I'd mistakenly indicate a miss where Ari or Scott would actually succeed in making diving contact with the birdie and then I'd have to deal with the consequences – like making a smashing sound for Ari throwing his racket in anger while glaring up at the booth.

That scene in *To You, the Birdie* is the most fun I've ever had making a sound for the stage. In many ways, with its total liveness and total unpredictability and the absolute requirement that I be totally present and working in concert with the actors, it is, to me, ideal sound design inside of ideal theatre. (This whole idea can be traced back to when Scott and I were roommates and had a ping-pong table. We played ping-pong after ERS rehearsals in the same room where we rehearsed in a loft we shared. There were three of us and whoever wasn't playing had the job of making sound effects for the game the other two were playing. The badminton birdie was pretty easy to follow by comparison).

AN INTERVIEW WITH JONATHAN DEANS

The scale and complexity of Jonathan Deans' sound designs for Cirque du Soleil, both in Las Vegas and on tour throughout the world, has no parallel.

They also continue a long tradition of stage illusion and circus performance that uses sound as an integral part of the magic. In the sheer numbers of loudspeakers, intensity of processing power and complexity of control, Deans' sound designs are unique, but his techniques and experience come from his theatre background. The technical design of the system, as he explains in this interview, is inseparable from the dramaturgical processes of sound design – indeed, not merely systems, but entire theatres are designed and constructed for some productions.

5.5   Interview With Jonathan Deans Conducted by Email on 1 February 2007
For This Volume

Ross Brown (RB): *The scale and scope of the sound systems design for Cirque Du Soleil – particularly in its Las Vegas operations – is huge and unprecedented. Can you give us a sense of what physical, human and time resources are involved?*

Jonathan Deans (JD): Each show is a little different but as a general answer, a unique theatre is built for each production. I am involved in the design and infrastructure and the time line is about three years per production. Technical rehearsals are planned to be anything from 12 to 16 weeks, not including any delays. My own resources are mainly my experience, swiftly followed by my sound colleagues, who often have to deal with an assertive sound designer who tries to accomplish something different each time a system is designed and built.

RB: *There's an old cliché that says the best sound design is the one you don't really notice, but I find it hard to imagine anyone not noticing the sound in Cirque du Soleil, or that ever being the intention. What would you want the effect of the sound design to be (to the audience)?*

JD: There are many ways to answer this depending on the actual production's needs. A well thought-out design should be unnoticed, like a classic musical such as *South Pacific*, *On Yer Toes*, or *Music Man*. This 'classic style' of musicals can also apply to newly written musicals. The actor's relationship to the music and the orchestrations will dictate the need for sound to be noticed or not.

Cirque du Soleil productions are set on a different set of rules for all of the designers and directors. The production is grown right in front of your eyes – and ears – as a group effort in realizing a performance that starts with no script. Sound with Cirque can be anything from a full-on intense experience to being totally transparent. Does the audience really hear what I do with sound? This is questionable, but certainly the enhanced emotional feelings are heavily contributed to by the sound's environment/mix. If done together as a creative team and done well, we will create a unique experience for the audience during that moment of time.

RB: *You started out as a child actor, working with the RSC and in the music industry before becoming a designer of sound for musical theatre. What is it about sound in theatre?*

JD: When I was about five years old, I would play with a gramophone and try to work out how it actually made sound. A few years later I learnt how to edit a two-track tape and record on my Ferrograph. I had a fantastic time as a child actor, loved the theatre and all that went with it. Later in my teenage years I was being asked to make up sound effects and operate the local show's sound cues. And it felt like I was contributing to the actor's performance from behind the scenes. Later I mixed my first musical where I was responsible for making the actors and musicians heard – or not. At that time I realized that I could heighten their performances by approaching sound mixing as a creative approach. Suddenly I had a new job and I have not been out of work since that realization.

RB: *Someone described sound design for musicals to me recently as a process of organizing fellow engineers and solving acoustic problems. Would you agree?*

JD: I was around in the UK when we started that pursuit of being recognized on the billboard, programmes and as a creative department. I am a little hurt that someone thinks that in the 60s and 70s we were just a group of 'fellow engineers'. What crosses my mind is Abe Jacob who is considered the Godfather of sound design for the legit theatre: this is commonly known by most of us in this field. His work was innovative in the creation of sound direction, layering, texture, colour and intention. Hmm, this sounds like I am describing a designer. Many billboards during at that time listed sound design as 'Sound by' but this is very misleading. Anyone who might be in the business of creating, directing, layering, texture, colour and intention might really fall under the title of designer.

Regarding plays, I certainly love a great play and would be honoured to get a play design project. I have in the past but these days I am rarely asked.

The few times I have been approached I recommended another sound designer who I thought would be a better choice. This does not really help the interview process!

RB: *A show like KA, directed by a theatre auteur Robert LePage, seems to combine all manner of theatrical conventions and devices along with the spectacle of Cirque du Soleil's spatial performance in a kind of hyper-theatrical narrative. This seems a bit like theatre sound design, but on a huge scale, and nothing like conventional sound-reinforcement or music event design. Talk me through the creative process: are you involved, creatively or dramaturgically in a devising process in the way one might expect of a more traditionally theatre-based production? Are you purely a creative problem solver responding to a brief?*

JD: A creative problem solver? I think that falls under the scope of the producer, director and all designers: in fact even the ushers have been known to have this trait. When sitting at the table over the course of many months with all of the KA creative team, we were invited to participate with ideas that would eventually impact the overall performance. Of course, when sitting with a director such as Robert LePage one's ideas can seem rather futile, but nonetheless, ideas are kicked around – or just kicked. In my domain I have complete creative input. Everything from presenting the idea, (like placing two speakers in every seat, which was a matter of me spending months in my studio and devising how to make this happen for 2,000 seats and preparing a demonstration with a multi-track sound effect and music playback) to getting my ideas across. Then having to choose what kind of sound should belong in this large theatre that will give our audience the unique experience that belongs to this type of performance and to the signature of Cirque. When working on a project I place myself inside the CAD drawing and imagine what wonderful things I could hear, and make myself fully comfortable in how I can achieve this in reality. Then I start the process of choosing the technical requirements that should belong to the storyboard and the theatre. It's not until after this process that I look at what this means regarding the actual equipment, quantity, cost and practicality. After this part of the design is complete I step into the built theatre and realize my vision, and have to make it a real world for all to share.

RB: *Your biog for Corteo includes the strapline: "When sound isn't focused, it's just noise." Do you mean literally – in terms of acoustic imaging or in a conceptual way?*

JD: Both. An example, although rather extreme: If you were to go to a football match and watch supporters cheer, sing and basically be loud, this would be totally acceptable: you see them, you see the reason why they are reacting in this manner and you most likely become involved yourself as part of the football crowd. Now, if you apply this same sound in a romantic restaurant during dessert and glass of cognac it would be considered an unacceptable noise as it has no focus with regard to the environment or situation. As I said, perhaps this analogy is a little extreme but you get the idea.

RB: *What professional ambitions do you have left?*

JD: I have many ambitions yet to accomplish. But when I have finished charging around designing productions – which is not for many years, I hasten to add – I want to be able to share my knowledge with future sound designers so they can get a head start with their own desires and not have to dig themselves out of big dark holes that could have been avoided because the wheel was invented many years ago.

Create something new and invent yourself.

Part II
Theatrically Organized Hearing

This Part will propose that *resonance*, the spatiotemporal buffer which 'holds' and savours the acoustic moment for a fraction of a second, is the place where the art and ideas of theatre performance meet with the flesh and bone of the audient body. As Smith says: 'In the theatre was to be found a degree of resonance unmatched elsewhere among body, society, psyche, and voice' (Smith, 1999, p. 284).

While the Greek origin of the word 'theatre' originally meant a place for viewing performance, the ancient Roman writer Vitruvius recognized that theatre is viewed from auditoria, which are immersive environments that affect the mood or feel of what is being observed. As the crafted words and music of drama project into space and journey to the ear of the receiver, they are transformed by the acoustic environment and they intermingle with environmental ambience and noise. Coughs, stumbles and splutters; bum notes and glitches – each 'imperfection' resounds within a reverberant field which treats words, music and noise just the same. Whether or not the ear recognizes the noise as well as the signal, theatre buildings re-sound significance and insignificance indiscriminately, showing them back to the audience as one surrounding field.

A chapter on sound understood according to phenomenology is introduced and motivated by a chapter that problematizes the categorization of sound design as scenography. Then we consider three historical examples of resonance in theatres, before considering, in Chapter 9, the dramaturgical effects of spatial acoustics in relation to scenography.

Chapter 6

Problems with Sound as Scenography

SHOWING

What is a sound design? Can it be exhibited in a design exhibition? Can a student hand one in in a box? Can sound design be archived? Or is it something than can only be discerned and judged *in situ* and in the moment of performance? Sound design is now becoming an established branch of scenography[1] within the professional organizations of theatre and in higher education. The International Organization of Scenographers, Theatre Architects and Technicians' (OISTAT) Scenography Commission is working at national and international level to raise awareness about theatre sound and see it fairly represented in exhibitions, conferences and museums.

Designers sometimes like to be able to look at each others' work, discuss it and give it prizes, and colleges that teach design often have to assess documentation and artefacts rather than time-based performance. Is sound at a disadvantage because you cannot put it on a plinth? Whereas set or costume designs might, to a certain extent, be appreciated while still in their prototypical forms as drawings or models, a sound design as a material plan comprises a set of papers and digital media (system schematics, cue sheets, annotated scripts, perhaps musical scores, show discs containing prerecorded material in digital form). Any 'sound' only becomes discernible when someone takes the time to play through the discs, and the only place that the total programme (speech, non-verbal human sound, non-human sound and music) can come together in their 'designed' proportions is in the ears of a theatre audience. Photographs cannot be shown of this; recordings or advance demos can only vaguely approximate the experience.

Design materials can help make an abstract proposition, but the process only becomes meaningful when it is heard in place (in the ambient context of a populated theatre and in the dramatic context of the play). Something similar might be true of lighting, or of costume and set design, but a costume

---

[1] Scenography is a term for stage design preferred by some people and used as standard in some European countries. It may include lighting design, set design and costume design, not as separate, departmental concerns, but as aspects of a concerted artistic approach to the creation of a scene, or stage picture, which might also include elements of 'scenographic performance'.

or a set is an object in its own right and makes a certain amount of sense even in isolation. Lighting has imaging software that renders, on a computer screen, a fair impression of what the design will eventually look like.

There is no comparable 'what you hear is what you get' software for theatre sound. Listening to demos and cues in advance does not convey what you will get in the spatial acoustic of the theatre, where the voices of the actors, the 'presence' of the audience and the acoustic of the room will have a transforming effect. Unlike music, there is no way of scoring, in advance, what the completed work will sound like. Experienced conductors can read a composer's score and 'hear' the music in their auditory imagination, but a compilation of sound cues resembles either a sound effects CD or a piece of *musique concrète*. A vivid auditory imagination and an annotated script remain the best ways of collaboratively plotting sound in advance, but a director will have to place more trust in the sound designer and the figurative vocabulary they use in their discussions than they might in other collaborators whose ideas they can see or read.

Archiving presents similar problems. Some sound designers create separate 'stand alone' montages to convey an analogue of the design, because straight show recordings do not work well. They do not work for the same reason that a simple fixed-camera video of a play does not work. Neither an audiovisual camera, nor a microphone, is sentient in the way that a human theatre-goer is. They are not 'present' in the flesh, and they do not have culturally or acoustically subjective psyches. A sonic environment is, to an extent, *produced by the subjectivity* of its inhabitants.

Anthropologists face similar issues when trying to document aural ecologies. For example, Stephen Feld, who coined the term *acoustemology*, makes CDs which try to capture, or model, the experience of being in an environment, like a rain forest, whose sounds define the cultures of those who live there (see Feld, 2003). His work has been influential in the development of understanding of the ways in which sound (and voice) 'place' humans in their environment, but the recordings have been criticized by some for reducing aural experience into artefact form to be judged according to music-based aesthetics; as Paul Carter explains in his essay 'Ambiguous Traces, Mishearing and Auditory Space' (in Erlmann, 2004), putting live environmental recordings on CD isolates them and makes them into something like art objects, framed by silence. In order to understand an acoustemology, Carter advocates that one must immerse oneself in environments, advocating a kind of 'dirty' hearing, or as he puts it, an 'attached' hearing within all of the noise of place. Framing with silence idealizes. The same is true of show recordings as documents of theatre experience: they are framed by silence and therefore listened to as quasi-musical artefacts: 'A detached hearing theorizes sounds arising out of silence and aspiring towards harmonization. The attached hearing advocated here considers that sounds begin and end in noise' (Carter, in Erlmann, 2004, p. 62).

One might assume it as a given that any archival document of an event is not the same as 'being there'. But an archival artefact is different from an artwork: its function is to *represent* an event in analogue. There is a risk, if the artefact becomes too seductive as art, that the event becomes misrepresented. It is an allegation sometimes made in relation to set design that the standard combination of model box and production photographs as a mode of representation in set design can lead to set designs that look like big model boxes or sequences of beautifully lit photographs. A clean and precisely made model is a seductive artefact, but can lead to a rigid, clinical or objective monumentality on the stage. Photographs and video can make a scene look good, but looking good doesn't necessarily have anything to do with its success or failure as a design. There are equivalent pitfalls with sound. A slick demo, or a cleverly mixed archival 'mix' can appeal as a listening experience but entirely misrepresent the show itself. The danger of assessing sound design through a demo/document model is that it affects the designs themselves. Sound mixes that sound good as standalone montages on CD, often sound over-complex in performance. Similarly, the use of studio production effects such as compression, spatial enhancement, reverb and so on, can make a sound design seem 'off the peg'. Better to introduce any digital sound processing live in the performance space, where one can gauge it in relation to the room.

RECORDING

With live concert recordings, there is a line between the documentation of a performance with a suitable amount of ambience, and the documentation of an audience experience with some music in the background. The very localized ambience of a bootleg recording, or an 'official' bootleg like *The Velvet Underground Live at Max's Kansas City* for example (Atlantic Records, 1972) made by a group of Andy Warhol's Factory coterie, at a table in a nightclub using a cassette recorder, is a great archival document of a cultural time and place in which music features, but not of the music itself. Essentially, it is an archive of a specific social listening context. Taken in conjunction with the studio recordings of the songs being performed, it is a valuable document, but one wouldn't want to have to rely on it as the only document of the musical material.

To an extent, theatre sound design – in its immersive spatial resonance, and particularly when it involves surround-sound effects, is a designed listening context as much as it is programmatic. Often it is not programmatic at all – one focuses on the spoken words and performed actions onstage, and doesn't consciously register the surrounding presence of ambient or underscoring sound.

One is able to hear but remain oblivious to one's local listening context due to a psychoacoustic process often known as the *cocktail party effect*. One is able, at a party, selectively to focus on what someone is saying in a conversation, and apparently 'not hear' all the noise going on around. If one recorded the conversation, the recording would be unintelligible, with much more ambient noise than one remembered. This is because microphones and recording devices do not listen, they hear. Humans do both, they are able to listen selectively, and 'zone out' irrelevant background noise, but they remain aurally alert all the while. If one were rapt in conversation at a cock-tail party, oblivious to one's surroundings, but someone were to drop a glass or mention one's name within earshot, it would immediately grab one's attention and one's head would turn round to identify the source of the interruption. This facility is part of hearing's primal function as an omni-directional early warning system, which predates but has accommodated, its communicative function of listening to language and other sonic signs.

In the theatre, it is often the case that the play is the cocktail-party inter-locutor, on whose words the audience hangs, and the sound design, resonat-ing in the surrounding space of the auditorium, is the clinking of glasses and chatter of the party, of which one is omnidirectionally but only subcon-sciously aware as a vague presence in the background. One becomes consciously aware of it only when it says one's name or drops a glass, so to speak. A good designer knows this and uses it. The trouble with sound-recording as a mode of documentation in theatre is that the sound design and other background ambience, like Andy Warhol's friends in Max's Kansas City, come out too prevalently and noticeably in the mix. One does not get a document of the programme in context, but of programme and context with equal weighting.

The relationship between the individual conscious attention and the envi-ronment changes continuously during the course of a live theatre perform-ance, and has a modulating effect on the way sound is perceived. The psychoacoustic relationship of the audient to sound in the theatre is more complex than a microphone or recorder could emulate without some kind of artificial sentient intelligence. In certain conditions, a sound can seem to come from its point of origin, in others, the same sound can seem to surround and immerse one in its resonance in the acoustic environment, and it can become clearer or less distinct depending on whether it features within the 'high-definition' zone of foreground audient attention, or in the low-definition zone of background noise.

There is, as yet, no agreed 'best way' to create or store a definitive docu-ment of theatre sound design. New spatial sound-field emulating and recording technology might help (although they rely on the listener's access to a properly calibrated surround-sound listening room). For now, perhaps the best bet is something similar to the Velvet Underground example given above: a highly subjective local recording of listening context, alongside a 'dry' studio recording. It's a lot to listen to. Model boxes and photographs have that other advantage of not being time-based.

Perhaps there is an inter-sensual model of theatre documentation to be developed that would suit both sound and visual design; some kind of immersive virtual modelling space. Certainly, there is interest among some scenographers, in moving their discipline away from permanence and monumentality implied in terms like 'visual theatre' or 'object theatre'. I know a scenographer who derives her creative energy from a somewhat paradoxical disciplinary resistance to objectivity. In a world that expects models, pre-production decisions and plotted meaning, she finds herself detesting 'miniature utopian visions – statuesque and deadly'; she would rather her audiences and performers 'wander in space, undecided' than look-on from a perspective she has decided for them. She talks a lot about *immersive space* and the *'resonant space* between the self and the other'. 'Meaning', she says, 'happens retrospectively if at all'. She describes her own creativity as immersive and uses music (any music, not the opera she is designing) to enable her to spend 'hours in an immersive [creative] space' (Joanna Parker, Central School of Speech and Drama Research Seminar, 22 October 2008). This is an aural approach to theatre design, even if the result is not sound.

This brings us to the second problem that sound has had in 'fitting in' with scenography: the traditional dominance of object-and-intent oriented *semiotics* as its primary pedagogic model. Sound tutors normally discuss sound design with their students in relation to allusional intent ('what are you trying to say with that sound? How does it relate to the author's intentions and the director's vision?'). It is more difficult to discuss the resultant effect of the whole design using these languages. Aside from the isolated, individual sign such as a door bell, the overall sound design rarely 'says' anything unequivocal, in the way that a set and costume design might within one consistent, visible concept. It might 'suggest' or 'make one feel like …' something, but its sum effect tends to be an atmosphere, or flavouring. And yet, in creative discussions with directors, in the development of sound design concepts and in the plotting of sound effects, a lot of care and attention is given to precise meanings, to codified schematics of sound, to witty allusion and clever symbolism. Most of this intention is futile. At best, sound designs seem to end up being remembered by audiences and critics as a set of vague adjectives: atmospheric, haunting, moody, effective, gloomy, plangent, ominous, portentous, creepy, irreverent, quirky, disconcerting, and so on, because sound is not 'read' for meaning like a cryptic crossword clue; its 'meaning' is relational.

As a sub-discipline of theatre design or scenography, sound designers have been encouraged to adopt the orthodox stage design approach, which is to develop a concept that is consistent with and coherent within an overall staging concept, emanating from the words of the text and guided by a unifying directorial vision. An individually plotted sound effect acts as a sign that interrelates within a wider system of signs. 'Meaning' is intended in the web of interactions between non-verbal sounds, spoken and musical sound, visual components and so on. The result, if all goes well, should be a total theatre text that the audience can read according to a manifest guiding idea or conceit. If a sound designer has done a good job then the design 'works' and the audience will understand what it all means, just as intended. But this cohesive and coherent, 'unified concept' model of design does not recognize the full potential of sound in theatre. It assumes that sound is only used in a programmatic way – as part of the overall 'programme' of sign-systems that is the mise-en-scène. Sound design has more to offer: as we have seen, it can be used to form a personal listening context; it can reach out from the production, and do very uncohesive and inconsistent things to the audience's predisposition toward the programme, to great effect. If it is scenography, it is a scenography of engagement *and* distraction rather than of the semiological 'gaze' and in order fully to understand its potential, the sound designer must first break free from what Serres described as the 'empire of signs'.

OUTSIDE THE EMPIRE OF SIGNS

Semiotics, the study of signs and symbols and their meanings, is often discussed in visual tropes, for example, writing and reading. In design orthodoxy, the scene becomes analogous to a written page, upon which the spectator trains an intellectual 'gaze' in order to read ideas.[2] However, in order to read something, one must be able see all of the words from the direction in which they were intended to be read. One therefore needs to be detached from the page, set back from it in order to see the sentence struc- tures and pagination. So too with visual theatre design: sense is derived on the basis of detachment from the scene. Sound, however, whatever events the sources of individual sounds might represent, is *in totum* an immersive environment. One cannot stand back from it and see the entire picture; one's aural attention does not have the equivalent of sightlines; the theatrical mode of listening does not gaze uniformly, but is, by nature, a state of contin- ual omnidirectional distraction.

I am not meaning to suggest that one can never 'read' an auditory text. There are, of course, oral texts: audiobooks, radio drama and so on, and verbal communications involve a kind of auditory reading. But our brains process verbal narratives differently to non-verbal sound, and language has been around long enough for them to have evolved so to do.[3] A radio play, tone-poem or a piece of *musique concrète* can also be 'read' as one narrative progression by dint of its acousmatic displacement, which sets it out on the containing 'page', so to speak, of the form and format of its mediation. In a radio play, sounds can be 'cut out' from their original context and put together in, syntactically, a sequence that describes a likely scenario (alarm

---

[2] For an overview summary of semiotics in relation to theatre, see Shepherd and Wallis (2004, pp. 236–40). For a specific semiotic theory of sound, see Van Leeuwen (1999).

[3] For a very readable account of psychoacoustics, which touches on this and other 'processing' aspects to hearing touched on in this chapter, see Moore (2003).

clock; sounds of peeing; toilet flush; teeth brushing; kettle filling; kettle whistling; radio on in background, cup of tea slurping in foreground; door slamming; silence). A sign sequence like this represents flowingly analogue reality in digital, bite-sized units. It is a low-resolution pixilation, or quantization of someone getting up and going to work. While it might 'read' in the sonically abstract (in a radio play for example) this kind of sonic narrative is hardly ever called-for in theatre, which is a flowingly analogue, less abstracted world.

Sound effects tend to read in a different way, in relation to *holistic moment* rather than in syntactical relationships with each other. Sonic theatre is experienced in the totality of verbal and non-verbal sound; words, images and gestures, which hold the attention while music, noises and ambient resonance contradict, comment on, reinforce, undermine or inflect the stories they tell, creating parallel, contrapuntal worlds. No sound is experienced in isolation.

This does not mean that sound design should not or cannot be created or analysed as a system of signs, but it does mean, I suggest, that the semiological trope of 'reading' a sonic sign system is misleading because of what it discounts. To read a text is to discount anything *off* the page and assume it has nothing to do with the meaning contained within that page. The negotiation of noise is part of the process of establishing meaning in sound (or of any signal perceived in an immersive aural field). To the extent that sight has a peripheral field, this might also be true of spectatorship as well as audience, but in the theatre, vision is trained by a range of mechanisms such as seating arrangements, proscenium arches, stage masking and stage lighting, designed to minimize peripheral distraction (although some riotously ornamental proscenium arches and adjacent theatre boxes are designed with deliberate opulence to buck this convention and remind the viewer of the status of the house). Hearing, however, is omnidirectional, while focused hearing – or listening – has only a vague directionality. There are no auditory equivalents to the visual concepts of blinkers, peripherals or scope other than in psychoacoustic effects such as *the cocktail party*, discussed above. Hearing's default 'first position' is one of central immersion rather than facial address. We do not need to point our heads at something in order to hear it and establish a relationship with it. The sense of surrounding presence has a bearing on what is being read and on the reader; aural awareness pulls the eye from the page. As Shepherd and Wallis point out:

> The audience is not simply a collection of psyches 'reading' the mise-en-scène: it is a set of bodies in relationship to one another and to the space that they are in, a set of eyes moving in their sockets. The 'I' also has an 'eye'. (p. 236)

Active scrutiny is constantly rebalancing itself with passive awareness. The seeing 'I' is simultaneously the hearing 'me' – an accusative rather than a nominative version of the self. It is through hearing and making sound that we know of our central place in the world[4]; and hearing and making sound are exchanges transacted between the self and the environment through the agency of the whole body. This brings us to *phenomenology*.

Phenomenology is the study of the world as it is experienced in the flesh-bound moment. It's a long word with a short history, beginning in the early twentieth-century, with the philosopher Husserl, as an attempt to free philosophy from the 'scientific' assumption that the world is best studied as something that happens 'over there' at the end of a blinkered tunnel of unidirectional gaze. Merleau-Ponty then developed the notion by focusing on the body as the immediate environment of all experience, and its effect on the way the subjective consciousness derives meaning from perception. This is harder to grasp, perhaps, with visual perception, than with sound, which is more obviously a tactile experience. Much of the complexity in Merleau-Ponty's writing comes from trying to accommodate what I would character-ize as a subjectively aural concept within a visual paradigm, and he gives surprisingly little attention to aurality. It is useful to be aware of phenome-nology as a way of thinking about perceptual engagement with the world, but this is perhaps not the place to become too diverted by its detail. Our interest here is in the way in which sound, in addition to being a carrier for linguistic and non-linguistic sign-systems, also affects the perception of meaning through its effect and affect on the human body.

Scenography is traditionally associated with perspective, whereas sound immerses not just the psychoacoustic mind, but the whole body. The body is aurally environmental, the inner, most dense part of the aural atmosphere which surrounds the *me*. It is a layer of atmosphere which has its own weather systems, produced by both internal and external factors. The body, as well as the intellect and the psychoacoustic mind, 'hears'. It has its own memory (the effect known as *anamnesis*) and sound has readily discernible, visceral effects on it, vibrating not only the eardrums, but the resonant cham-bers and the fleshy organs of the body. As we saw in Chapter 3, in the medi-aeval notion of *musica humana*, physiological and psychological health depended on a harmonic balance between the various energy centres and important organs of the body, much as the health of the cosmos – *musica mundana* – depended on harmonic relationships between the spheres. This aural notion of corporeal harmonic balance also underpins some traditional Chinese approaches to medicine. It is a measurable fact that different parts of the body have different dominant resonance characteristics – most of which are at infrasonic frequency levels (without the range of hearing) but which can be felt, either consciously or subconsciously. The body, as a whole, resonates at 2Hz when lying down, between 4 and 5Hz when standing

---

[4] In particular, through speech, as Bruce R. Smith says 'Whether we follow Aristotle and conceive of the existential being as "soul", or Lacan and think of it as "ego", it is the sound of the subject's own voice that centers the subject's "I" in the world.' (1999, p. 146).

(relaxed) and at 5 and 6Hz when sitting. Heads will also resonate at between 20 to 30Hz (within the hearing range) and eyeballs at 40 to 60Hz. Chest walls resonate, typically, at 60Hz, spinal columns at 8Hz, pelvic areas at 8Hz and so on (NASA-STD-3000/Vol1/Rev.A quoted in Devereux, 2001, p. 51). Within a theatre of sound, the overall effect is, therefore, not only one of audition but of complex corporeal vibration, of some organs, and relationships of organs, responding differently in sympathy with different frequencies and amplitudes of sound. Under most circumstances we are unaware or only subliminally aware of this, but the effect has been associated with 'sick building' syndrome and other nauseating effects in environments where there is a lot of low-frequency sonic energy, and also with the tingle of excitement produced in dynamic, human soundscapes such as the football terrace, where applause and vocal sounds excite the aural body in complex ways across the full frequency spectrum, both empathetically through anamnesis and sympathetically through acoustic resonance. We shall see, later in this chapter, that the resonance of the body at 110 Hz – the musical note A2, or A two octaves below middle C, which is a typical frequency of the male 'hum', 'activates' the body in a very noticeable way and is employed in various instances of ritual practice.

All of this bodily resonance, however, is incidental to the primary activity of listening to theatre, it goes unnoticed, or at best it is a slight feeling, possibly experienced as a kind of mood. Empathetic and sympathetic corporeal effect may not 'read', but play an important role in sound's ability to affect the way a scene or a theatrical moment 'feels'. When one considers that part of the effect of sound is a physical one, produced through the flesh by vibration in the surrounding medium of air, then the term 'feel' becomes a literal one. Sound can literally make one feel the drama.

A low foreboding drone, whether musically produced or derived from a sound such as thunder or industrial noise, may be read as a sign (a storm is coming; the local factory is casting its aural shadow over the human drama; Lawrence's Mrs Holroyd opens the door of her cottage and we hear the sound of the winding gear in the pit). But part of the exciting effect, like the tingling effect of an organ pedal note, is purely visceral. The sound is speaking straight to the adrenal gland and other internal organs through the physical interactions of air, flesh and bone. Arguably, theatre sound understood according to phenomenology has more disciplinary similarity to Voice or Movement Studies than Scenography.

AUDITORY ENGAGEMENT/AURAL DISTRACTION

Our next 'problem with sound as scenography' is that hearing has evolved specifically to attend to surrounding fields of noise, to be the 'distracting sense' where vision is the 'concentrating sense'. Let us remind ourselves of the difference between listening and hearing. Listening is focused hearing – active auditory attention that attends to one thing at a time or follows a particular, 'monophonic' flow (which might be an ensemble of sounds). I have noted that spoken words, especially, will command continuity of attention more than non-verbal sounds. What might appear to be simultaneous attention to multiple signals (for example in musical counterpoint) is in fact attention to one primary foreground signal (or figure), within a polyphonic background context. The attention may switch from signal to signal – or line to line – very quickly, with the effect being that several contrapuntal melodies can be 'tracked' at once, if not all listened to at once. Counterpoint is discernible because when we are listening to one thing, we still hear others. This facility is primeval; our brains are programmed to let hearing interrupt focused attention at the slightest suggestion of danger, or even of uncertainty, in our surrounding, aural environment. This, within the division of specialist duties in the *sensorium*,[5] is hearing's role.

This aural 'availability to distraction' is both a problem and an opportunity for the theatre sound designer. Theatre convention tends to assume 'eyes front' attentiveness, and to presume that peripheral noise is extraneous and therefore to be ignored in terms of any potential dramaturgical intent. Auditoria are noisy places, so this constant circumstantial awareness is continually tugging at the coat-tails of forward-facing attention. Most of the time auditorium noise can be ignored, because it is clearly irrelevant, random, accidental and so on, but the audient remains alert to it, and occasionally becomes very annoyed by it. Silenced and darkened auditoria, stage lighting and theatre architecture all police the conventional assumption that the auditorium is an insignificant place (literally a place that does not signify) and that the mise-en-scène is the sole object of the audience's collective attention. Counter-conventional use of unexpected audience plants, vomitorium or rear auditorium entrances, the sudden use of house lights during the performance and, in some instances, the use of surround sound, all *reinforce* the convention by making a *performance of breaking it* for theatrical effect. In the normal course of theatrical events, the audience is supposed to be so transfixed by the scene that it forgets itself and its circumstance; but this ideal state of devotion, the famous 'willing suspension of disbelief', is an ideal which forgets the phenomenology of bodily presence within the auditorium.

As individuals, audience members are perpetually in a state of being more or less distracted. They itch, they need to go to the toilet; people around them scratch and leave to go to the toilet; they can't remember whether they left the gas on; they find themselves transfixed not by a coherent scenic whole, but by a bit of wobbly scenery, or the sweat around the actor's armpits (is that the character's sweat, or the actor's?). They are reminded of personal memories and they go on personal anecdotal tangents.

---

[5] Boethius' notion of the synaesthetic *totum* of perception, developed in seventeenth-century philosophy both as a way of conceptualizing perception and as a metaphor (the Newtonian notion of the world as God's *sensorium*).

Not all of these distractions are auditory, but I would class them all as aural. In each case, either bodily presence or the auditory imagination is superimposing itself on the reception of the play, and tinkering with the perception of any meaning.

The opportunity for the sound designer is in understanding and controlling this. Sound is particularly distracting because that is what it has evolved to be, and the sound designer knows that she can subvert meaning within the aural field of hearing even while the audient continues to listen attentively to the words of the drama or watch the actions of the play. The auditorium may be a presumably insignificant place, but it is a very powerful aural zone in which the sound designer can construct contrapuntal contexts to signals and figures of the staged performance. In addition to this dramaturgical counterpoint, the sound designer can also take advantage of an area of circumstantial uncertainty. By this I mean the slight doubt as to whether something was intentional or not which keeps an audience interested in their surroundings. A subtle use of surround sound will work precisely *because* it distracts the audience with a sound that may or may not be of significance. When an audience cannot be entirely certain whether a siren, or a drip, or an appliance hum or noise, or even an echo, is a 'real' part of the auditorium environment, or a potentially meaningful piece of sound design, it enjoys the performance in a heightened, bristling state of aural attentiveness to its surroundings. In other words, the teasing of an audience with sonic suggestions or auditory ambiguities can be theatrically exciting, and therefore change physiological and psychological registers of reception.

The idea of 'design through annoyance', of aural mischievousness within presumably insignificant areas of conventional theatre psycho-geography, is a hard one to reconcile with traditional semiotic scenography, although auditorium intervention is of course by no means unheard of in visual design. The fact remains, though, that in design school studios and within the rehearsal room sound can be extremely annoying. This is not a problem a costume designer experiences with the fabrics of her design. The processes of sound design require technologies to be tested and designs to be rehearsed in auditory space that is also used for conversation, concentration and for social breaks. Actors struggling to remember lines curse the attention-grabbing underscoring that unexpectedly appears beneath their rehearsals; directors struggling to inflect dialogue with subtle meaning curse the mistimed or the wrongly calibrated sound cue. Everything that enables sound as a potent part of dramatic production – its ability to subvert meaning, to provide dramaturgical counterpoint or to heighten aural theatricality – also has the potential, in equal measure, to drive people up the wall.

Chapter 7

Live Listening: The Aural Phenomenology of Theatre

> Theatre is continually becoming that it is becoming; each human being is
> at the best point for reception. (Cage, 1978, p. 14)

In this quotation, Cage is describing sound's anthropocentric phenomenology. He is placing the human body at the centre of a spherical theoretical model of sound. Phenomenology is the study of objects, signs and meaning as they are experienced *around*, *through* and *in* the living body; or of the way the environment impinges on the body. The previous chapter suggested that to think of sound as scenography was, so to speak, to try to insert a round peg into a square hole. This chapter, then, beginning with the phenomenological theory of Don Ihde, describes sound's roundness in relation to the human body, in the architectural theory of Vitruvius in the next chapter and in the concept of atmosphere (derived from the Greek word meaning *ball of vapour*).

The notion that sound might have a shape at all might seem puzzling. Auditory space is defined not by the cubic dimension of its containment, but by the radial compass of hearing. Auditory space emanates spherically from the listener at its centre. One might think of it as the space contained within earshot.

Within this auditory sphere, sounds themselves begin their lives as inflating spheres of acoustic energy and then spread out and resonate as part of the spherical sonic environment. *In totum*, sound then, comprises spherical objects within a spherical subjectivity. Sound is round.

In his *Experimental Music: Doctrine* of 1955 (contained in the collection *Silence*, 1978) John Cage describes it thus:

> Urgent, unique, uninformed about history and theory, beyond imagination, central to a sphere without surface, its becoming is unimpeded, energetically broadcast. There is no escape from its action. It does not exist as one of a series of discrete steps, but as transmission in all directions from the field's center. It is inextricably synchronous with all other, sounds, non-sounds, which latter, received by other sets than the ear, operate in the same manner. (Cage, 1978, 14)

In the theatre, this energetic broadcast engages the audience instantaneously *within* the field of the performance. The audience is acoustically encircled or surrounded by the performance; Bruce R. Smith makes an analogy between this phenomenology and the shape of the Elizabethan public theatre, the famous 'wooden O' referred to in the Prologue of *Henry V*:

> Instructed by phenomenologists of sound like Don Ihde, we can 'see' the acoustic field by imagining the Prologue standing at the front edge of the stage, near the geometric centre of The Globe. As he projects his voice in all directions, he defines a circle. Beyond the reach of his voice stretches a horizon of silence. Along with the speaker, the auditors stand well within the circle defined by that horizon. Actor and audience share that same field of sound. If the actor stands at the centre of that shared acoustic space, each individual auditor stands nonetheless at the center of his or her own field of hearing – a field that includes the actor's voice but is not limited by it. The radius of sounds each auditor can hear is defined by its own encircling horizon of silence. For the space of the play, each individual auditor's radius of hearing is narrowed. As each of the 'gentles all' focuses his or her attention on the speakers onstage, sounds outside the acoustic field of the play become, quite literally, peripheral (Ihde, 1976, p. 170). The result is, or can be, a totalising experience of sound that surrounds each hearer completely, penetrating his or her body through the ears, immersing him or her in the playful patterning of speech. (Smith, 1999, p. 271)

THE PHENOMENOLOGY OF AUDITORY EXERIENCE

Don Ihde is one of surprisingly few phenomenologists to concentrate on sound. His best known work on this subject is *Listening and Voice: A Phenomenology of Sound* (1976). In it he explores many of the themes I have been discussing above. He is particularly interested in the air that we breathe as the medium of the sounds that we hear and make.

> We know that we live immersed in a vast but invisible ocean of air which surrounds us and permeates us and without which our life must necessarily escape us. For even when we humans wander far from the surface of the earth to that of the moon or deep into the sea, we must take with us packaged envelopes of air which we inhale and exhale. But in the words about breath there lurk ancient significances by which we take in the haleness or health of the air which for the ancients was spirit. From breath and the submersion in air also comes inspire, 'to take in spirit', and upon a final ex-halation we ex-(s)pire, and the spirit leaves us without life. … But the air which is breathed is not neutral or lifeless, for it has its life in sound and voice. Its sound ranges from the barely or not-at-all noticed background of our own breathing to the noises of the world and the singing of word and song among humans. The silence of the invisible comes to life in sound. For the human listener there is a multiplicity of senses in which there is word in the wind. (Ihde, 1976, p. 3)

In the following abridged extract from his earlier essay 'Parmenidean Meditations', Ihde reflects on sound and sphere in relation to the following quotation from the pre-Socratic philosopher Parmenides the Eleatic

(c. 510–450 BC): 'Being is complete on every side, like the mass of a well-rounded sphere, equally balanced in every direction from the centre.'

(It is not necessary to be familiar with the ideas of Parmenides to appreciate the extract).

7.1   Abridged Extract from Ihde, D. 'Parmenidean Meditations', *Journal of British Society for Phenomenology*, 1, 3, October (reprinted in Ihde, 1973)

The Shape of Sound is Round

Sound comes in two primary spatial dimensions. Sound is directional and sound is encompassing. And, at first curiously, neither dimension is lacking in any given experience of sound, although one of these dimensions may 'stand out' in relative prominence over the other depending upon the situation and the intention in the situation.

First, directionality: In our ordinary course of affairs we are quite aware of sounds which appear directionally. If the automobile horn honks behind me I quickly jump out of its way. I hear the sound of the typewriter down the hall. There are my two colleagues arguing again and they are in David's office this time instead of Ed's. In fact, expanded examples rightly amaze us with the clarity and distinctness possible in relation to directionality. Georg von Békésy in his studies upon localization cites the fact that the building of straight roads in eastern European forests depended upon just this ability. One man would stand on one side of the woods and yell loudly and the second would proceed straight towards him marking trees on the way thus creating a straight path. And in WW I, aircraft location, in a day when sounds were more clearly sounds of the aircraft, was accomplished by means of two extended trumpets set into the ears to locate the direction of the aircraft before its visual spotting. A variation of this same technique has been used by the Vietnamese in recent years. By standing at the bottom of a bomb crater, an 'unnatural' natural receiving bowl, the guerrilla is able to detect the direction of coming planes minutes before they are spotted and thus warn his company of their approach. In many aspects of ordinary affairs we focus upon sounds as directional.

But the encompassing characteristics of sound are never absent, even if placed on the fringe by our attending consciousness. The ticking of the clock, though coming from the dresser, also surrounds me. By merely shifting the focus of my attention I can note, within limits in this ease, the dimension of encompassing which the ticking displays.

At the opposite end of the continuum where the encompassing characteristics of sound are most clearly present stands the example of listening to music. Well built stereos and well built auditoria are designed so as to maximize an immersion in sound. I am surrounded by the symphony which at an optimal peak is so total that I find it difficult to tell whether it is 'in the middle of my head' or 'out there' – the usual inner and outer distinctions become blurred. It is in this phenomenon that the round shape of sound is first suggested and the hoary head of Parmenides lurks below us.

But I must not allow a resurrection too soon lest his spectre frighten us from seeing other relevant aspects of the phenomenon before us. If sound is both dimensional and encompassing and if one characteristic seems to stand out in certain experiences and the other in different experiences we have yet no basis for relating these differences to consciousness in its structural characteristics.

Between the optimal immersion in music and the concentric focus upon direction stand a whole series of auditory phenomena. Attend for a moment to a catalogue of auditory occasions within a given duration of consciousness. Given, all at once, are a plethora of sounds. The furnace is roaring; the clock is ticking; the page of my wife's book is flicking; the dog is barking; the traffic on the road is humming; the birds are singing; etc. Here I note three things. First, all of these things are going on at the same time but I have great trouble paying attention equally to them at the same time. Indeed, as I catalogue I find the focus of my attention switches subtly from one to another. But at the same time the other sounds are noticeably present on the fringes of my awareness. Second, I note that this catalogue is of sounds, entities with which my field is filled, atoms as it were, of sound. Third, insofar as these sounds appear directionally they are on a common sense level all 'sounds of ...', i.e., the auditory expressions of entities. Directionality appears as essentially connected to sounds.

Now a new question poses itself – can I note any field characteristics of Sound? And, if this is possible, what are the characteristics of the auditory field strictly as a field? The observation itself seems very difficult to make. It runs counter to my usual habits of attention. Usually I am focused upon this or that entity; I am concerned with this or that thing. In Heideggerian language, I am 'forgetful' of the ground of things, of the Being of beings.

At first my attempts are crude and additive, I attempt to construct the field of sound. The sound of the clock is to the right; the sound of the dog is slightly behind; the traffic to the left; etc. By this crude process of addition and perhaps by making inferences I light upon the possibility that one field characteristic of Sound is its 'roundness' – the field of Sound encompasses me. This structure of the auditory field, however, need not be arrived at in this indirect way because it is also 'given at a stroke' as Merleau-Ponty might say and we have already noted it in the paradigm example of sound in its encompassing dimension. The experience of music accomplished this 'immediately'. If you will understand me carefully and remain within the Husserlian notion in which examples, even a single example, may give an intuition of an essence, then I might well say that music is a privileged instance in which field characteristics of Sound are revealed.

One such characteristic of the field of Sound is its encompassing of me, of my consciousness. But there are other field characteristics as well. Sound is a plenum, always full even if that fullness displays different textures and intensifies. So long as I am conscious (and am not stone deaf) Sound is present. Sound is, in this sense, continuous as well. Even in the desert and in [an echo] chamber there are still small sounds. In terms of the field of Sound, 'I' am the centre around which the constant field of Sound extends indefinitely as a 'roundness.' The shape of Sound is round and I am in the middle. Parmenides rises. But is 'round' too strong? Is it merely metaphorical?

Because if it is round it must have a boundary, a horizon, no matter how indefinite and hard to locate. Where does Sound 'end'? What is the horizon of Sound?

The Horizon of Sound is Silence

As soon as the question of a horizon of Sound is raised the limitations upon the ordinary uses of space and time also come into view. As I move towards 'time' in its phenomenological sense in auditory experience the 'spatiality' of Sound begins to take on a certain strangeness for common sense. A certain Heideggerian making-strange-of-the-familiar begins to intrude. I make this approximation by introducing the thesis that silence is the horizon of Sound.

I begin with sounds, the entity terms of auditory experience. What happens with a sound? In the Parmenidean sense, appearances 'come into being and pass from being.' This is clearly the case with sounds. 'BOOM' – the explosion startles as it suddenly appears and almost as suddenly disappears. More gently, the sound of the train comes from nothing, gradually slipping into consciousness and when down the track in the other direction gradually fades out of presence. It comes from 'nothing' and disappears into 'nothing.' What is the 'nothing'? The 'nothing' is silence, the horizon of sound is silence. There is a boundary which at the edge of sound passes over into non-experience.

Take the case of the 'top' and 'bottom' of the ability to hear sounds. If we momentarily import the universe of discourse used by the acoustician, we are able to hear sounds 'up to' a certain frequency and 'down to' a certain frequency beyond which they pass into – silence. The same boundary phenomenon occurs with volume. A horizon is reached at the low end of the scale such that a barely discernible sound finally disappears – into silence. And, in the days of hard rock music, certain loudness at the edge of our hearing ability where sound gives way to pain brings a certain 'silence' in which sounds 'disappear.' Before and after a discrete sound's existence there is 'silence' and all gesturing towards the boundaries are gestures towards silence.

But we are dealing here with sounds as entity terms for which silence is clearly relative, relative to the particular sounds. This is the Parmenidean 'coming into being and passing from being' which applies to entities and not to the field as field. Sounds are the inconstants which occur against the background of Sound as the constant field of conscious experience. But nevertheless, one reaches a boundary here, too. In every direction I find a horizon to the sphere of Sound, the horizon is 'all around.' That horizon is the 'edge' which passes ever into silence. But silence is not a presence. In fact, silence is not given, but is a limit concept. Silence as the horizon of Sound is never given, but is reached. It may be noted, but not named in the Parmenidean sense, for, when reached it is the way of not-being which the goddess noted for Parmenides as the limit. 'That it is not and that not-being must be, cannot be grasped by my mind; for you cannot know not-being and cannot express it.' Silence is inexpressible; it is not-being. It is the horizon which 'surrounds' Sound. But I am no longer sure that the 'all around' is spatial in the ordinary sense at all. It is rather my 'lived space' which is "surrounded" by the horizon of silence.

ATMO–SPHERE

The Aesthetics of Atmosphere

To have a sound design described as *atmospheric* feels like being damned by faint praise. Mood music or atmospheric sound, like the use of smoke or dry-ice, is often critically belittled as though it is somehow cosmetic to the drama.[1] Sound and music are often said to 'provide atmosphere' for plays. This seems to me to be a respectable, indeed, vital part of the theatrical technê; nothing lives without atmosphere. So why should something that can so patently change the audience's perception of a play, which can obscure, alter or enhance meaning and manipulate emotional response, be afforded such scant and often dismissive critical mention?

The word *atmo-sphere*[2] (ball of vapour) itself echoes Ihde's auditory phenomenology of air and spheres, but it is also associated with the *feel* of place. The kinds of metaphors used to describe that *feel* are culturally produced through language and discourse, and themselves have an effect on the *feel* as it is experienced. We talk of the mood of a place, but environments do not have moods, people do. People somehow project mood into an environment. Phenomenologist and physicist Gernot Böhme (1995, p. 33) defines atmosphere as the effect of 'the relationship between ambient qualities and a person's feeling of wellbeing or otherwise'. The interesting thing is that most of the time people's projected moods seem to agree with each other.

> One talks of a pleasant valley, of the depressive mood before a storm, of the tense atmosphere in a meeting, and it is easy to agree on what these phrases mean. If atmospheres are moods, which one feels in the air, then we are describing a phenomenon which is familiar to everyone; moreover, the potential source material for discussing and characterizing atmospheres is nearly inexhaustible. One speaks of a sombre atmosphere, a foreboding atmosphere, an exalted atmosphere, but one speaks also of an atmosphere of violence or holiness, and one even speaks of the boudoir atmosphere, or a petit-bourgeois atmosphere, or the atmosphere of the twenties.
>
> [...]
>
> What is unique and also theoretically complex is that the term describes a typical in-between phenomenon. Atmospheres stand between subjects and objects: one can describe them as object-like emotions, which are randomly cast into a space. But one must at the same time describe them as subjective, insofar as they are nothing without a discerning Subject. But their great value lies exactly in this

---

[1] [whereas it could be said to be enacting the fact that it is not the drama – Series Ed.]

[2] The *Oxford English Dictionary*, at the time of my writing, dates the first use of the word 'atmosphere' in relation to a sonic mood. as recently as a 1941 BBC manual, which uses the words in relation to 'background sounds' that evoke a particular mood, impression or setting, In fact, Napier uses the word in 1936; as does Isaacs in 1933, writing of '*atmospheric* music ... used in Shakespeare's time'.

inbetweeness. Atmospheres combine what was traditionally divided up into *Production Aesthetics* and *Reception Aesthetics*. It is possible to generate atmospheres, of course, and there are developed art disciplines dedicated specifically to the creation of atmospheres. These involve the deployment of what are clearly objects plus all kinds of technical aids, whose presence, however, does not serve its own end, but serves to create atmospheres. Stage design is the paradigmatic example of this approach to atmospheres. On the other hand, however, atmospheres are experienced affectively, and one can only describe their characteristics insofar as one exposes oneself to their presence and experiences them as bodily sensations. (Böhme, 2000, p. 15)

At the heart of Böhme's 'Aesthetics of Atmosphere' is the notion of the 'discerning Subject' – a sentient corporeal presence around which is arranged a 'constellation of surroundings'. It is something 'one feels in the air' hanging like a pall of smoke between subject and object. Indeed, in the theatre, a lighting designer might permeate an auditorium with a thin haze of smoke to create an atmosphere. Its location appears to be neither *here* (wholly within *my* psyche) nor *there* (wholly part of the surrounding environment). Atmosphere is not a purely subjective mood, nor is it an independently measurable, objective substance. We feel it around us and it affects what we do, but we also affect it:

> Bodily space as the space of actions is experienced essentially as possibility, as scope (*Spielraum*). The space of moods is physical expanse, in so far as it involves me affectively. The space of moods is atmospheric space, that is, a certain mental or emotive tone permeating a particular environment, and it is also the atmosphere spreading spatially around me, in which I participate through my mood. (Böhme, 2000, pp. 4–5)

Ambience and Mood

In their respective definitions of the function of sound seen in Part I, Burris-Meyer and Collison talk of atmosphere, while Bracewell talks of mood. In *Sound and Music for the Theatre*, Kaye and Lebrecht (1992) talk of 'ambiance' [sic]. Are these terms interchangeable?

Ambience and atmosphere seem to be more closely related terms – ambience being a specific atmosphere characteristic of a particular place. Atmosphere is more a generic condition of density or semi-opacity: one might cut the atmosphere with a knife, but not the ambience. Mood, it would seem, is something that humans bring to a place. Böhme suggests that one participates in atmosphere though mood – which he claims has a spatial dimension (one might say it is auratic – something which the subject gives out or projects into the space around them, while atmosphere or ambience are aural – immersing and affecting the subject). If one said there was a mood in a room, one would normally infer that it belonged to people in that room, whereas an atmosphere or ambience belongs to the environment.

In theatre, then, mood music might be used to create a mood in the audience so that they interpret the narrative or scene in a different way, whereas atmosphere or ambience might be used to set a scene. Traditionally, 'atmospheres' are washes of sound – rain, wind or crickets – which run under a scene. However, particularly with the use of reverberation or echo, individually cued sounds can add up to a pervading armosphere. An example of this might be the sound design for *Festen*, which Paul Arditti describes in Part I. Susannah Clapp (2004) refers to 'the faint sound of dripping water, the faraway laughter of a child ... informative as well as evocative'. In being informative as well as evocative, the sound design appears to contribute dramaturgically to the sense or meaning of the play as well as creating mood-enhancing or altering receptive conditions for it. This seems to take atmosphere or ambience beyond the traditional role, damned by the faint praise of the clichéd critical adjectives (spooky, doom-laden, portentous and so on). In his review for *The Guardian* (22 December 2004) Michael Billington wrote of *Festen*: 'It's the sounds one remembers most. The clink of a spoon on a wine glass. The laughter of a child. The gush of running water. All these reverberate through *Festen*.'

Arditti says that in fact the number of sounds was fairly minimal and not continuous as many people seem to remember. They seem to connect, according to Billington, and become a continuous atmospheric environment to the play, in the reverberant field of subjective auditory memory.

The use of artificial reverberation, partly through convention, has become a perennially effective (although at times potentially trite) way of achieving opacity or density of aural atmosphere (much as a smoke machine might do for lighting). Indeed, perhaps the most common means of achieving atmospheric sound effects in theatre does not involve the production of sounds at all, but their resounding in enlivened space.

LIVENESS

Resonance, Reverberation and Echo

The term *resonance*, from *resonate*, literally, to *re-sound*, is generally used to describe any noticeable spatial sonic effect, including echo and reverberation. In acoustic theory, however, these three terms have more precise meanings. They each relate to slightly different ways in which a room resounds or responds to a sonic impulse.

Reverberation is the diffuse effect of spatial and temporal extension, as reflected sound waves bounce back and forth between the walls or surfaces of a room or a containing space. Each reflection diminishes in power as an amount of the original energy is absorbed, and the multiple arrivals of these reflections at the ear 'blur' into one diminishing prolongation. David Collison (1982, p. 182) defines it as 'the persistence of sound within a space after the source of that sound has ceased'. Reverberation replays sound, but also tells the subject something about the physical nature of the environment. The longer the reverberation time (the time it takes for the reverberation to decay to the point of inaudibility), the larger the room is psychoacoustically inferred to be. Artificial reverb creates the illusion of a larger space by *implying* that the room is bigger than it really is. Artificial reverb 'presets' are normally categorized as room types: *room, hall, church, cathedral, club* and so on.

Reverberation appears to continue its originary sound (like a comet's tail, it has been said). *Echo*, on the other hand, is separated from its originary sound and appears as one or more discreet 'repeats'. The effect can be like an auditory mirror. In Ovid's telling of the Greek myth, Echo was a sprite or wood nymph who lived in the hills and who became infatuated with the vain young man Narcissus. Echo could not pluck up the courage to speak first to Narcissus, and when Narcissus spoke was only able, in a state of panic, to repeat back the exact words that Narcissus used. When she went to embrace him, Narcissus pulled away, and devastated, Echo was doomed to wander the hills until her body passed away and only her voice remained, repeating anything that it heard.

In musical production, artificial reverb and echo are used to give a sense of enhanced spatiality. They introduce ambience to a sound that would otherwise be too 'clean' or 'dry' by implying acoustic space around either the whole mix, or around certain elements within the mix (for example, the voice or the drums).

The term *resonance* while used as a general description for spatially responsive acoustic effect, including echo and reverberation, more specifically refers to the way in which enclosed spaces appear to 'ring' with sound; that is to say, the way a space accentuates or prolongs some sonic frequencies more than others. If reverberation is the diffuse effect of sound bouncing back and forth, then resonance is a sound bouncing back and forth at one particular pitch more than others. This is the effect of a phenomenon called the 'standing wave', which happens when the wavelength of a certain frequency of sound corresponds proportionally with one of the volumetric dimensions of a containing space. Standing wave resonance occurs in dense objects (strings, anvils, and as we have seen, heads, eyeballs and livers!) as well as in volumes of air. It is most noticeable in rectilinear, hard-surfaced rooms (try singing a scale in your bathroom – you will find that some notes ring more loudly than others). One of the jobs of architectural acoustics is to try to make sure that rooms resonate in ways that are fit for purpose. If a room is to be used for speech or music, they try to make sure that it is neither too boomy nor too shrill and that the ratio of 'wet' (resonant) to 'dry' signal is not too low. In electroacoustic sound systems, it is possible to equalize the frequency response using filters which normalize the way energy is perceived across the whole spectrum. In acoustic halls, this needs to be done physically using baffles and cavities to prevent the formation of standing

waves. A certain amount of resonance, as we will see when we look at auditorium design, can create a warm feeling, but too much can hinder speech
intelligibility.

Live Space

Resonance, reverb and echo (let us refer to these with the single word *resonance*) aesthetically modify the way sound is perceived. Acousticians talk
about a dry sound (without resonance) and wet sound (with it). A room
might be similarly described as a dead space or a live space. When considering a room for intelligible speech or aesthetic feel, acousticians talk about
that room's degree of *liveness*, by which they mean a combination of its energetic frequency response and reverberation time and level. A *live* room
responds longer and more loudly to a sound than a *dead* room, which either
absorbs energy (rather than reflecting it) or baffles reflections in order to
cancel them out. In order to localize sound (get a fix on its point of origin)
the brain relies on a certain amount of spatial reflection: too little, and there
is insufficient spatial information psychoacoustically to triangulate the point
of origin. In most situations, however, there is an amount of environmental
liveness within which to orientate oneself. Since humans are unable to visit
and survive outer space, the closest one can get to completely 'dead'
acoustic space is the *anechoic chamber*: a totally 'suspended' (acoustically
isolated) space, where resonance and reverberation have been completely
negated by absorption and baffles. It is an unnatural and disturbing environment. 'One speaks and the sound seems to drop from one's lips to the
floor. The ears strain to pick up evidence that there is still life in the world'
(Schafer, 1994, p. 256).

'Silence', when observed in a totally soundproofed and absorbent
anechoic chamber, reveals the noise of the subject's own body. Alphonso
Lingis (1994, p. 94) describes how John Cage experienced the 'rustling,
throbbing, whooshing, buzzings, ringings, and squeakings with which the
movements of his muscles and glands resounded with the ripples and
rumbles of the never-ending movements of the atmosphere'. As well as
being sonic, his body also became the only resonant part of the environment.
As a composer, the experience caused Cage to rethink his entire relationship
to sound:

> For, when, after convincing oneself ignorantly that sound has, as its clearly defined
> opposite, silence, that since duration is the only characteristic of sound that is
> measurable in terms of silence, therefore any valid structure involving sounds and
> silences should be based, not as occidentally traditional, on frequency, but rightly
> on duration, one enters an anechoic chamber, as silent as technologically possible
> in 1951, to discover that one hears two sounds of one's own unintentional making
> (nerve's systematic operation, blood's circulation), the situation one is clearly in is
> not objective (sound–silence), but rather subjective (sounds only), those intended
> and those others (so-called silence) not intended. If, at this point one says 'Yes I do

not discriminate between intention and non-intention' the splits: subject–object, art–life, etc., disappear, an identification has been made with the material, and actions are then those relevant to its nature. (Cage, 1978, pp. 13–14)

Theatre's Liveness, Presence and Aura

There is something in the anthropomorphic metaphor of calling a space 'live' which seems to relate to the other use of the word live in relation to theatre: liveness as opposed to pre-recorded; simultaneous; concurrent; in the moment. It may be a tenuous link, but I think the ways in which a live acoustic space impinges on the body, subsumes or even engages it in resonant vibration, connect to that 'special' liveness which some people regard as partly definitive of theatre (as opposed to other mediated or plastic arts). Theatre is not just live because it is happening 'now'; it asserts a live presence on the audience (much as a live room, in prolonging or emphasizing a sound, asserts its presence). This is a very mysterious concept and some people are cautious of it. Philip Auslander, in his (1999) book *Liveness* claims that the concept of *liveness* has become subsumed within the cultural economics of the entertainment industries, and that 'live theatre' is experienced only in relation to the dominant cultural forces of our time, which are the mediatized ones. He is sceptical about claims that theatre has a special *aura* or *presence*. In my view, though, theatre does sonically resonate in a characteristic way, by virtue of the size of its typical spaces, the relatively low acoustic levels, and the conventional silence and stillness of its audience. This resonance, and the audience's aural relationship to it (as opposed to the performance's auratic appearance to the audience) do assert a physical feeling of accentuated 'presence' or prolonged moment which might be experienced as seemingly mysterious 'liveness'.

8 *Resounding Theatres*

This chapter looks at three examples of how some of the phenomena discussed in the previous chapter are produced and controlled by theatre architecture.

The first example does not concern theatre *per se*, but ritual practice and the way resonance was used to create a metaphysical effect for the performance of religious Neolithic burial rites. The transformative effect of resonance on the sung voice becomes a common feature in many subsequent religious practices, but rather than follow that history, the second example looks at resonance (and lack of it) within ancient Greek theatre, as described by the ancient Roman writer Vitruvius. The third looks at the wooden O theatres of Elizabethan London in relation to Vitruvian ideals.

STONE AGE SOUND DESIGN

The Magic Glow of Designed Resonance

> First, by whatever course of design and construction, all six of the diverse configurations visited sustain clearly discernible acoustical resonances in the vicinity of 110Hz, well within the male voice range. (Jahn, Devereux, and Ibison, 1996, p. 658)

In 2001, a popular Channel 4 documentary *Secrets of the Dead: Sounds from the Stone Age* suggested that various ancient sites of ritual practice, both in America and Europe, were acoustically designed to resonate theatrically in response to pitched chanting and percussion. Kivas are large, covered, circular ritual or ceremonial chambers which are partially or fully sunk into the ground and are used to this day by Pueblan peoples in the Four Corners region of America for ceremonies connected to *kachina* belief systems. As 'theatres', they are dark or semi-dark, smoke-filled places, where chanting, storytelling and ceremonies were traditionally performed under the influence of hallucinogens. Vocal intonation plays a significant part in the ritual practices of kachina belief systems, as it does in many religions, and many kivas seem to resonate particularly around 110Hz (or the A below middle C), which is at the low end of the typical male vocal range. According to the documentary and Paul Devereux's associated book *Stone Age Soundtracks: the Acoustic Archaeology of Ancient Sites*, this accentuated resonance 'in the vicinity' of 110Hz seems, from archaeological evidence, to have been a deliberate characteristic of *kiva* design for over 3,000 years, and one which, it was claimed, occurs in other designed places of ritual practice in several other, unconnected, cultures.

The effect of this architecturally accentuated 110Hz resonance is a warm acoustic 'glow' around that frequency area, it is audible but it is also palpable: the glow is felt within the body as well as heard in the ears. Within the circular kiva spaces, the build-up of standing wave resonance around (male) chanting creates an engulfing sensation wherein physical vibration and sound seem to combine in one powerful feeling of spiritual transformation or energetic trance.

Intrigued by evidence of Stone Age acoustic design in America, Paul Devereux along with Professors Michael Ibison and Robert Jahn undertook a pilot study of six ancient Neolithic chambered tombs in the UK and Ireland. The results showed that the same accentuated 110Hz resonance occurred in each site. They published the results of this pilot study in the journal of the *Acoustical Society of America* (and later in *Antiquity*) also noting that there were, in several of the sites, drawings that looked like wave patterns, suggesting that somehow the ancient architects of these chambers were knowingly employing acoustic theory. These sites, it is thought, were used not only for burial, but for performing religious rites. If true, the 110Hz theory suggested that they might have been specifically designed – tuned, if you will – for ritual sonic practices similar to the kachina trance rituals, in which chanting at 110Hz literally seemed to 'invoke' a supernatural presence within the chamber. This remains a common feature of religious services and rituals and one which features within all major faiths:

> It was the physically sounded word of God that transformed Christ's 'mystical body' from a wafer in the Roman rite into an assembly of people in the Protestant liturgy. A preacher, like an orator, accomplishes that feat through the totalizing deployment of his voice (Ihde, 1976, p. 267)

Resonance between 100 and 120Hz assists this 'totalizing' effect of the male voice and is a designed feature of church, temple and mosque design dating from at least the middle ages. Perhaps on account of its seemingly metaphysical visceral effect, sound features prominently within religious scripture, liturgy and forms of prayer. For example:

> In the Upanishads the 'primal sound' is called Sabda Brahman, the sound of Lord Brahma, the cosmic sound whose power resides in all words that express the essential. In the Vedas, it is the anahad, the 'unlimited tone'. And for the musicians and sages of India since the times of the Moguls, Nada Brahma is the primal sound, understood as 'Brahma-sound', 'world-sound', or 'god-sound'. In order to

understand it, one needs Nada Yoga: drill and exercise and training through sound. Sufis call the primal sound Saute Surmad, the tone that fills the cosmos. Muhammad perceived it when he was enlightened in the cave of Gare-Hira. So Islam also knows the sound that says, 'Let there be ...' Sufi Han-at Inayat Khan writes: 'This sound is the source of all manifestation. ... The knower of the mystery of sound knows the mystery of the whole universe.'

The Hebraic-Jewish world has a sense of these matters too. The trumpets that brought down the walls of Jericho are symbols of the power of the primal sound and of primal music. The 'trumpeting cherub' is a Hebrew and Christian prime concept, and what he blows is primal music.

Of course, mantras also exist in the realm of Christianity. Amen, the Hail Mary of the rosary, Hallelujah, Hosanna, Kyrie Eleison – these are all mantras. The last named – 'Lord have mercy' – is the 'Jesus prayer' of the Orthodox tradition, used by wandering monks, many of whom meditate on it for years. (Berendt, 1988, p. 38)

A full exploration of sound and religion would require another volume, but, in relation to our subject of sound and theatre, the ancient connection between acoustic resonance and supernatural presence (be it a divine holy spirit, or the presence of the deceased) is worth noting, as are the ways in which acoustic and 'worked' sonic effects have played a part in all kinds of religious services and ritual events that involve theatrical, priestly ministration to an audient congregation.

The discovery of apparently designed resonance in Stone Age burial chambers is not the only form of sonic 'theatricality' evident in sites of ritual practice from this period. There are also 'whispering holes' and other apertures through which the sound of the wind or of the human voice could be channelled and resonated with similarly supernatural effect (see Ihde's comments on 'spirit', breath and sound, quoted in the last chapter). More detailed research by archaeologist Aaron Watson and acoustician David Keating, both of Reading University confirmed that ancient burial chambers seemed not only to be 'tuned' to the performance of sound within them, but to have *designed* properties of 'Helmholtz resonance', which, in effect, made them sound-making instruments.

Helmholtz resonance is responsible for the surprisingly loud sound that is made when air is blown across the mouth of a bottle. The act of blowing causes the air to vibrate in the bottleneck, producing an audible tone. This action sends patterned shockwaves into the volume of air in the main 'jar' portion of the bottle. Air is elastic (or bouncy) and the waves rebound, combining their peaks at the fundamental standing-wave frequency of the bottle, which has the effect of energizing or amplifying the sound which is forced back out of the bottleneck as seemingly amplified tone. The audible pitch produced is dependent on the relationship of the size of the cavity to the size of the aperture. It is the same acoustic phenomenon responsible for the amplifying effect of any instrument comprising a resonant sound box and a projective aperture: an acoustic guitar for instance.

Helmholtz processes are also used to maximise energy at very low, *infrasonic* levels (*infrasonic* means acoustic vibration that is below the frequency level at which our ears can process it as sound – normally around 20 vibrations per second, or 20Hz) They are responsible for the operation of bass subwoofers, familiar in dance clubs, which produce tangible, sympathetic vibration in the body. Infrasonic Helmholtz resonance can be one of the most viscerally disturbing/moving of acoustic effects, with the potential to alter the pulse and the breathing (as anyone who has spent time in a club may recognize). Some people attribute the sense of spirituality experienced in resonant churches to the infrasonic vibrations of large organ pipes (a phenomenon not unknown by the architects of such spaces).

Helmholtz resonance seems vaguely alchemistic: the amount of acoustic energy that seems to resonate within or emanate from the chamber seems to be more than that which was put in: the effect exceeds the cause, apparently, so it might well be tempting to infer some supernatural force at work. Keating and Watson found designed Helmholtz resonance applied in different ways in the various tombs that they studied. Whispering holes – aside from offering apertures through which to speak to the dead, also had the bottleneck effect of Helmholtz resonance. Essentially they acted as mouthpieces though which the tombs could be played like musical instruments, either by wind blowing across the openings, or through the excitation of the air within the tombs by voices or drums. The resonant response of the chambers seems like ghostly or divine spirits responding or joining in with the ritual. Similar effects are found in the ancient sites of oracles in Greece.

In other sites, the effect of drumming within a certain space within the tomb-system produced a Helmholtz bass response that was routed through passages and tunnels to connected tombs, while remaining virtually unheard above ground – in other words, the sound of drumming appeared to come from nowhere, or at least with no visible source, which is to say it is what we might now call *acousmatic* (see Devereux, 2001, pp. 100–1). This, as we saw in the Butterworth extract, was powerful theatrical magic to the pre-Edison ear.

Watson and Keating discovered the most dramatic Helmholtz effect in the tomb *Dwarfie Stane*. They found a passage and two chambers tomb hewn into an enormous sandstone rock (8.5 metres long, 4.2 metres high and 2.4 metres wide). The passage is 2.2 metres long, but barely 0.7 metres high, and not much wider, while the chamber or cell is almost 2 metres wide and slightly higher than the passage. The closing stone for the passage entrance lay outside the passage, but when in place would have left a 'whispering hole' through which a sound could be projected. Watson and Keating found it quite easy to use their voices to set up a resonant frequency, which seemed to be taken on by the rock and to develop a character of its own. Not only did this vast rock seem to produce sound, it seemed to shake:

When this happened, the sound appeared to become expansive and substantially fuller. At the same time, the massive stone block, and the air within it, appeared to shake vigorously. This vibration was also evident to listeners positioned outside the entrance and standing on the roof. Using sound in this way, one person can induce many tons of stones to appear to come alive in a manner which would be difficult to achieve by any other means. (Devereux, 2001, p. 102)

This was an illusion – the shaking rock was in fact a hollowed out resonance chamber – but it seemed like magic and would have made the ancient priest, or whoever invoked the shaking rock, seem supernaturally powerful.

The connection I am making between ritual funereal practices and theatre is intended to be illustrative of the theatricality of resonance in places where performance and audient congregation are governed by ritual convention and administered by a priestly performer. But I like to think there may be a more progenitorial link between chanting in resonant funeral spaces and theatre *per se*:

> In early days the tragic chorus and its dithyramb were closely attached to the tombs or shrines of heroes, and were only performed on festival occasions at sacred spots, as was the case with the Mysteries and Miracles of mediaeval Europe. Thespis detached his chorus and dithyramb from some particular shrine, possibly at Icaria … (Ridgeway, 1915, p. 11)

Alternative and Complementary Theories of Intelligent Sonic Design

Aside from the religious theatricality and feelings of spirituality produced by the experience of resonance at certain frequencies, some people claim that certain sonic frequencies are significant because they represent cosmic 'magic numbers'. These include the vibratory intervals, structural proportionality and orbital cycles of phenomena as diverse as DNA, planetary orbits, pulsars, genes, oxygen and other elemental atoms, crystals, leaves, trees and the human body. It is often observed by people who, like me, probably don't really understand it, that the *dual resonance* model of theoretical physics, or 'string theory' as it is popularly known, is a sonic analogy of the universe. The notion that the universe might be 'tuned' by intelligent design excites some imaginations. A succession of sub-Pythagorean mathematicians from Nikomachos of Gerasa in the second century AD, through Johannes Kepler (1571–1630), to 'new age' scholars such as Hans Cousto, have attempted to create music from cosmic magic numbers by 'octavizing'[1] natural measurements. Thus, we have Kepler's primordial harmonies (octave, fifth, fourth etc) derived from earthly observation and measurement of planetary movement, and several other systems of orbital 'day' and 'year' and 'moon' frequencies. According to these, planets have both day tones and

---

[1] For example, if one were to double the number 1.71875 six times, one would arrive at the audible frequency of 110Hz , seven times, at 220, eight times at 440 etc. All of these numbers are, if one wishes, the note A.

colours and year tones and colours; solar systems can be heard as chords; if a planet has a moon then its lunar cycle can be octavized up to a 'moon tone'; and so on (see Berendt, 1988, pp. 84–105 for more on all of this). Depending on which cosmic 'tuning' theory you want to use, 110Hz or the note A might be a moon tone or a sun tone or even the pitch of the planet Venus. If you Google '110Hz conspiracy' or variations on this theme, you will find many suggestions of cosmic significance for the tone 110Hz which connect it to the ancient god-name YHVH, the great flood of Noah, healing crystals and much else besides. Similar is true of many other frequencies. Berendt seems to be a fan of G as earth's 'day tone' and also describes the cultural significance of the Indian tone *sa* (136Hz), which is the basis of traditional Indian instrumental tuning systems and in the chanting of the primal word / sacred mantra OM.

VITRUVIUS ON ARCHITECTURE

Aural Pleasure

It is not unsurprising that 110Hz seems to recur in Stone Age sound design, if you consider that the main sound sources in the ritual practices performed within them would in all likelihood have been male voices and drums, and that by tuning the room to 110Hz, the architects were effectively 'turning the bass up' on proceedings and creating a warm sonic glow within the bodies of those present. Whatever its significance, it should be remembered that this, after all, can be a pleasurable sensation.

Aural pleasure, as well as sonic functionality, has a place in theatre design. C. J. Phipps' Theatre Royal Bath or the more reverberant Theatre Royal Nottingham, for example, both have a warmth in their acoustics which one 'feels' in one's body. This is deliberate, and has nothing to do with hearing the words intelligibly. A warmly resonant environment is intended merely to enhance the pleasure of the audience.

Stone-built Greek theatres are commonly associated with the functional clarity of their speech transmission, which is achieved by allowing sound to emanate unhindered in its spherical way from the 'orchestra' playing areas throughout the amphitheatre. Unlike the *Dwarfie Stane*, the stone used in Greek amphitheatres is not hollow and does not resonate internally. When full of absorptive human bodies, these theatres are virtually free from sonic reflectivity, save that of the *skene* front which helps throw the sound of the performance forward into the auditorium. Great for diction, perhaps, but low on theatrical 'atmosphere' – and, as Landels points out, not helpful for the actors:

> One reason why the acoustics are so good in ancient theatres is that the design, with semicircular auditorium and no roof, virtually eliminates any echo or

reverberation. For the spoken word this is essential, especially at very low power levels. And though the actor can easily make himself audible throughout what is by our standards a very large theatre indeed, he must take this on trust: there is practically no response from the auditorium. (Landels, 1967, p. 891)

Êcheia Resonators

These Greek acoustics were praised by the Roman writer Vitruvius. Marcus Vitruvius Pollio (c. 75–25 BC) was both an architect and engineer whose treatise *De Architectura* was rediscovered in fifteenth-century Italy and became one of the major inspirations for Renaissance, Baroque and Neoclassical architecture. Vitruvius' understanding of acoustics is remarkable for the time. In *De Architectura* he analyses the acoustics of ancient Greek theatres (of which there were several antique examples in his native Italy) and correctly identifies many of the acoustic principles that made them so famously clear for diction. But he also remarks that they lack the warmth of resonance found in Roman wooden theatres. Perhaps because he cannot accept that the otherwise miraculous Greeks would have overlooked the importance of aural pleasure in this way, he spends a lot of time speculating on the function of bronze vases known as *êcheia*, whose fragments were found distributed around ancient Greek auditoria in Italy.

These, according to Vitruvius, were meant to resonate in sympathy with the voices of the chorus or actors when they hit certain notes. The vases were pitched to resonate at different frequencies and were arranged in harmonic relationships to one another. The effect would have been to prolong and accentuate the tonality of music or voice (rather than the diction). As Vitruvius puts it, upon hitting these vases, sound 'will wake an harmonious note in unison with itself'. This theory is plausible because we know (through Loraux 2002, and others) that Greek drama had an acoustemological meta-text with precise coded meaning attached to certain musical timbres and vocal phonemes (which were, it is suggested, also deliberately enhanced by the wearing of resonant wooden masks – see below).

Less established, however, is the physics. We have no intact *êcheia* to test nor any sufficiently precise specifications in order to recreate them, but some scholars believe that their effectiveness in relation to this purpose was possibly speculation on the part of Vitruvius. Vases similar to those Vitruvius describes have been found concealed within cavities in the walls of Renaissance churches and the Turkish mosques of Sinan the Architect (possibly inspired by Vitruvius' theories). Scientific testing has shown the resonant effect of such devices to be very localized, extremely minimal in terms of energizing the overall room acoustic (see Arns and Crawford, 1995), and sometimes even counterproductive (suggesting that the vases were sometimes used as resonance cancelling devices). Nevertheless, Vitruvius' vases seem to have existed and according to the latest digital modelling, could theoretically, if positioned and manufactured very precisely, have worked (see Godman, 2005).

The Acoustic Properties of Wood

Vitruvius' comments on the wooden resonance of his contemporary Roman theatres are just as important as his observations on Greek stone built theatres. He notes that their resonant, reflective properties 'may be observed from the behaviour of those who sing to the lyre, who, when they wish to sing in a higher key, turn towards the folding doors on the stage, and thus by their aid are reinforced with a sound in harmony with the voice.' Wood reflects sound pleasantly, absorbing some harsher frequencies and returning a warmly modified reverberation to the listener. It also turns sub-stage spaces, seating boxes and sub-auditoria spaces into resonance chambers. Wooden resonance is soft and warm and if Vitruvius felt that this resonance was missing in stone built Greek auditoria, then his *êcheia* would surely not have been a substitute. Aside from the doubt which surrounds their efficacy, their metallic, harmonically pitched resonance would sound very different from the kind of wooden resonance that Vitruvius experienced in his contemporary Roman theatres.

But one should not let the curious *êcheia* debate cloud Vitruvius' main architectural legacy, which was to inspire Renaissance theatre builders. In relation to our subject here, we should note the particular importance he attached to achieving an acoustic quality that balanced functional clarity and intelligibility of sound within an aesthetically pleasurable degree of resonance.

8.1 Extracts from Vitruvius (1914) *Ten Books on Architecture*, trans. M. H. Morgan (Cambridge, MA: Harvard University Press)

Book V, Chapter III: The Theatre: Its Site, Foundations and Acoustics

[In paragraphs 1–3 Vitruvius has discussed health and safety and aesthetic issues involved in deciding where to site a theatre].

4. The curved cross-aisles should be constructed in proportionate relation, it is thought, to the height of the theatre, but not higher than the footway of the passage is broad. If they are loftier, they will throw back the voice and drive it away from the upper portion, thus preventing the case-endings of words from reaching with distinct meaning the ears of those who are in the uppermost seats above the cross-aisles. In short, it should be so contrived that a line drawn from the lowest to the highest seat will touch the top edges and angles of all the seats. Thus the voice will meet with no obstruction.

5. The different entrances ought to be numerous and spacious, the upper not connected with the lower, but built in a continuous straight line from all parts of the house, without turnings, so that the people may not be crowded together when let out from shows, but may have separate exits from all parts without obstructions. Particular pains must also be taken that the site be not a 'deaf' one, but one through which the voice can range with the greatest clearness. This can be brought about if a site is selected where there is no obstruction due to echo.

6. Voice is a flowing breath of air, perceptible to the hearing by contact. It moves in an endless number of circular rounds, like the innumerably increasing circular waves which appear when a stone is thrown into smooth water, and which keep on spreading indefinitely from the centre unless interrupted by narrow limits, or by some obstruction which prevents such waves from reaching their end in due formation. When they are interrupted by obstructions, the first waves, flowing back, break up the formation of those which follow.

7. In the same manner the voice executes its movements in concentric circles; but while in the case of water the circles move horizontally on a plane surface, the voice not only proceeds horizontally, but also ascends vertically by regular stages. Therefore, as in the case of the waves formed in the water, so it is in the case of the voice: the first wave, when there is no obstruction to interrupt it, does not break up the second or the following waves, but they all reach the ears of the lowest and highest spectators without an echo.

8. Hence the ancient architects, following in the footsteps of nature, perfected the ascending rows of seats in theatres from their investigations of the ascending voice, and, by means of the canonical theory of the mathematicians and that of the musicians, endeavoured to make every voice uttered on the stage come with greater clearness and sweetness to the ears of the audience. For just as musical instruments are brought to perfection of clearness in the sound of their strings by means of bronze plates or horns [Greek: *êcheia*], so the ancients devised methods of increasing the power of the voice in theatres through the application of harmonics.

[In *Chapter IV* Vitruvius describes harmonic theory. For the sake of brevity I have excluded this section.]

Chapter V: Sounding Vessels in the Theatre

1. In accordance with the foregoing investigations on mathematical principles, let bronze vessels be made, proportionate to the size of the theatre, and let them be so fashioned that, when touched, they may produce with one another the notes of the fourth, the fifth, and so on up to the double octave. Then, having constructed niches in between the seats of the theatre, let the vessels be arranged in them, in accordance with musical laws, in such a way that they nowhere touch the wall, but have a clear space all round them and room over their tops. They should be set upside down, and be supported on the side facing the stage by wedges not less than half a foot high. Opposite each niche, apertures should be left in the surface of the seat next below, two feet long and half a foot deep.

2. The arrangement of these vessels, with reference to the situations in which they should be placed, may be described as follows. If the theatre be of no great size, mark out a horizontal range halfway up, and in it construct thirteen arched niches with twelve equal spaces between them, so that of the above mentioned 'êcheia' those which give the note *nete hyperbolaeon* may be placed first on each side, in the niches which are at the extreme ends; next to the ends and a fourth below in pitch, the note *nete diezeugmenon*; third, *paramese*, a fourth below; fourth, *nete synhemmenon*; fifth, *mese*, a fourth below; sixth, *hypate* meson, a fourth below; and in the middle and another fourth below, one vessel giving the note *hypate hypaton*.

3. On this principle of arrangement, the voice, uttered from the stage as from a centre, and spreading and striking against the cavities of the different vessels, as it comes in contact with them, will be increased in clearness of sound, and will wake an harmonious note in unison with itself. But if the theatre be rather large, let its height be divided into four parts, so that three horizontal ranges of niches may be marked out and constructed: one for the enharmonic, another for the chromatic, and the third for the diatonic system. Beginning with the bottom range, let the arrangement be as described above in the case of a smaller theatre, but on the enharmonic system.

4. In the middle range, place first at the extreme ends the vessels which give the note of the chromatic *hyperbolaeon*; next to them, those which give the chromatic *diezeugmenon*, a fourth below; third, the chromatic *synhemmenon*; fourth, the chromatic *meson*, a fourth below; fifth, the chromatic *hypaton*, a fourth below; sixth, the *paramese*, for this is both the concord of the fifth to the chromatic *hyperbolaeon*, and the *concord of* the chromatic *synhemmenon*.

5. No vessel is to be placed in the middle, for the reason that there is no other note in the chromatic system that forms a natural concord of sound. In the highest division and range of niches, place at the extreme ends vessels fashioned so as to give the note of the diatonic *hyperbolaeon*; next, the diatonic *diezeugmenon*, a fourth below; third, the diatonic *synhemmenon*; fourth, the diatonic meson, a fourth below; fifth, the diatonic *hypaton*, a fourth below; sixth, the *proslambanomenos*, a fourth below; in the middle, the note mese, for this is both the octave to *proslambanomenos*, and the concord of the fifth to the diatonic hypaton.

6. Whoever wishes to carry out these principles with ease, has only to consult the scheme at the end of this book, drawn up in accordance with the laws of music. It was left by Aristoxenus, who with great ability and labour classified and arranged in it the different modes. In accordance with it, and by giving heed to these theories, one can easily bring a theatre to perfection, from the point of view of the nature of the voice, so as to give pleasure to the audience.

7. Somebody will perhaps say that many theatres are built every year in Rome, and that in them no attention at all is paid to these principles; but he will be in error, from the fact that all our public theatres made of wood contain a great deal of boarding, which must be resonant. This may be observed from the behaviour of those who sing to the lyre, who, when they wish to sing in a higher key, turn towards the folding doors on the stage, and thus by their aid are reinforced with a sound in harmony with the voice. But when theatres are built of solid materials like masonry, stone, or

marble, which cannot be resonant, then the principles of the 'êcheia' must be applied.

8. If, however, it is asked in what theatre these vessels have been employed, we cannot point to any in Rome itself, but only to those in the districts of Italy and in a good many Greek states. We have also the evidence of Lucius Mummius, who, after destroying the theatre in Corinth, brought its bronze vessels to Rome, and made a dedicatory offering at the temple of Luna with the money obtained from the sale of them. Besides, many skilful architects, in constructing theatres in small towns, have, for lack of means, taken large jars made of clay, but similarly resonant, and have produced very advantageous results by arranging them on the principles described.

Coda to Vitruvius Section

Swedish mask maker Torbjörn Alström has found that wooden masks modelled on ancient Greek designs have the effect of amplifying and projecting the non-verbal performance of wails and shrieks that formed a traditional part of Greek theatre. In collaboration with voice teacher Mirkka Yemendzakis and mask constructor Thanos Vovolis, Alström fashioned masks based on archaeological finds and pictorial representations of Greek masks. Unlike those more normally encountered in modern staging of classical Greek drama, these masks had relatively small oral openings that seem to have been designed to project tonal sound by Helmholtz resonance. Alström writes about this in *The Drama Review*:

> Vocal resonance masks afford additional possibilities for emphasizing specific vocal qualities and can even facilitate special vocal effects. When the voice is able to orient properly in a vocal resonance mask, effects such as the highlighting of overtones can be achieved. Furthermore, the voice is experienced as fuller than otherwise. A wide range of acoustical expressions becomes available, not leastwise in coordination with other performers in resonance masks. The combination of the mask's focusing on the voice and the effects achieved within that focusing sometimes approach a hypnotic result. Here, one can easily experience a parallel to the shamanic use of the mask. In those cultures in which song has been instrumental in reaching a state of trance, it seems likely that mask resonance has been one of the tools used to achieve the hypnotic state of consciousness. (Alström, 2004, pp. 133–4)

Again, resonance enhances vocal sound in a way that produces effects associated with shamanistic trance, as we saw in the previous section on ancient ritual sites. The Helmholtz relationship of the mouth aperture to the cavity between the face and the interior of the mask seems to have been calculated to emphasize certain frequencies (which Alström describes as predominantly in the low-mid and bass areas, with some high frequency reinforcement):

> Working with the vocal resonance mask onstage contributes to the spectrum of unique expressions available to the performance arts. Together with the performer's physical creativity, the mask can sharpen and deepen a scenic illusion by affording

the voice previously unexplored possibilities. The voice speaks directly to the listener's inner world. Not only does work with resonance masks open opportunities for new acoustic experiences, but it also enhances the listener's perception of the spoken words themselves, and of the songs performed. (Ibid., p. 135)

The effect was a sonic persona, the equivalent of the visual effect of mask. But could the êcheia vases conceivably have been tuned specifically to respond and amplify transmissions from these masks? If so, the masks might be regarded as a prototype of that characteristically modern form of sonic performer persona, the stage microphone.

PRIVILEGING THE AURAL: SHAKESPEARIAN ACOUSTICS

Far more than for us in the twenty-first century, the Elizabethan audience experienced drama as a live acoustic phenomenon, and with a much more sophisticated ear. (Johnson, 2005)

The remarkable theatre acoustics of the Elizabethan 'wooden O' theatres seem to have achieved a near-perfect balance between speech intelligibility and enveloping, wooden resonance. In private productions too, wooden-fitted indoor sounding-chambers privileged both the sound of the text and the aural experience of the audience (although in subtly different ways – the round public theatres having a 'broader', more panoramic sound, and the rectilinear indoor wooden theatre having, ironically, a rounder sound). Were it not for the high status attached to acoustic design in the theatres of the time, which enabled the vocal performance and pleasurable reception of complex poetic drama, the Elizabethan age might not have produced the great literary theatre for which it is remembered. Circular public theatres such as the Globe created an environment in which audience and performers felt invigorated by the acoustic presence around them, and yet the design of the wooden, plaster and thatch surroundings allowed them to hear the intricate wordplay of the drama intimately amidst the noise of an outdoor theatre that still retained much of the ambience of a pageant. The theatre acoustic offered a balance between circumstantial aural excitement and focused listening that was familiar to contemporary London ears from the streets, taverns and markets, and within which the drama would have felt alive and relevant to the contemporary cultural moment. This was no accident. Bruce R. Smith suggests that the public theatres of the time were designed first and foremost as 'instruments for the production and reception of sound' (Smith, 1999, p. 207) and were consciously built, along Vitruvian lines, to be suitable arenas for the performance of a drama which, like its classical Greek forebear, consisted both within the verbal text and within an acoustemological meta-text of sound, music and sonic allusion. They may have originated in courtyard theatres or bear-pits, but the wooden Os were designed by architects to be the ideal sonic arenas in which to 'complete' a dramatic work through its sounding (Ibid., pp. 208–17). Theatres were sonic instruments, and such was the attention to sound in the years leading up to the turn of the seventeenth-century, that where a hall (for example, at court or in a university college) had unacceptable acoustics for theatre performance, temporary sub-structures made of wood were built, in order to contain and control the resonance.[2]

Theatre sound, to a certain extent, echoed the rapidly developing urban soundscape in its acoustic characteristics and diversity of noises. The balance between absorption and reflection in a wood/plaster/thatch environment is typically softer to the ear than the harsh reflectivity of environments of concrete, glass or marble to which the modern ear is used, and it allows for more differentiation of sound. Elizabethan cities resonated with speech or the singing of work songs, the noises of animals and wheels, the near and far sounds of commerce and the distant sound of ancient parish bells, but not as a cacophony: each of these sounds would have been individually discernable as part of a broad, urban panorama rather than a general urban drone. The sound of a 'noise' (band) of musicians might occupy a position just here, within this panorama, while the calls of a fishmonger were clearly just there and the clang of the blacksmith's anvil was just over there; and thus it would be onstage: music coexisting alongside the sounds of the speech, stage effects and the surrounding noises of the audience, just as it would within the daily urban earshot of the audience. The architecturally controlled resonance of the round outdoor public theatres would accentuate this effect:

> Thanks to the absence of a roof over the yard, auditors in the yard and in the galleries would have found themselves in a perceptibly different relationship to the auditory events going on all around them. In a cylindrical space, listeners can locate sounds horizontally far more accurately than they can in a space enclosed on six sides. Applause sounds on the left and the right, not all around; loud laughter comes from over there, a rude comment from over there. Performers in the reconstructed Globe in London have commented on the way audience response can start in one part of the theater and then spread laterally to the rest. The experience of broad sound comes not only from the actors onstage but from one's fellow auditors. (Ibid., p. 214)

Coda: Hi-Fidelity

The Elizabethan environment of thatch, plaster and wood had exceptional sound imaging and resonance and reverberation balanced, rather than

---

2 Including the pre-Inigo Jones version of the Banqueting House – something that anyone who has tried to listen to a speech in the echoey acoustic of the surviving version of that room might wish still existed!

competed with, the 'original' signal (e.g. the voice). This is what the acoustic ecologist R. Murray Schafer calls a 'hi-fi system'.

> A hi-fi system is one possessing a favorable signal-to-noise ratio. The hi-fi sound-scape is one in which discrete sounds can be heard clearly because of the low ambient noise level. The country is generally more hi-fi than the city; night more than day; ancient times more than modern. In the hi-fi soundscape, sounds over-lap less frequently; there is perspective – foreground and background: 'the sound of a pail on the lip of a well, and the crack of a whip in the distance' – the image is Alain-Fournier's to describe the economic acoustics of the French countryside.
>
> The quiet ambiance of the hi-fi soundscape allows the listener to hear farther into the distance just as the countryside exercises long-range viewing. The city abbreviates this facility for distant hearing (and seeing) marking one of the more important changes in the history of perception.
>
> In a lo-fidelity soundscape individual acoustic signals are obscured in an over-dense population of sounds. The pellucid sound – a footstep in the snow, a church bell across the valley or an animal scurrying in the brush is masked by broad-band noise. Perspective is lost. On a downtown street corner of the modern city there is no distance; there is only presence. There is cross-talk on all the channels, and in order for the most ordinary sounds to be heard they have to be increasingly ampli-fied. (Shafer, 1994, pp. 43–4)

The definitive work on spatial imaging is Blauert (1997) *Spatial Hearing: The Psychophysics of Human Sound Localization*.

9 *Alternative Realities*

In the last two chapters we looked at theatre's 'live' acoustic space as the aural arena within which performance is made. One might call these the 'real' aural circumstances of theatre. We now look at how sound contributes to the creation of alternate time and space within the theatre, within the mise-en-scène and within the imagination.

THE SONIC SCENE

Out of the Round: Of Roofs and Flattage

The Olivier Theatre in London is modelled on the Greek theatre of Epidauros in all but one key respect: it has a roof. As a result, the acoustics – far from displaying the legendary clarity and transmission of an ancient Greek amphitheatre – have been problematic to audiences, actors, directors and sound designers alike. Expensive electroacoustic reinforcement systems with multiple microphones and loudspeakers have been installed and abandoned; many different configurations of sound baffling have been tried to rid the theatre of its uneven coverage, its strange echoes, acoustic 'deadspots' and over-resonant 'hotspots'. These days, the expertise of the sound department has managed to get the Olivier sounding better than ever before, but Vitruvius would not have considered it ideal.

In Shakespeare's time, the stone-built, paved, roofed, Blackfriars Theatre had a different, more 'live' acoustic than the outdoor amphitheatres, but the acoustic experts of the time made it work, with wooden cladding, screens and false ceilings. The 'feel' would have been entirely different from the panoramic sound of the Globe:

> The sound the speaker sent out into the hall would not immediately have been returned to the center, as it would have at the Globe, but would have struck the back wall, bounced to the sides, and only then returned to the center. This dispersal effect would have been enhanced by the multiple planes of the galleries. However deep they may have been, whether or not they ran the full perimeter of the room, the galleries provided a series of differently angled, resonant wood surfaces that contributed to the dispersal of sound in its full range of frequencies. … With or without a vaulted ceiling, the rectilinear surfaces of the Blackfriars

Theater would have produced a 'round' sound quite different from the 'broad' sound of the Globe – just the reverse of the effect suggested by the physical shapes of the two structures. (Smith, 1999, p. 217)

There are many good reasons – the weather being one of them – why London theatre moved indoors and its buildings and their acoustics began to change. The Masque was perhaps only a somewhat rarefied, expensive form of theatre experienced by the wealthy elite, but its effect, as we have seen in Part I, had led to the incorporation of more music into the production itself and a more marked emphasis (not least in production budgets) on scenic painting and machinery. While, following the Interregnum, only two theatres were licensed for the performance of plays, one of these was, at first, in a converted tennis court. We know that from the start, there was competition around which one could provide the most spectacular stagings, and it is apparent that sound had become a lower priority. As their buildings grew incrementally larger, and then as new theatres began to appear at the Haymarket in London and in regional centres such as Bristol, Bath and Liverpool (in the late seventeenth-century) they were built to house mixed seasons of spoken drama and music theatre (Semi-Opera and Restoration Spectacular at first, although in practice, theatres could not afford to stage many of these) and then, increasingly, Italian Opera. Music and speech have different ideal acoustics, resulting in compromise.

Italianate fashions for illusionistic, painted scenery and ingenious scenic 'reveals' demanded an 'end on' perspective on the 'scene,' viewed through the frame of the proscenium arch (although for quite a long while, following the Restoration, much of the verbal play – particularly of comedy – was done downstage of the proscenium on an extended forestage or 'apron' that retained many of the intimate 'thrust-stage' attributes of the amphitheatre). In the rush to impress the eye, care for the ear – so important in theatre architecture less than a century before – seemed to have lost priority. The first Drury Lane theatre, opened in haste after the Restoration, had terrible acoustic problems, which Pepys describes:

The house is made with extraordinary good contrivance, and yet hath some faults, as the narrowness of the passages in and out of the Pitt, and the distance from the stage to the boxes, which I am confident cannot hear; but for all other things it is well, only, above all, the musique being below, and most of it sounding under the very stage, there is no hearing of the bases at all, nor very well of the trebles, which sure must be mended (8 May 1663). (Pepys, S, Diaries http://www.pepys.info/1663/1663may.html, accessed 21 March 2007)

Compared with the Globe, which could seat a thousand, the early, roofed Patent theatres were small, but grew with each rebuilding (and they had a habit of regularly burning down). Eventually they reached capacities of between two and three thousand and competed with each other to be the biggest and most visually splendid. With this increased air volume, acoustics became increasingly problematic for spoken drama. In this 1706 extract from *An Apology for the Life of Mr. Colley Cibber, (Volume I)*, the actor complains about how theatre managers Sir John Vanbrugh and his associate the poet William Congreve ('music has charms to sooth a savage breast') neglected the 'auditor' (of spoken texts, at least) in favour of the 'spectator':

> As to their other dependence, the House, they had not yet discover'd that almost every proper quality and convenience of a good theatre had been sacrificed or neglected to shew the spectator a vast triumphal piece of architecture! And that the best play, for the reasons I am going to offer, could not but be under great disadvantages, and be less capable of delighting the auditor here than it could have been in the plain theatre they came from. ... This extraordinary and super-fluous space occasion'd such an undulation from the voice of every actor, that generally what they said sounded like the gabbling of so many people in the lofty aisles in a cathedral – the tone of a trumpet, or the swell of an eunuch's holding note, 'tis true, might be sweeten'd by it, but the articulate sounds of a speaking voice were drown'd by the hollow reverberations of one word upon another. (Cibber, 1889, pp. 321–2)

Theatre architecture would, in due course, get to grips with the challenges of cathedral-like dimensions, re-learning a lot of the techniques used at the Blackfriars Theatre in Shakespeare's time. For a thorough account of some of these I recommend Michael Barron's *Auditorium Acoustics and Architectural Design* (1993).

The general trend was towards larger auditoria, whose 'liveness' was harnessed (by baffles, reflective surfaces and resonant lanterns or domes) to aid in the projection of the stage sound outwards into the auditoria. The roundness of the Blackfriars and the broad, detailed panoramic soundstage of the Globe gave way to the sonic equivalent of the picture window, the audience sitting in a muted room over here, listening to a bright and lively other room over there. These changing theatre acoustics, I suppose, played a part in changing performance styles and audience aural behaviours. Within the Globe, there may be areas of restricted view, but not of restricted audi-tion. Not so in huge, multi-storey theatres. 'Actorly' vocal projection, rein-forced by semaphore-like gesture,[1] becomes necessary when attempting to communicate with the rear of the upper circle through a narrow slot, but confronts those in the stalls or at the font of the circle with an outsized and overly loud performance. For the audience at the rear of the auditorium, local circumstantial noise can be almost as loud as the actor's voice, and the level of the reverberation in relation to the 'dry' signal can obscure the intel-ligibility of the stage sound.

---

[1] The theory has also been suggested to me that the large gestures worked to mobilize the musculature in a way which enhances the capacity of the voice. It is also the case that these large gestures don't necessarily relate just to architecture but to convention as well. The 1590s mocked the ranting of the 1580s without the theatres changing very much.

A Coherent World Beyond

In the proscenium arch theatre, the audience faces the same way, more or less. There is a consistent front, back, left and right, and all of the programmatic sound of a play emanates from a rectangular opening at one end of the auditorium. The development of this finite, contained sound-field opened up new possibilities: the creation of a framed auditory 'scene' accompanying the visual stage picture, and imagined sonic worlds extending beyond the confines of the set.

Elizabethan productions had essentially been staged 'in the round' or on a 'thrust' stage, with some of the audience sitting behind the playing area as well as to the sides. End-on proscenium arrangements now meant that *stage left* was consistently *auditorium right* for everyone in the audience and so on, and with more or less consistent sightlines, hidden wing space could now be utilized, sonically, to create the impression of extended space, which would work more or less consistently for everybody in the audience.

New dramatic space was thus created – an imaginary, unseen world alluded to by *noises off* that could seemingly extend way beyond the probable confines of wing space. Many people will remember their first childhood trip 'backstage' at a theatre, and their surprise to find only a few feet of real space where they had imagined so much more. From the audience's perspective, an actor can exit stage right, and sounds subsequently emanating from off-stage right are assumed to be continuing action in some unseen 'other' space – equally, if not more vividly 'real' as that on stage.

The mise-en-scène could be now be worked within a world extended by virtual sound-space. Sounds heard from behind each of the doors of a farce give a sense of many different unseen rooms – the visible stage set being only one of them. A stage door could open and close on a grand off-stage party, complete with music, the murmur of chat and the tinkle of glasses, far more lavish than anything that could be visibly staged, but in reality, only being thrown in a yard-and-a-half of wing space. The illusion of distance became possible (a distant mob, an approaching storm, the sound of a string breaking). The practical noisemakers of the pre-electroacoustic era appeared in the wings and backstage areas and crammed them full of paraphernalia. To this day, however, even though loudspeakers are often visibly mounted on proscenium arches, the majority of sound effects will be played though unseen loudspeakers placed in the wings and behind the 'back wall' of the set.

Indeed, a conjurer would most probably advise against having visible loudspeakers on proscenium arches and there is a very simple experiment that shows why. If you place a dummy domestic radio set or gramophone on the floor of a theatre stage, and then play music from a hidden speaker somewhere in the room, the ear will be very easily fooled into thinking that the sound is coming from the seen 'prop' sound source. This effect can be magical, as it reportedly was with de Loutherbourg's 1781 Eidophusikon automated panorama attraction, where a hidden bass drum beat could be transformed into a distress canon merely through the suggestive power of visual context:

> The vessels, which were beautiful models, went over the waves with a natural undulation, those nearest making their courses with a proportionate rate to their bulk, and those farther off moving with a slower pace. They were all correctly rigged, and carried only such sails as their situation would demand. Those in the distance were coloured in every part to preserve the aerial perspective of the scene. The illusion was so perfect, that the audience were frequently heard to exclaim, 'Hark! the signal of distress came from that vessel labouring out there and now from that.' (Hardcastle, 1823, p. 299)

This is a trick that sound designers use all the time – and the hidden loud-speaker does not even need to be particularly near to the prop source for it to work. The same effect, however, works in reverse. If the intention of the sound designer is to create an unseen world 'beyond' by playing sounds through a hidden speaker in the wings, but there is a visible speaker present on the proscenium arch, the audience will be fooled into thinking that the sound is coming from front of house, and the effect will be diminished.

Ironically perhaps, in the 'radio' era when the sleek, industrial design of technology epitomized modernity, loudspeakers were sometimes mounted on proscenium arches by theatre managements just for show. Even today, many unscrupulous manufacturers and hire companies will try to convince naïve sound designers that they should specify and hire front-of-house speakers in order to achieve 'even coverage' which is not really necessary unless, like a musical, the whole production is being amplified. If an unamplified actor can be heard from all seats in the auditorium, than a single, well-positioned onstage effects speaker will be too.

Great Reckonings in Littler Rooms Within Little Rooms

With the retreat behind the proscenium and the disappearance of the forestage apron, the scene was acted out in a room more or less separate from that inhabited by the audience. The stage now 'sounded' different from the auditorium and this difference in acoustic 'feel' reinforces the visual sense, in proscenium theatres, that the room in which the play is enacted is detached (or at least semi-detached) from the room in which the audience sits.[2] This detachedness was eventually one of the reasons why modernism sought to break through the proscenium, although the aural aspect is not often mentioned.

---

[2] [This all relates, for what it's worth, to different theatrical projects: as Williams says, naturalism worked to interpenetrate bodies and environment; melodrama deals in a heroic body] – Series Ed.

There are some things to be said, though, for picturesque theatre and sound. Not only is there much theatricality to be had in the hidden world around the stage picture, but some acoustic features of the enclosed stage are also to be relished as vibrantly 'theatrical'. The harder, more reflective surroundings (wooden floor, hard wood or painted canvas flattage, false ceilings perhaps and the resonance of the fly tower) tend to make the stage-space discernibly more 'lively' than the softly furnished and flesh-filled auditorium. This acoustic liveness (reinforced by darkened auditorium and stage lighting)[3] can give a sense of heightened reality onstage (remember Vitruvius's example in the previous chapter of the lyre player turning upstage to harness the reflectivity and resonance of the wooden stage doors in first-century BC Roman theatre).

Sub-spaces can be created within this heightened sonic stage. A spatially constraining 'box set' can produce its own 'boxy' acoustic – which can be entirely appropriate. John Bury's design for Peter Hall's 1990 production of *The Wild Duck* had a false ceiling as well as three walls, and within that, a yet smaller room representing Hedwig's attic, where she kept her wounded duck. This presented a range of acoustic scale: the attic space was a room within a room (the larger set) within a room (the stage space) within a room (the theatre space). Touring with the show as sound operator, I experienced this in a variety of theatres from the Theatres Royal at York and Bath to the cavernous Manchester Palace, where the acoustic effect of Bury's set was most noticeable. By comparison with the acoustic 'background' of the Palace's extensive wing space, fly tower and huge auditorium Ekdal's house was cosily domestic and Hedwig's attic a quiet sanctuary. As the drama unfolded, however, any cosiness transformed into claustrophobia.

From Scene to Screen

Many of the cinematic conventions of sound, which, ironically, now influence theatre sound design, are predicated on an end-on auditorium with a rectangular proscenium opening on one end wall, beyond which is an infinitely imaginable space. The projected rectangular image formally replicates the proscenium 'window' onto the alternative world upstage of the 'iron' line (the iron safety curtain). In the early days of film, sound belonged on the audience side of that line; the image remaining resolutely mute and the sound coming from (just about) visible musicians who inhabited the lower depths of the auditorium. By the time cinema was ready for synchronized, recorded sound, theatre had evolved a sophisticated dramaturgical understanding of the effect of sound emanating through this one window, but the early technologies of film not only allowed for none of the subtlety of the

---

[3] Darkened auditoria began to be used during the nineteenth-century to concentrate the effect of controllable gas lighting, which was introduced in 1803. Gordon Williams (2003, p. 47) notes that they there were still undarkened theatre auditoria by the time of the Great War in 1914

practical effectsman, but the technical requirements of microphone placement in order to capture actors' speech placed new limitations on the cinematography. Cinema needed to find creative talent to exploit the potential of
sound beyond the initial 'wow' factor of hearing actors speaking, and in the
fierce competition between studios to find directors, properties masters,
noise makers and musical directors, theatre experienced a brain drain.
Theatre directors like Rouben Mamoulian, who studied under Stanislavski
and was famous for his intricately arranged stage soundscapes, were head-
hunted by Hollywood to produce 'talkies' that could compete artistically
with the 'silents', which threatened to reclaim their audiences. Through a
less naturalistic use of sound, gleaned from the melodramatic and sonically
picturesque traditions of the theatre, Mamoulian was able to free the camera
to move around the set. For examples, see *Applause* (1929), *City Streets* (1931),
Dr. Jekyll and Mr. Hyde (1931–2).

SURROUND SOUND

The resonant auditoria of theatre's aural Elizabethan golden age immersed
the audience in a warmly resonant field of sound and noise. Then, 300 years
of theatrical evolution set about detaching audience from the programmatic
sound of the production and acoustically muting auditoria, creating two
more-or-less separate acoustic spaces: one for performing, one for listening.
The advent of electroacoustic sound reinforcement and playback then introduced a new aural space, which sometimes coincided diegetically with the
immediate 'real' theatre space (in the case of replayed sound effects) and at
other times hovered extradiegetically between the audience and the play
(underscoring, the voice of the unseen narrator.) At first, this intermediate
electroacoustic space was generally confined to a zone at the stage end of the
theatre room – presented through proscenium loudspeakers and onstage
effects speakers. As we saw in Part I, audiences adapted their conventional
auditory competence and were able to understand both of these 'registers' of
audition as one 'intermediate' auditory space.

There were early experiments with auditorium 'surround sound'. In his
biography of George Devine, Irving Wardle describes the following, from a
1940 production of *The Tempest*:

> [Devine] also used optional amplification, so that at some moments the isle could
> be full of sweet sounds, and at others the auditorium could be flooded with musi-
> cal tumult. The opening scene presented a ship based on a medieval painting
> which also pitched the characters about in the storm, while out front
> Goldschmidt's orchestration of Mozart's C minor Piano Fantasy was coming at
> the audience from all directions over loudspeakers. This kind of environmental
> treatment was ahead of its time, and when it reached the public there were those
> (like Harcourt Williams) who felt that poetry was being displaced by stage
> management. (Wardle, 1978, p. 86)

At first, auditorium sound seemed problematic, as Harcourt Williams suggests, because it seemed to make the artifice of the *theatre* too evident. At this time, the technê of production was trying to keep as 'invisible' as possible in order to let the literary merit of the play appear as unmediated as possible (see Rebellato's *1956 And All That*, 1999, pp. 86–99). This opposition towards anything that might distract from the words persisted as a default orthodoxy until the end of the twentieth-century (and some might say beyond that).

Immersive, 'surround' or auditorium sound had been used experimentally from time-to-time, but became more frequently used in the 1990s. This partly reflected a broader cultural shift. The experience of new surround sound technologies in the home and in cinemas had not only made surround sound easier for the audience to accept, but also made it a 'must have' consumer accessory. The desire to extend the electroacoustic metaspace into the auditorium was therefore not only an artistic one but also a commercial one. Audiences now not only accept, but expect electroacoustic sounds coming at them from all sides when they are watching drama. In other words, the imaginary auditory world of the play has been reintroduced into the auditorium which for hundreds of years had been off limits.

The initial approach was therefore cautious and the use of surround sound was limited to certain moments that seemed conventionally permissible:

> As a general rule, most sound occurring within a production tends to be localized within the area defined by the stage picture. However there are many times when it is viable to 'immerse' an audience in sound. Blackouts and dark scenes which imply a dramatic visual world above and behind the audience support the use of surround sound.[4] Fantasy scenes, and dream scenes are also favorably disposed to the use of surround sound. Any scene which makes use of the entire visual space around the audience (or at least within their peripheral vision) may support the use of surround sound. (Thomas and Bell, 1995, p. 22)

Its other early use was to create an illusion of alternate resonant space. Surround speakers could be used not only for replaying sound effects and music, but for carrying artificial echo and reverberation, or for using subtle delays and other techniques that emulate different spatial effects. For example, sound might be spoken onstage, picked up by a local microphone, and fed through a digital sound processor. The reverberative, diffuse 'tail' of the sound could then be 'routed' to the auditorium loudspeakers, the result being the impression of a transformed auditorium listening space.

> If the audience is kept relatively unaware of the acoustic of the theatre, the Sound Score Designer now has a hemisphere with which to work. Sounds can be made

---

[4] Note in this chapter that we will use the term surround sound for lack of a better one. However, it should not be confused with the way the term is used in film sound. It simply means the audience is 'surrounded' by the sound.

to sound further away than the supposed boundaries of the theatre, and sounds can be made to appear closer. Sound can also be used to mask the physical auditory space and create an apparent auditory space that is different (such as is attempted with electroacoustically enhanced reverberation systems), or to create an impression of spatiality that is not relative to any known acoustic (such as a film surround sound system). (Ibid., p. 21)

The use of surround sound is now commonplace. The film theorist Michel Chion has even written about the effect of the 'silence of loudspeakers' placed around the auditorium;[5] the absence of electroacoustic sound in the auditorium now seemingly as noticeable as its presence. It is worth emphasizing though, that theatre and film sound are different. The theatre auditorium, while quieter (of late) by convention and design than once it was, has nevertheless always been a more resonant and more noisy place than the cinema. Its programmes are generally quieter.

Many people are aware of surround sound from the 5.1 and 7.1 digital sound encoding used in public and home cinema. Standardized formats such as Dolby Digital and DTS are desirable when a sound editor is mixing a film that is to be distributed to thousands of cinemas. This standardization does not apply in theatre, where sound systems are designed for specific, one-off productions (although with the spread of 'franchise' musicals worldwide, the notion of the standardized, pre-programmed soundtrack is perhaps not so far-fetched). Usually, theatre surround-sound has no reason to be limited to 5.1 or 7.1 formats[6] and may be mixed live to any number of speakers placed anywhere the sound designer wishes. The standard reference work on such systems is *Surround Sound: Up and Running*, by Tomlinson Holman (2007).

DESIGNING SURROUND SOUND AT THE MANCHESTER ROYAL EXCHANGE

Contemporary sound designer Steve Brown describes below his approach to designing immersive sound in-the-round at the Manchester Royal Exchange Theatre. Brown was one of the first people to use a system called Timax, which uses minute differentials in timing between the speakers in order to invoke the psychoacoustic Haas effect and achieve spatial sound imaging.

The Haas effect – or precedence theory – says that we will only perceive

---

[5] See Chion, M, 1999 'Silence In The Loudspeakers Or – Why, With Dolby Sound In Films, It Is The Film Which Is Listening To Us,' in *Framework: The Journal of Cinema and Media* :40 – available online at http://www.frameworkonline.com/archive.htm, accessed 15 September 2008.

[6] 5.1 indicates six discrete channels of sound supplying five speakers, or zones of speakers, placed around the auditorium – normally three front, two rear, and one non-directional bass sub-woofer. 7.1 systems have two additional 'rear-side' satellite speakers.

the first of two or more identical sound-waves arriving in our ears (up to a time differential of about 50 milliseconds, after which we start to hear the beginnings of an echo). The same sound, in other words, might be played through 50 loudspeakers at once, but if one of them arrives slightly earlier than the others, we will only seem to hear that one loudspeaker. By electronically delaying the other 49 speakers, the sound designer can move the sound image around the array.

This system has the advantage of being effective wherever one sits in an auditorium (rather than playing to one 'sweet spot' which is a limitation of systems, such as traditional 2-speaker stereo, that rely on level differentials).

9.1   Abridged (With the Permission of the Author) from a Presentation made by Steve Brown to the June 2003 OISTAT Scenofest

---

The Royal Exchange Theatre is a unique space. The theatre is a seven-sided theatre-in-the-round, constructed of steel and glass, it seats up to 750 people on three levels and is sited inside the building which was once Manchester's famous cotton exchange. The theatre is actually a space-within-a-space: a module inside the cotton exchange space built in 1976. The outer space in which the theatre is situated – the cotton exchange itself – was built in 1914 and is said to be the largest single room in the world. Although the theatre was built in 1976 it was completely refurbished between 1996 and 1998 after being severely damaged by a terrorist bomb.

Designing sound in the main house of the Royal Exchange Theatre is, I believe, a unique experience because you can easily place your sound behind, in front of, above and below the audience as well as locate your sound both inside and *outside* the auditorium. You can almost place your sound anywhere, and it's as near to 360 degree immersive surround sound as I believe you are currently likely to get.

Because the sound designer is able to place sonic information around both the audience and performer and has the ability to pan between these various locations, it allows the design to have movement, depth and spatial dimension.

The members of the audience occupy the same space as the actors. At the Royal Exchange, in fact, the audience enter the auditorium through the same doors that the actors will use when making their entrances and exits during the performance. I believe that this is important for a number of reasons; most significantly, it immediately breaks down the invisible barriers, which we all know a proscenium arch constructs. It is truly a space that is equally shared between the observed and the observer. The actors and audience see, experience and hear exactly the same things. It's this shared ownership of the theatre space and the shared theatrical moments that are encountered within it, that, I feel, makes theatre-in-the-round such a fulfilling experience. In a proscenium arch theatre (much like watching television or viewing a film in the cinema) you merely watch a performance, with theatre-in-the-round you can be fully focused and feel totally involved with all the occurrences and perform-ances relating to the production you are watching. For me it's the ultimate theatrical experience.

As far as surround sound is concerned, some people worry and argue that equal audio coverage of the auditorium is necessary. This may well be the case with music or miked voices, but this certainly shouldn't be the case with sound effects or soundscapes. The audience will all see all the various visual components of a production from different points of view, depending on where in the auditorium they're sitting, so, it stands to reason that the sonic elements should also be heard from different perspectives. Indeed it's this localization of the sound that in many cases explains and gives reason to certain aspects of a play. From the time when Roman gladiators fought tigers in specially constructed arenas through to the major sporting events of today such as the World Cup Final or Super Bowl, audiences have often felt more involved when surrounding the action. It is human nature to surround an event whether it is a person lying on the ground needing help or some street entertainment. A proscenium arch theatre merely displays whereas theatre-in-the-round truly contains.

All theatres that are constructed to be instruments designed for the production and reception of sound (whether this is simply to aid an actor's un-amplified voice, providing a canvas for designing sound effects on or playing music, in a theatrical context) ask to be thought about in a different way than those that are merely picture frames built for the mounting and viewing of spectacles. I believe that the Royal Exchange is such an instrument.

I first discovered the importance of, and began thinking about, being able to immerse the audience in a sonic landscape quite a few years ago when I found myself in Japan. I first became aware of the power of separating sound sources and how spatial effects can enhance a production when I visited the Kabuki-Za Theatre in Tokyo. The enormously wide Kabuki stage seemingly had musicians placed care-fully behind it, so that the rhythms and sounds made by the various instruments were perfectly placed in order to give a perfect and interesting, spatial effect. After the performance I couldn't help thinking about how difficult this would be to achieve within the confines of a normal, narrower, European proscenium stage. I remember thinking about this effect for some time and decided that I wanted to find a method of being able to achieve similar spatial effects.

But probably, more importantly, later during the same visit to Japan, I found myself, unexpectedly, in what I would consider a typical Japanese garden. I was sightseeing and travelling around Tokyo on a subway train; it was rush hour and filled with commuters. I was finding this particular journey stressful and noisy and wanted to leave this manic environment for a while. So, I randomly got off the train and left the station. Whilst exploring the district I found myself in, I stumbled upon what I can only describe as the most peaceful place on earth! I discovered a garden, which I later found out had been carefully designed by a group of Buddhist monks. They had created a space without distractions, certainly a feat of skill in a bustling city such as Tokyo! This Zen-like garden was a perfect combination of visual and aural beauty. The gentle sounds produced by the breeze blowing through trees, the occasional

notes from a wind chime, perfectly placed and musical sounding stones under a gently running stream: it was just a perfect and calm sonic landscape. What struck me most about this is that in a matter of minutes my mood and feelings had been changed from feeling anxious, alert, confused and unhappy to feeling calm, relaxed and completely in control of my senses. As I began to think about this more I realized that both of these extremes in my mood had been created, in no small way, purely by the sound in the world that surrounded me. My mental state and, importantly, my feelings about my surroundings and myself changed.

I've always known and tried to understand why certain pieces of music had an emotional effect on me, but this was the first instance where I really realized that normal everyday sounds could have a similar effect.

So, I decided to try and use the effect that this experience had on me, when possible, in my work. I wanted to be able to control the feelings that an audience may have when watching a production in a similar way that these extremes in sonic environments had affected my thoughts and feelings. To me this is of much greater importance than simply creating sound effects. Since that day my major influence has been the world and the fantastic poetry of the sound that surrounds it. That is not to say that I will always choose naturalistic sounds to (hopefully) enhance a production, but sometimes I will often simply attempt to find sounds that will reflect the mood of the piece and have some kind of emotional impact on the audience, as well as aid the story being told.

I now understand how much our feelings are influenced by the sonic landscape that surrounds us. What I heard that day, on the subway and in the garden was, to my mind, musical, but instead of hearing familiar instruments the sounds and rhythms were caused by everyday objects. This was the turning point in my professional life when I became convinced that the correct spatialization of the correct sound, in a theatre production, was the key to enforcing the emotional power and supporting a playwright's work.

It's now obvious to me that I should use well-constructed sound effects, as well as music, to trigger emotional responses in an audience.

The techniques I use can vary from production to production. But I always work to achieve true surround sound and not electronically simulated surround sound (such as proprietary cinema-orientated encodings such as 5.1).

I really don't want to have to think about the technical and artistic constraints that this may put on me. The action on stage is always three dimensional and I believe that whenever possible the sound should be as well. I also realise how lucky I am to work mainly in a theatre in which I'm able to approach my work in this way. Our world is totally immersive, and the challenge I set myself is always to create an audio reflection of this fact. It may not necessarily be total authenticity that I'm after in terms of the sounds I use, but I do want to be able to, when required, produce an uncompromised sonic experience.

Sound plays a prominent part in all of our lives; it is one of the most important tools that we use to make sense of our experiences. Sound defines our perceptual, emotional, spiritual, and psychological spaces. It also helps us to understand our environment and ourselves. It most often achieves this by surrounding us and not by simply coming from a single point source. Because of this I believe it stands to reason that sound should be an important part of any piece of theatre (after all most theatre aims to reflect our lives, feelings, hopes, dreams and fears), and certainly, the role of the sound designer should be considered and valued on the same terms as that of a scenic or lighting designer.

I tend to use what I can only describe as a *prism method* for deciding which sounds I should use or when creating the palette of sounds which I feel I might use in a production. This helps me in deciding what separate sonic elements I need in order to achieve a depth and spatial dimension to my work. So, I start by simply dissecting each overall sound into its component parts.

We all know that a prism divides white light into red, orange, yellow, green, blue, indigo and violet. I try to apply a similar principle with my soundscapes. We also know what primary colours are and I try to find the primary sounds which are required to achieve the particular effect I'm after. If one was to record soundscapes directly from everyday life, there would be far too much audio information to absorb. Such recordings rarely work in a theatrical context. An urban soundscape might break down into many elements: a subway train, footsteps, sirens, traffic, street vendors, pedestrians and some roadworks. All this played back together sounds like a cacophony: there is far too much going on. If we ever used this effect it would be a distraction and if we were to surround the audience with it we would pull the focus away from the stage. So using my audio prism I need to decide which of these sounds hold the key to achieving the environment that I'm trying to achieve. Maybe using the subway, emergency vehicles and traffic will place us firmly on the street and although in reality we would hear all the other sounds they are simply not needed in order achieve the desired effect. Certainly anything with dialogue, such as the street vendor, I feel, shouldn't be used if this soundscape was to be used under-scoring a scene.

So I have my basic components, but I often need to dissect these even further: for instance, the traffic. If we put this into my imaginary prism we get maybe cars, buses, trucks, motorbikes. I then dissect these further – are they stationary? Do they move? If so, at what speeds? Is this a busy street or a quiet street? And so on. I eventually come to a conclusion of what exactly I'm trying to create and what components I need to create this.

In terms of how I place these sounds within a surround sound environment – well, that is nearly always dictated by the set design and the direction of the piece, and really no more than a little simple logic and common sense is needed to correctly place these sounds within the overall environment. I usually map the landscape that I'm trying to create initially in my mind, before transferring this information to my rough plan.

At the Royal Exchange a general rule of thumb is that if the action onstage is an interior, all the exterior sounds will usually come from outside the auditorium. I also need to decide how to place these sounds on a vertical plane. Once again this is all often down to basic logic, some more simple examples; thunder, birdsong and aircraft obviously are usually placed above the audience and street sounds, for instance, at stage level etc.

Going back to my experience in Japan, I believe that you respond emotionally to changes in the soundscape without necessarily being conscious of hearing them. So, if a director asks for some garden sounds to underscore a particular scene and you supply him with a simple recording of some random bird song, which you intend to play from one or two loudspeakers, you are doing the audience a huge disservice. You may consider this sound is there just to simply signify that this scene is taking place in a garden. If that's all you think is required then that's fine, but details, such as choice of birdsong you might use can be crucial in setting the overall mood of the scene. For a 'simple' garden scene at the Royal Exchange I will have a number of loudspeakers above the audience, each playing a different birdsongs, which will change and evolve as a scene progresses.

Other sounds such as grasshoppers, cicadas and crickets will come from stage level loudspeakers (often placed under seats). This kind of rhythmical sound can be crucial if trying to build tension. As these sounds often imitate the beating of a heart, subtle changes in speed can change the atmosphere dramatically. I often reflect a rhythm of a scene by subtly changing the speed of the noises these creatures make. So apart from obviously setting the location, I always aim to reflect and complement the scene when creating such effects. The power of sound in these situations should never be underestimated – even if the audience is barely aware of it.

Placing the audience among the sounds in this way and ensuring that the audio comes from the correct direction can ensure that the mood and an emotional response is created. Weather is often another important device: changing wind tones and velocities can really have an enormous effect.

I often imagine *sounds* such as cicadas, clock ticks and birdsong in a musical context. Other sounds such as wind, rain and crowds I often try to imagine as randomly created *noises*. I then decide what needs to be ambient and what needs to be concrete. A mixture of randomness and rhythm often works well when creating ambience and atmospheres. Successful ambient or atmosphere effects are obviously required to be of a non-predictive and non-repetitive nature.

I've found that with surround sound, certain effects can have what I can only describe as a 'wow' factor. Simply, many members of the audience will not have experienced or expected to hear sound in this way while sitting in a theatre. They simply go 'wow' before considering the purpose of the effect, if indeed they consider it at all.

I enjoy the fact that the point of effects like these are so often missed and I'm usually confident that the effect has done its job. The opening of a production of *A Midsummer Nights Dream*, which I designed a few years ago, had such an effect. As the house lights faded, the sound of a car chase started outside the theatre. These cars screeched and revved as they made their way circling the theatre behind the audience. It was quite a noise. The effect ended as the cars tooted their horns three times (as homage to the fact that Shakespeare's plays always started with three blasts of a trumpet) and crashed. This effect, although simple to create, is still talked about today. It was a 'wow' effect, but also set up some important information: the period, the style, and of course, that the production was in the round.

RICHARD K. THOMAS ON *THE SOUNDS OF TIME*

Thomas is Professor of Sound at Purdue University in America and a practicing sound designer who has written extensively on his art, notably for *Theatre Design and Technology* – the journal of the United States Institute of Theatre Technology. Along with Steve Brown and others, he has campaigned through organizations like OISTAT (an international organization of theatre architects, technicians and scenographers) for sound design to be recognized fully by the international theatre community as one of the 'creative' professions of theatre.

Until this point, we have not specifically addressed sound as a spatio-temporal environment – a field in which time and space are inseparable. In this previously unpublished essay, Thomas considers the interrelation of visual and aural perception in the theatre in terms of the twentieth-century physics of 'relativity'. Thomas writes, here, and in other essays (many of which can be accessed through Charlie Richmond's excellent online collection of theatre sound articles to be found at http://www.richmondsounddesign.com/bibliographies-articles.html) as a composer. His references to the scenographic tradition of Craig and Meyerhold, and in particular to Appia, betray his instinctive composer's sensibilities that theatrical space, or the 'stage' on which theatrical performance is made, is 'fluent' rather than monumental. Space *is* moment, so to speak, and the 'moment of performance' is a spatial continuum or 'plenum' which manifest through *movement* at an ontological level (the constant and universe-defining wave-movement of light, and the molecular wave-movements of sound). Thomas locates his thought-provoking observations within a history, suggesting that Modernist developments in dramaturgy during the twentieth-century trace changes in contemporary understanding of the physics of the universe. As understanding of the non-linearity of the universe develops, he predicts, theatre sound will play an increasing part in the dramaturgies of the future.

9.2   Richard K. Thomas: *The Sounds of Time*

Introduction

> Cinematic strength derives from the multiplier effect of sound and visual being brought together. (Kurosawa, 1983)

In this essay we will compare the roles that the ears and eyes play in apprehending the outside world, and then explore the relationship between the ear and the brain in perceiving dramatic performance. The great similarities between how the ears and the eyes gather information about our external world lead to an investigation of the critical *differences* between how these organs function, and how they interact, complement and depend on each other in four dimensional space-time. We will discuss how the ears have evolved primarily to perceive the temporal dimension using the unique temporal relationships established between the ear and the brain. Finally we will explore how twentieth-century advances in our understanding of the relativity of the temporal dimension provide significant clues about how theatre works, and the implications for the theatre and the composition of a theatre sound design.

The Similar Physical Properties of Light and Sound

There are a surprising number of physical similarities between light waves and sound waves. Both are propagated waves that share the common properties of reflection (angle of incidence equals the angle of reflection), diffraction (both sound and light waves are able to 'bend' around objects, and some frequencies are able to bend around objects better than others), absorption and transmission. Both sound waves and light waves undergo Doppler shift, a phenomenon in which the frequency of a moving source changes with its velocity. Both the eye and the ear receive their information in the form of a peculiar combination of frequencies transmitted from a source in *waves*. Both sound waves and light waves have a finite region of wavelengths that human organs can detect. These wavelengths both derive from the general equation $\lambda = c/f$. The ears and the eyes come in pairs, and serve the same function in both cases: the perception of space. The brain processes temporal information from both the eye and the ear with an approximate integration constant of 1/20th of a second; slow the moving film projector to show less than 20 frames per second, and the human eye perceives individual images; delay auditory reflections to the human ear by greater than 1/20th of a second, and the ear hears individual sounds. The human ear differentiates frequencies in the basilar membrane in a manner similar to how the rods and cones of the human eye differentiate frequencies.

We often use the same word to describe how the ear and the eye perceive combinations of frequencies: *colour*. Very rarely does a single frequency exist by itself in nature. The sinusoidal waveform the function generator produces, or the colours generated by a prism are both colours that very rarely occur in nature. The combination of all sound frequencies mixed in equal amounts produces 'white' noise, and the combination of all light frequencies mixed in equal amounts produces 'white' light. The perception of colour by both eyes and ears is subjective and relative; the perceived colour of light and sound are both dependent on their surrounding temporal and spatial colours – otherwise all songs would be 'in tune', and no colours would 'clash'. Humans vary in their ability to perceive visual and auditory colour. 'colour blindness' is related to 'tone deafness' in that in neither case, can a person differentiate between the relative frequencies of two light or sound waves (respectively). Finally, the nerve endings in the human retina (rods and cones) are subject to fatigue from over stimulation in a manner similar to the nerve endings along the basilar membrane.

As a final example of the close relationship between sight and sound, consider the test first offered by John Booth Davies (Davies 1978). I have personally tested this hypothesis on students in classes for decades and on professionals and lay persons in my travels around the world. The results are astonishingly consistent regardless of age, race or culture. We ask the participants to consider two shapes that look similar to those in Figure 9.1 (in actuality, they don't have to be these shapes, one just needs to have round corners, and the other needs to have sharp edges).

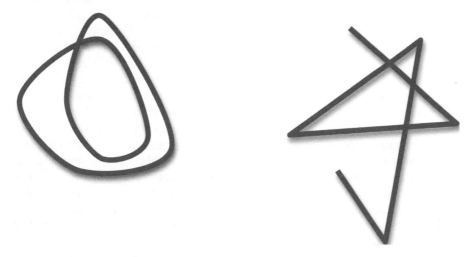

Figure 9.1

Tell the subjects that one is called *takete*, the other, *uloomu* and then ask them to match the appropriate name with the appropriate figure In most cases (even among varying cultures), people will call the left 'uloomu' and the right 'takete'.

In the end, we understand that the eyes and ears have evolved to perceive the visual and the auditory, yet bear a marked resemblance to each other in terms of how they function.

Understanding 'c': Light and Sound Compared

There are two striking differences between sound and light that differentiate their function. The first difference is the velocity (c) at which sound and light are transmitted. Sound travels considerably slower than light – 1,130 feet per second as opposed to 186,000 miles per second. This slower speed creates sound wavelengths that vary between 3/4 of an inch and 50 feet, while light wavelengths vary between 16 and 38 millionths of an inch. This slow speed also creates sound waves perceptible from about 20 to 20,000 cycles per second, as compared to about 311,000 to 737,000 gigacycles per second for light. This difference in speed plays an important role in how the eyes and the ears interact with the brain. It is especially significant because the speed at which light travels is generally understood to be Einstein's upper velocity of the universe: 186,000 miles per second. It is a constant, and does not change. The speed of sound, on the other hand, varies greatly depending on the density of the medium conveying it.

The second significant difference between sound and light lies in their relationship to mass. Light is conveyed solely through a temporal medium (i.e., cycles per second). It requires no mass in order to be transmitted (relying instead on the mass-less photon). The reliance on mass-less particles for transmission makes light perfectly suited to *reveal* mass through the organ of the eye. Mass inserted between the source of a light, and the eye distorts the image, or renders the source invisible. Sound, on the other hand, depends greatly on the mass that conveys it; its speed varies according to the density of that mass. Sound does not travel in a vacuum, because it requires mass to convey it. Light travels in a vacuum, because it does not require mass to convey it. In order to create sound, we must move molecules (typically, of air) in time. It does not matter if we move molecules of air, or wood, or water, we can still create sound as long as we keep moving the molecules. The molecules never lose their original properties. They do not physically become sound, they remain air, wood, water, or whatever they were before they propagated sound. Since the transmitting medium (typically, air) does not normally affect the temporal aspects of sound transmission (i.e., remains constant like the speed of light in a vacuum), the reliance on mass particles for transmission makes sound perfectly suited to *reveal* time through the organ of the ear. Vibrating mass makes sources audible, often in situations where the sources have been rendered invisible by the same mass that conducted the sound.

This fundamental relationship between sound and light then, is such that *light* reveals *mass in space* by defining it relative to *time*, and *sound* reveals *time* by defining it relative to *mass in space*. Here we have the fundamental dichotomy between the primary sensory experiences we use to apprehend both the general world and the world of theatre; one set of organs, the eyes, have evolved to allow us to better apprehend mass and spatial relationships, and the other, the ears, have evolved to better apprehend time and temporal relationships.

It comes as no surprise, of course, that these relationships exist. The visual arts have focused almost exclusively on spatial relationships throughout most of recorded history, whether it be painting, sculpture, architecture, etc., and have developed a sophisticated language to communicate spatial concepts, including length, width and depth, colour, hue and saturation, shadow and light, etc. The audible arts through most of recorded history developed their vocabulary in the language of time, especially in music, and have developed a sophisticated language to communicate temporal concepts including tempo, meter, rhythm, phrasing and duration. Neuroscientist Michael Thaut (2005) affirms time's significance in sound:

> One of the most important characteristics of music – also when compared with other art forms – is its strictly temporal character. Music unfolds only in time, and the physical basis of music is based on the time patterns of physical vibrations transduced in our hearing apparatus into electrochemical information that passes through the neural relays of the auditory system to reach the brain. Music communicates critical time dimensions into our perceptual processes.

The manner in which auditory artists subdivide and organize sound corresponds closely to both the respiratory pulses of the human autonomous nervous system (e.g., heart rate, blood pressure) and the neural rhythms of the central nervous system. It is no accident that common musical tempos correlate with the pulses of average people at rest (60–80 bpm for example, adagio, literally meaning, 'at ease'), walking (80–100 bpm – andante), exercising moderately (100–120 bpm – moderato), and running or pushing the limits of ones cardio-respiratory system (greater than 120 bpm – allegro). Daniel Mauro (2006) proposed that: 'The brain's neural language is grounded in temporal principles which are mirrored in the basic ingredients of musical rhythm. Specifically, three facets of neural processing evident in the brain (frequency, synchrony, temporal pattern) are reflected in three essential properties of rhythm (tempo, meter, phrasing)', and argued that 'it is this fundamental relationship between music and neural function that underlies the brain's exquisite sensitivity to music.'

The evolution of the human ear to apprehend these fundamental rhythms in sound creates a special conduit to human experience directly through the brain. This relationship between the brain, sound and time became increasingly important in the twentieth-century theatre when our fundamental understanding of the nature of the relationship between space and time itself suddenly changed.

Space-Time and Art

The close relationships between the eyes and space, and the ears and time are not, of course, mutually exclusive, for the eye can perceive temporal relationships, and the ear can perceive spatial relationships. The twentieth-century found artists beginning to discover new potentials in exploring time in the visual arts and space in the auditory arts. Lighting designers like Tharon Musser discovered, as assistant Jeff Davis put it, 'light was a living entity that moved in time and space, as did the drama,' and became a master who could 'move light and the stage picture in a synchronized rhythm with the dialogue and the performance' (Unruh, Rennagel and Davis, 2006). The development of film allowed pictures to move, and established the need for an artist that specialized in time, the motion picture editor.[7]

At the same time that visual artists began to explore time visually, sound artists discovered space – first in stereo, and subsequently in multichannel surround sound. Modern sound designers discovered the remarkable ability of surround sound to envelope their audiences in a newly discovered three-dimensional world of sonic spatiality. What began as a single channel of monaural sound, became stereo, and then 5.1, and then 7.1, 9.1, and even 10.2. Tomlinson Holman (2001) reported suggestions that it would 'take about 1,000,000 channels to fully capture one space and reproduce it in another in all its detail …'[8]

---

[7] It must be noted that, despite the advances in video editing, film editor David Yewdall (2007, p. 160) reported that director Jim Cameron still required audio 'temp' tracks when viewing visual edits for *The Abyss*, because he felt that 'you can't really know if the cut is working until the sound effects are in.'

[8] Yet, despite the advances in the spatial palettes of modern sound design with 5.1 and 7.1 systems, the dialogue typically remains locked in the centre channel because audiences find that shifting the auditory spatial perspective of multiple camera angles in a scene is distracting, even though the changing visual perspective is not.

It is probably no accident that advances in the physicist's understanding of the close-bound relationship between time and space should play a key role in blurring the more traditional roles of the eyes and the ears in the twentieth century and beyond. One of the many remarkable conclusions reached in the twentieth-century, was that space and time are so closely related that they depend on each other in a continuous, flowing object called 'space-time'. Stephen Hawking (1998) describes space-time as a 'four-dimensional space whose points are events', and concludes that 'We must accept that time is not completely separate from and independent of space, but is combined with it to form an object called space-time.'

Space and time are so closely related that we routinely use the terms interchangeably. For example, we routinely interchange concepts of space and time when we speak of travel. We refer to a city as being a certain number of kilometres away as readily as we refer to the same city being a certain number of hours away, depending on the mode of transportation. In either case, we define space in terms of time and time in terms of space, and do so interchangeably. Certainly there exists in our own intuition, a strong relationship between space and time.

If time and space cannot be separated, and the eye is the primary perceiver of space, and the ear the primary perceiver of time, it follows that maximum apprehension of the world around us (especially in art) is best accomplished through the simultaneous use of both the eyes and the ears. What is the role that the ear, and its stimulus, sound, plays in apprehending space-time, and the consequences for the theatre that ultimately sound, as the chief apprehender of time, must therefore be responsible for providing?

The Relationship between Physical Time and Dramatic Time

The most important temporal part of the theatrical experience is the fundamental manipulation of time in which playmakers engage. Aristotle promoted the Unities of Time, Place and Action. The dramatic theorists of seventeenth-century neoclassicism developed strict rules limiting the passage of time in a play: the events of the play must transpire in a single 24 hour period. These restrictions essentially created a close relationship between the flow of time as monitored on a clock and the flow of time in the drama. The limiting of dramatic time has manifested itself repeatedly in the history of theatre, and remnants of it still dominate modern realism in the theatre today.

Nevertheless, theatre has continually strayed from the so-called unities, however, as the need for playmakers to explore the human condition unbounded by them trumped artificially imposed forms. Set designers have been preoccupied with developing a staging system to create space that must conform to changing dramatic time and place, throughout most of the history of drama. The periaktoi of Sophocles, house-platea staging and pageant wagons of medieval drama, perspective scenery of the sixteenth- and seventheenth-century theatre, elaborate stage machinery of the eighteenth-century, evolution of lighting in the nineteenth-century and the modern theatre (with its fly system, traps, wagons, projections, etc.) all evolved to allow a more fluent dramatic space and time to spring to life in a physical theatre space bounded by conventional time.

Shakespeare developed another method for reconciling the physical space and time to the dramatic one. Granville Barker pointed out that Shakespeare 'required a fluid stage where space and time changed freely and quickly' (Barker, 1995, p. 13). To accomplish this fluidity of dramatic time and place Shakespeare limited the physical space and time (for example, scenery, costumes) to that which could keep pace with his dramatic needs. Shakespeare dispensed with attempts to create an illusion of reality in his visual world in order to more freely manipulate space and time dramatically. In the late nineteenth and early twentieth centuries scene designers such as Appia, Craig and Meyerhold discovered new forms to embrace Shakespeare's more fluid use of space and time.

Then, at the dawn of the twentieth-century, Albert Einstein created a revolution that fundamentally liberated time: he discovered that time was not an absolute phenomenon, but was relative to every individual. His theory also fundamentally explains the essential nature of the dramatic experience, and implies how sound may work on a theatre audience.

Einstein's General Theory of Relativity predicted the possibility of travelling through time. The fundamental equation governing the manipulation of time is c (velocity) = d (distance)/t (time). Einstein showed that if the speed of light is constant, travelling at 186,000 miles/second, then clearly time must vary according to the relative velocities of individuals; the faster one travels, the slower time progresses. If one were able to travel at the upper limiting speed of the universe, time would stand still. If one were able to travel faster than this speed, time would go backwards.[9] Time, then, is different for objects travelling at different speeds. In other words, time is relative to every object, or, in our case, individual.

Imagine departing from earth on a space ship that travels at speeds close to the speed of light. Notice that from our vantage point inside the spaceship, we aren't moving (as long as we are travelling at a constant speed), and the hands on our watches are ticking at normal intervals. However, upon returning to earth, we find that we have travelled far into the future of those that remained on earth, even though the hands on their clocks were ticking normally also!

Theatrical productions also transport audiences back and forth in time. Consider, for example, Shakespeare's classic play *Antony and Cleopatra*. In Acts III and IV, Shakespeare transports the audience through 28 different locations over a period of three days! Is there a similarity between the time travel that Einstein speaks of and the time travel of a theatre audience?

The Frame of Reference

To understand the relationship between the relativity of time and the theatre experience, we must understand the concept of 'frames of reference'. A frame of reference

---

[9] Not only has this relationship been demonstrated experimentally, but modern technologies, such as global positioning systems (GPS) depend on reconciling this relativity of time in order to operate accurately (Hawking, 1998, p. 34).

is a 'set or system (as of facts or ideas) serving to orient or give particular meaning' (*Webster's*, 1963, p. 332).

What is the frame of reference for a theatre audience? When the audience enters the theatre, the frame of reference is the physical theatre space itself. The audience shares this frame of reference with the cast, crew and other production personnel. In this physical frame of reference, the audience is aware of their discomfort with their seats, with the coughing sounds of the audience, and with the linear time which all of the audience shares, referenced to their watches, that says that the performance will begin at 8.00 p.m., and conclude at 10.30 p.m.

But at the start of a performance, a very special thing happens: the lighting changes, the sound changes (as the audience quiets), and the production team immediately sets to work to *change the frame of reference* from a physical one, to a dramatic one. In this frame, the audience is transported to the dramatic setting of the play. They are soon made aware of how time functions in this world. Traditionally, the *exposition* of the play establishes this frame of reference.

Simultaneously, the audience is faced with the paradox of two frames of reference: the first relative to the space and time they share with the rest of the audience, the second relative to the dramatic space and time governed by the performance. In the common frame of reference, space and time are relative to an outside reference (for example, a clock). In the dramatic frame of reference, however, space and time are unique to each individual: for some members of the audience, time in the play passes quickly, as if mere seconds have elapsed. For others, time passes more slowly, as if more time has elapsed than the watch referenced to the physical frame indicates. Notice how much more closely Dramatic Space and Time conform to Einstein's understanding of time (that is, it's relativity to each person) than the more commonly agreed upon passing of time as measured on a clock.

We all know that plays somehow transport us back and forth in time; we have all experienced this phenomenon as audience members *immersed* in the action of a play. We might object, however, that our journey in dramatic space and time is not a form of *time travel* because this journey doesn't really *physically* occur. Einstein showed that this journey really does occur because time must be measured within the appropriate frame of reference for each individual. Remember our space traveller who left earth travelling close to the speed of light and then returned having aged much less than those left behind? This was possible because the traveller's frame of reference was based on a different relationship between velocity (that is, the ratio of space [distance between two points in three dimensional space] to time, [or 'c']) than those left behind. Notice how changing the frame of reference for a theatre audience from a common one to a dramatic one accomplishes the same function. Time in the physical 'c' is different than time in the dramatic 'c', in the same way that time for those left behind is different than time for the space traveller. The frame of reference experienced in either the spaceship or the theatre compresses the time of the other world to a much shorter duration.

Our own brains concur with this conclusion, by providing us with our own unique memories of having somehow travelled through space and time in our experience of the drama. Einstein embraced the idea that relativity included human perception when he told his secretary how to explain it to reporters and laypersons: 'An hour sitting with a pretty girl on a park bench passes like a minute, but a minute sitting on a hot stove seems like an hour' (Calaprice, 2005, p. 247).

The Importance of the Relativity of Time to Sound Design

The relativity of time to each individual suggests that one of the more important functions of the production team is to manipulate the individual perception of time by the theatre audience. Sound, as a time art, is an essential tool for manipulating the relative temporal experience of theatre audiences.[10] Composers, sound design-ers, actors and directors use sound in the theatre to establish time frames in theatre productions. They organize sound by subdividing time using the tools of tempo, meter, duration and phrasing, and create rhythms that transport listeners into the dramatic frame of reference, literally creating unique experiences for each audience member through the manipulation of time. They use these tools because they directly stimulate and interact with fundamental functions of the brain.

Theatre practitioners have long understood this extraordinary potential of sound to influence the audience. Aristotle observed that we do not always have complete control over what we hear or how we interpret it, and recognized that the way in which something was said had an important influence over whether the listener believed what was said to be true. Aristotle believed that man constantly sought perfection, and, since our inability to have complete control over our hearing or its effect upon us prevented us from achieving perfection, there must be a 'defect' in human listeners (Aristotle, 1931, pp. 11–12). Aristotle's defect turns out to be the art of sound design, and lies in the ability of sound to exploit that 'defect' in audiences.

Nineteenth- and twentieth-century sonic artists also understood the unique power that sound has over a theatre audience. After a lifetime of work, Richard Wagner came to the conclusion that 'into whatsoever alliance music may enter, it never ceases to be the highest, most redeeming art' (Gutman, 1968, p. 290). Pioneering theatre sound designer Harold Burris-Meyer was fond of saying, 'you can shut your eyes, but the sound comes out to get you.' Whether it be music or sound design, artists understand the unique power of sound to invade our subconscious regardless of the focus of our conscious attention. Once connected, sound *compels* us to experience time frames created by others subjectively, that is, as *real* experi-ences, even though the intellectual communication or the visual experience may have no bearing in truth or reality. Sound provides such an extraordinary experience of being transported in time, precisely because it takes control of our own very personal perception of time. It is an extremely powerful agent that convinces us that our experience of the intellectual communication and the visual space of the drama are real, because they conform to our perception of time. The words to a patriotic anthem ring much truer when we apprehend the anthem set to the powerful persuader of time expressed in music. Pop lyrics set to music are cherished for the

---

[10] Visual artists are more typically challenged with a spatial objective – creating the *place* of the action.

way in which they express extraordinary truths about the world around us, regardless of the veracity of the lyrics. In the theatre, sound has the incredible power to blend the disparate worlds of the actor, the text, and the mise-en-scène into a very real experience for the audience – so real, that the truth of the intellectual communication is hard to deny. Theatre *feels* real because audiences *really* experience it. Sound design can be a very powerful *and* dangerous thing, as governments and authority figures have long understood. This power depends on the direct conduit to the brain provided by sound and the relativity of time to each individual.

For modern drama, the discovery of the relativity of time seems to have been accompanied by a complementary explosion in the freedom to manipulate time in dramatic form. Less than 500 miles from Einstein's Zurich to Freud's Vienna, the beginnings of Modernism developed simultaneously with the physicists' discovery of the relativity of time. Peter Barry (1995, p. 82) describes this sudden willingness to experiment with time in literature: 'There was a rejection of traditional realism (*chronological* plots, *continuous* narratives relayed by omniscient narrators, "closed *endings*", etc.) in favour of experimental forms of various kinds ... The Modernists placed a new emphasis on subjectivity.' Subjectivity in the theatre is empowered by the relativity of time, and its ally, sound; both provide a uniquely different experience for each audience member. In theatre, the freedom to portray *time* as a malleable component of the dramatic experience gave the dramatists opportunities to create much more complex experiences than in traditional linear drama. Barry also notes that the modernists developed a 'new liking for *fragmented* forms, *discontinuous* narrative, and *random*-seeming collages of disparate materials' (p. 82). All of these techniques indicate a non-linear manipulation of time. As our understanding of the relativity of time developed in the twentieth-century, we began to experiment with it more and more in such movements as Dadaism, Expressionism, Absurdism, Surrealism and Post-Modernism.

The coinciding of the discovery of the relativity of time to each individual with the increased emphasis on subjectivity in the twentieth-century theatre created tremendous opportunities for sound designers to contribute more to the theatrical experience. Linear dramas of the nineteenth and twentieth-century (realism) had minimal need for sound and music to organize and validate time, since the objective of the drama was to follow the seemingly linear time experienced by the audiences (although this time was almost always still compressed). Instead, sound and music were used to control the experience of time that was already there, for example, in opera and musicals. In the twentieth-century directors began to reject the simplicity of that relationship, as film director, Kurosawa noted: 'I changed my thinking about musical accompaniment from the time Hayaska Fumio began working with me as a composer of my film scores. Up until that time film music was nothing more than accompaniment – for a sad scene there was always sad music. This is the way most people use music, and it is ineffective' (Ebrahimian, 2004, p. 87).

As nonlinear drama developed to explore the uniquely individual relationship between the audience and time, it began to rely more and more on the ability of sound to organize time into a perceptually 'real' experience. Sound has the power to not only organize the visual experience, but provides its own frame of reference that makes the visual journey viable. The visual art may provide the fantasy, but the audible one makes the fantasy a reality. So as theatre design moves more and more into realms of the nonlinear, sound has an opportunity to play a greater and greater role. Where the principles of traditional *dramatic* structure play critical roles in linear drama, the principles that govern *musical* structures become more imperative in non-linear theatre.

Time, Sound, and the Twenty-First-Century

In the performing arts, we encounter the energy of the dramatic life force through the ability of our eyes and ears to perceive sight and sound. Without sight and sound, and the continuum of space and time they reveal to us, the mise-en-scène would remain inert, dark and silent, and out of our grasp. Twentieth-century science has provided new revelations about the relativity of time that suggests extraordinary possibilities in the evolution of theatrical form in the twenty-first-century. These possibilities proceed from an understanding that sound is an extremely valuable tool used to control the individual's perception of time, and consequently, of the individual's subjective experience. For sound designers and composers working in the theatre, the understanding of the relationship between sound and time provides extraordinary glimpses into the powers that may be unleashed by the sound score.

John Levack Drever on Sound Effect – Object – Event

Chapter **10**

This chapter serves as a *coda* to the book. Commissioned for this volume from the acoustic ecologist, composer and sonic artist John Levack Drever, it reprises the main themes of the volume.

10.1   Endemic and Exogenous Sound Practices in Theatre and Beyond

---

> ... fragile music which seems to grind the most precious metals, where springs of water bubble up as in a state of nature, where columns of insects march through the plants, where the sound of light itself appears to have been picked up, where the sounds of deep solitudes seem distilled into crystal swarms. (Antonin Artaud (1931) *On Balinese Theatre*, in Artaud (1974), p. 42)

INTRODUCTION

Radiating outwards and onwards from the physical/geographical position and moment in time of initial oscillations, in everyday listening sound seldom arrives at the pinnae by a direct path exclusively. Inevitably it will traverse a range of media, be that gas, sold, liquid; transduced into electric current, converted from analogue to digital and back again; encounter shifting thermal gradients, atmospheric turbulence, physical obstruction and mechanical noise; rebound off surfaces (not to forget the ground as a pervasive reflective and absorbent surface) in its turn generating potentially 'millions of resonances' (Blesser and Salter, 2007, p. 250).[1] Traces of these numerous, various, simultaneous and staggered journeys, albeit initially departing from a more or less discrete singular point and instant, are dynamically inscribed into the fabric of the sound – split, attenuated, postponed and/or redoubled. And akin to a flowing stream, the sound's *source* 'screened from our gaze' (Smalley, 1992, p. 515).

Cognition strategically oscillates through a continuum of modes, from listening to hearing. Hearing is passive and involuntary, while listening is selective, discretionary,

---

[1] The characteristics of which are determined by the quality of those surfaces in relation to the spectral constituents, the relative amplitudes, strengths of the spectra and the dimensions of the space.

partial, primordial and forensic; we rate, group and transform. Hearing involuntarily prompts listening: 'a silent intelligence that directs us to what we think matters. And what matters occupies our attention' (Norman, 2004, p. 77).

Sound may be fashioned for another's attention, or simply a haphazard by-product of a natural or industrial process. Background noise or sound signal, regardless of intention (or lack), competes for attention and apprehension. Affected, transported, enveloped, isolated, perplexed, and informed, we can ignore and/or can be overwhelmed. Correctly or otherwise, we attribute a metabolism of sounding bodies construed by past experience or influenced by extra-auditory causality, nevertheless constantly affording acoustic profiles of depth, distance and proximity for consideration. Attention may *zoom in* on the essential qualities of particular fragments or strata and/or the ensuing spatial choreography that unfolds as sonorities from the same and disparate causes assemble and collide. Such is the auditory condition on listening to one's prevailing sounding environment in the everyday.

Albeit reinforced by a battery of PA positioned throughout the auditorium, from the *point-of-audition* of the audience member, the conventional contemporary theatre soundscape is a more highly determined and rarefied form than that of routine listening practices. Here, ritualistic cultural convention prescribes a focus on the sound that seemingly disseminates from the locus of the visual frame of the stage, while suppressing cognition of peripheral *noise* emanating from neighbouring audience members or spilling in from the outside world. Like cinema (Deleuze after Fano, 2005, p. 225), the theatre soundscape is formed of a continuum of aural phenomena. Within the continuum we can distinguish distinct types:

> [N]oises (which isolate an object and are isolated from each other), sounds (which indicate relationships and are themselves in mutual relation), phonations (which cut into these relations, which can be shouts, but also genuine 'jargons', as in the talking burlesque of Chaplin or Jerry Lewis), words, music. (Deleuze, 2005, p. 225)

The relative dominance of each type shifts from genre to genre and from act to act, but it is uncontroversial to claim that in theatre words tend to reign, with music assuming a secondary and supportive role. This chapter is concerned, although not necessarily exclusively, with the remainder: *noises*, *sounds* and *phonations*. While theatre sound design has a rich and diverse endemic lineage of its own played out in Aeschylus, Shakespeare, Chekhov, Brecht, Kabuki, Balinese Theatre, and so on, today, albeit unconsciously, a wide range of conventions that are adopted/adapted, derive from beyond theatre theory and practice. For a sound designer to fully harness theatre audition with poise, nuance (e.g. *trompe l'oreille*), awe and vitality as exemplified in the epigraph by Antonin Artaud's aspiring description of his sonic epiphany on experiencing Balinese Theatre (at the International Colonial Exposition, Paris, 1931), it is necessary to incorporate analysis of extant practice from within theatre, excavation of historical precedence and elucidation on corresponding disciplines that prioritize sound and the practice of listening. This chapter will expound on three related approaches to the practice of listening and sound making; the latter two of which have only recently found a significant resonance with the language of scenography and dramaturgy:

1. *Sound effect* (commonly referred to as *sfx*): widely practiced in theatre through-out history and cross-culturally (although ruled by genre-distinct conventions), and in the late part of the twentieth-century has been more and more allied with hegemonic televisual and cinematic practices.[2]
2. *Sound object*: from the compositional field of *musique concrète* in Paris in the late 1940s. Founded on Husserlian phenomenological precepts, it fed into a general practice of sonic art, aspects of which permeate standard audio studio practice today.
3. *Sound event:* from the interdiscipline of acoustic ecology developed in Vancouver in the early 1970s. A concept that extends from noise abatement, environmental and architectural sound design, qualitative social science and soundscape composition/phonography.

It must be underlined that these approaches are not mutually exclusive, in fact a syntheses or a reading around of these concepts may prove more practical use than any one approach may offer. Moreover, like any categorization, the groupings are acutely influenced by historical contingency and in practice are much less discrete as this text may imply. And of course once reworked in theatre the blurring of such categories and consequent mutation is manifold.

In theatre all these approaches are primarily dependant on mechanical reproduc-tion of sound – from today's perspective almost exclusively electroacoustic. The incorporation of electroacoustic technologies provides means to cue, amplify, record, transform, concatenate, synthesize and playback sound. And with the right know-how its articulatory potential is theoretically unbounded, encompassing and surpass-ing linguistic semantics. From a filmic perspective, Andrei Tarkovsky expressed an aspiration, which he arguably achieved through his collaborations with sound designer/composer, Edward Artemiev, for example, *Solaris* (1972) and *Stalker* (1979):

> We wanted sounds to be close to that of an earthly echo, filled with poetic suggestion – to rustling, to sighing. The notes had to convey the fact that reality is conditional, and at he same time accurately to reproduce precise states of mind, the sounds of a person's interior world ... It can be hidden behind other noises and remain indistinct; like the voice of nature, of vague intimations ... It can be like somebody breathing. (Tarkovsy, 1998, p. 162)

THE UMBILICAL SOUND EFFECT

On the face of it the status of the *sound effect* in theatre and the dramatic arts in general, in the language of Peircian[3] semiotics (Peirce, 1955), is *indexical*; where

---

[2] 'It is absolutely clear that our current cultural formation is saturated with, and dominated by, mass media representations in general, and television in particular' (Auslander, 1999, p. 1).

[3] I opt for the semiotics of Charles S. Peirce due to his conception of, 'signs on the basis of images and their combinations, not as a function of determinants which were already linguis-tic' (Deleuze, 1989, p. 29).

sound, or a period of relative silence[4] does not refer to itself, rather it functions as an initial *sign* (the *representamen*) in the service of another *sign* (the *interpretant*) in terms of causation. The understanding is that there is actual contiguity or physical connection between what you hear (that is, the selective sensuous translation of vibrating air molecules) and what gave rise to that sound: its cause, for example, telephone, wolf, storm, rifle, baby, wind. 'One identifies a particular sound as indicating the presences of an object or person, or as reflecting a specific state of the environment' (Truax, 2001, p. 163). Such identification is formed through, 'the *lived experience* of the sign's users' (Nattiez, 1990, pp. 7–8). Thus the efficacy of a sound effect is contingent on a shared 'lived experience'[5] of the audience and producers alike. The sound in this regard is basically a container that transports a sign, thus 'once the information has been received, the sound itself is "disregarded"' (Truax, 2001, p. 163).

This approach to sound design is commonsense as it engages our primed evolutionary apparatus of striving to assign sources. Pierre Schaeffer (1910–95), the founder of *musique concrète*, refers to this level of listening as 'primitive' (Schaefer quoted in Chion, 1983, p. 8), provoking fundamental questions in our intellect: 'What is it? Who is it? What's happening?' (Chion, 1983, p. 8). In his comprehensive quest, *On Sonic Art* (1996), Trevor Wishart ponders on the evolutionary roots of what Michel Chion (after Schaeffer) has classified as *causal listening* (Chion, 1983, 1994): 'one needed to be able to differentiate between harmless herbivores and dangerous carnivores, predator and prey, friend and foe' (Wishart, 1996, p. 129).

We can all recognize that the vestiges of this listening mode still prevail, functioning as a cursory response to attending to transients in the air that manage to punctuate the omnipresent gauze of background noise.[6] Struck by the *mêlée* going on in the Paris streets in the early 1930s compared with the relative silence and seclusion of the theatre, Artaud in fact stressed that, 'the noise background is what theater lacks the most':

> and this is why the noises and screams that come from backstage are so ridiculously mangy and grotesque … One should never try to have ten extras sound like a ten-thousand-men crowd. To produce such an effect, one must use recordings of real noises whose intensity could be regulated at will by means of amplifiers and loudspeakers disseminated all across the stage and the theater. (Artaud, A., 'Deux projets de mise en scène' (1931), *Oeuvres Completes*, vol. 2, pp. 148–9, quoted in Hollier, 1997, p. 36)

And Artaud endeavored to do just that! With the technical and artistic aid of Roger Désormière, Artaud presented his version of *Les Cenci* at the Folies-Wagram, 6 May 1935, which going short of using actual church bells pealing above the audience's

---

[4] A discussion on the power of relative silence in radio drama can be found in the chapter, 'Silence: dead air and ambient noise' in Shingler and Wieringa (1998, pp. 54–5).

[5] The notion of 'lived experience' here includes exposure to theatre, cinema, TV and radio.

[6] For an informed discussion on auditory spatial awareness as evolutionary artefact see Blesser and Salter (2007, ch. 8).

heads as desired,[7] incorporated the playback of the bell of the Cathedral of Amiens, which, 'resounded from the four corners of the auditorium before the curtain was raised' (Kirby, V.N., quoted in Blin et al., 1972, p. 108).[8] To bridge the noise gap between street and theatre, in his mise-en-scène direction for Roger Vitrac's Coup de Trafalgar (finally performed in 1934) he proposed that: 'From the very beginning of the Act, a background noise will be established in order to make one feel the constant presence of life outside' (Artaud, A., 'Deux projets de mise en scène' (1931), Oeuvres Completes, vol. 2, p. 147 quoted in Hollier, 1997, p. 35)

Denis Hollier, reflecting on this technique, suggests: 'By opening the theater to the outdoor noises, Artaud's sound system was meant to force ... the sound of life outside, into the space of the theater' (Hollier, 1997, p. 35). But this was not merely a matter of relative sound pressure levels but noise as a metaphor for the political struggles being fought out in the streets of Paris at the time (Hollier, 1997, p. 35).

INAUGURATION: *THE JUDGE* (1890)

The first documented use of recorded sound as *indexical* sound effect in theatre was the emanations into the auditorium of an off-stage sound resembling that of a baby's cry – apt that a baby's cry should be given the honours – in Arthur Law's The Judge on 2 August 1890. The programme proclaimed that the sounds were that: 'of a real infant recorded by an Edison Phonograph on Monday, July 21st' (Stedman, 1976, p. 125).

Such a statement affirms the *indexical* status, assuring contiguity from actual baby crying *via* mechanical inscription onto a wax phonogram, and consequently played back off-stage in a theatre 11 days later, observing the script's direction of baby crying in the wings.

Despite its disembodied presence, the physical object of the phonograph was construed by some as the performer as opposed to the *actual* baby whose cries had entered the horn of the phonograph, as testified by a reviewer for the Marylebone & Paddington Independent: '[T]he Phonograph ... undertook the role of a fretful baby's howls and acquitted itself admirably' (Marylebone & Paddington Independent, 24 July 1890 quoted in Stedman, 1976, p. 125).

We can speculate on the director's intentions:

* In its day the use of such technology would have been of high novelty even pioneering value.[9]

---

[7] Artaud wrote of his desire for, 'bells ten meters high that would have surrounded the public in the middle of a swirl of vibration and forced it to surrender' (Interview for L'intransigeant (1934), Oeuvres completes, vol. 5, p. 299 quoted in Hollier, 1997, p. 34).

[8] The performance also included playback of amplified footsteps, sounds recorded in a factory, a metronome ticking at different speeds and shouting and whispering voices, with the inclusion of a live performance of the Ondes Martenot employed to help evoke the sound of a tempest (Blin et al., 1972).

[9] The Judge predates the celebrated recording made for charity by Edison's representative in Britain, of the voice of Florence Nightingale to the veterans of the Charge of the Light Brigade (30 July 1890).

- It is an attempt at a *literal* rendition of the script's instruction. Such a *naturalist* reading may well have been influenced by Edison's marketing prowess. In *The Phonograph and its Future* written by Edison in 1878, he made a number of pronounced claims for this emerging medium:

> [T]he phonograph demonstrates the following as *faits accomplis*: ... The reproduction with all their original characteristics at will, without the presence or consent of the original source, and after the lapse of any period of time. (Edison, 1878, p. 530)[10]

The sound of a baby crying in *The Judge*, however, is not a baby's cry *per se*; it is a *mechanical reproduction* of a baby's cry *via* the medium of a phonograph. The sound quality of this rudimentary apparatus would have been marked by a very poor signal-to-noise ratio, before we even consider the limited power of propagation of the phonograph's playback[11] within a packed auditorium.[12] Aspects of sound quality were not completely overlooked (*overheard*) by the audience: Clement Scott, writing for the *Illustrated London News*, maintained that the cry was: 'infinitely worse than nature' (2 Aug 1890, quoted in Stedman, 1976, p. 125). Having said that, Barry Truax reminds us that: 'Prior to audio reproduction, no sound had ever been heard with lesser or greater sound quality' (Truax, 2001, p. 165).

Perhaps then we can assume that an audience of 1890 would have been more susceptible to accepting this signal as credible baby cry, than an audience of today accustomed to negligible signal-to-noise ratio reproduction. In fact we may surmise that rather than disregarding the noise on the recording, an audience of today may well concatenate the 'noise' and 'signal' – the particular quality of added noise and subtracted signal connoting the patina of its antiquated medium of reproduction. This *forensic* reading again points to the prevailing *naturalist* concept of the *sound effect*. In the context of the standard audio-visual practice in cinema, Michel Chion develops this salient issue: 'the mike must remain excluded not only from the visual and auditory field (microphone noises, etc.) but also from the spectator's very *mental representation*' (Chion, 1994, p. 93).

THE OPERATION OF SOUND EFFECTS TODAY

So how do we demarcate *sound effects* from the enveloping *acoustic arena*[13] (Blesser and Salter, 2007; Truax, 2001) of the theatre auditorium? It is customary for

---

10 In the same article he starts to use intoxicating terminology such as 'fidelity' in relation to the phonograph. Such language lingers around audio-media today.

11 Having said that a baby's cry would have been an ideal choice of sound for this medium as warned by Edison: 'if reproduction is to be made audible to an audience, considerable force is requisite in the original utterance' (Edison, 1878, p. 530).

12 'In 1900, Wallace Sabine calculated that the [sound] absorbing power of the average woman was equivalent to 0.54 square meter of open window' (Thompson, 2002, p. 374).

13 '[A] region where listeners are part of a community that shares an ability to hear a sonic event. An acoustic area is centered at the sound source; listeners are inside or outside the area of the sonic event' (Blesser and Salter, 2007. p. 22).

the management of *sound effects* to fall under the jurisdiction of the *sound designer*, a role distinct to that of composer, scriptwriter and performer/actor, etc. Therefore within this definition we are not necessarily including musical score, sound track or semantically linguistic utterance. Having said that, music and spoken word often find their way into the concern of the sound designer, when some form of further manipulation or treatment is called for, such as the use of voiceover. For a widely shared definition of *sound effect* we may refer to *The Oxford English Dictionary*: 'A sound typical of an event or evocative of an atmosphere, produced artificially in a play, film, etc. … The various aids and contrivances (appropriate "noises off", lighting, etc.) used to accompany and vivify the production of plays, films, or broadcasts' (*OED*, 2007).

Within this definition lies a conundrum: 'vivification' of the dramatic arts facilitated by the application of 'artificially' produced sound. This conundrum is in sharp contrast to our earlier semiotic classification of the *sound effect* of the baby's cry in *The Judge* as indexical; 'artificial' connoting the severing of the umbilical linkage. This opinion is supported by Chion's maxim: '[S]ounds … can be made in any and every way' (Chion, 1993, p. 53)[14] Whether we accept such a radical claim, it has been known for some time that theoretically we can synthesise any sound without the presence of the signal we seek to represent.[15]

And yet, despite this indexical fracture, in practice *sound effects* are delivered with such slight-of-hand confidence that we tacitly recognize it as *natural*, ceasing to acknowledge the *artificial* nature of its ontology. In this regard, again from a cinematic orientation, Chion goes as far as to say: 'The naturalist conception of sound continues to infuse real experience and critical discourse so completely that it has remained unnoticed by those who have referred to it and critiqued the same transparency on the level of the image' (Chion, 1994, p. 93).

As well as theory, this attitude suffuses pedagogical approaches to the practice of sound design.[16] In Robert L. Mott's (1990) textbook, *Sound Effects: Radio, TV, and Film* he asserts: 'Our perception of natural sounds has become so influenced by ideology about sounds that we are often disappointed with reality' (Mott, 1990, p. 85). As a corollary and reinforcing this attitude to sound and listening, Mott encourages the sound designer to eschew the 'natural' in favor of the 'characteristic': 'natural sound … manipulated in such a manner to achieve a desired effect' (*ibid.*).

---

[14] And of course when we are considering sound design for science fiction or action movie for example, there is often no extant model outside of media practice to refer to, or unconceivable to reproduce authentically. Hence some form of creative mocking-up of a credible accompanying sound is required. For example, in *Indiana Jones* the sound linked with the giant boulder rolling down the cave scene, is "a Honda Civic station wagon rolling down a gravel slope with the engine off"' (Sonnenschein, 2001, p. 58).

[15] Herman Helmholtz (1821–94), writing after Joseph Fourier (1786–1830), in his tome, *On the Sensations of Tone* (1877), scientifically proclaims: 'any form of vibration, no matter what shape it may take, can be expressed as the sum of simple vibrations' (Helmholtz, 1954, p. 34).

[16] The ultimate status for the *sound effect* we may surmise is its sublimation into Baudrillard's all-pervasive account of postmodern culture of *Simulacra and Simulation* (1994).

This 'desired effect' is derived from, 'what a sound should be according to som one's perception of sound' (*ibid*.). Considering the predilection for 'characteristic sound effects, the theatre sound designer has two means of preparing material for playback in the auditorium:

1. bespoke sound design through the practice of studio and field recording, and sound synthesis, with further manipulation as required; or
2. recourse to trusty off-the-shelf sfx catalogues.

Unlike the baby cry in *The Judge*, however due to budgetary restrictions and priorities placed elsewhere, the later prevails; recourse to catalogues is *de rigueur*. The danger is that this can result is a highly conventionalized sound design practice primarily derived from or referred to a well-rehearsed repertoire of *sound effects*. This practice is particularly pronounced in film sound design.

The commercial viability of primarily cinema-derived sound effect libraries are reliant on continued reuse of material. A portfolio of catalogues such as http://www.sound-ideas.com provides efficient access to vast sound effect libraries developed and implemented by major production studios, for example, Hanna-Barbera, Lucas Film, Twentieth Century Fox, Warner Bros. and Universal Studios. Via an online search engine accessed though key-words, tried and publicly (even globally) tested material awaits revival, based on the sound designer and director's rule of thumb, 'does it work?', in other words, does it effectively serve the narrative and dramatic flow, without drawing attention to itself (*ibid*., p. 86).

Despite the often tangential relationship with audio-visual causality in the 'real world', once posited and consequently repeated in another play, film or radio drama, inertia sets in, as representational configurations settle and ossify into a global system of audio-visual codification, *ad infinitum*. *Semantic listening*, defined by Chion (again after Schaeffer) as, 'listening that refers to a code or a language to interpret a message' (Chion, 1994, p. 28), (for example, spoken language), consequently overrides *causal listening* here. A sound effect's efficacy, therefore, is contingent on a circular system, incorporating the heritage of hegemonic production houses, distribution and dissemination networks, and the audience's exposure to such output. This is exemplified by the recurring motifs established by the BBC and Hollywood production houses. Immediately distinguishable sound effects such as 'Castle Thunder', first used in *Frankenstein* (directed by James Whale with Boris Karloff playing the Monster) in 1931, reverberates throughout countless films, radio dramas, musicals and theatre. 'Castle thunder' is a highly legible symbol that conveys an indelible message.

With a particular focus on radio drama, Tim Crook cites:

> [T]he notorious BBC Seagull that has more appearances and fewer royalties than any other item in the history of human dramatic communication … There are jokes among sound designers now about the ubiquitous use of the BBC baby from a certain sound effect CD. (Crook, 1999, p. 72)

These are extreme examples (and are often implemented ironically for those 'in the know'),[17] but it demonstrates the closed cycle that a particular combination of sounds and their concomitant signs can enter.

The practice of proprietary studio and field recording, editing and synthesis, although radically different modes of production, often fall under the mimetic dominance of the mass media *sound effect* archetypes. With the encroaching influence of sound design convention experienced through Western cinema, even the Kabuki's *geza* which is traditionally characterized by highly conventionalized/*unnatural* use of off-stage sound and music, have conformed to cinematic conventions:

> The only attempt to use sound literally and thus project the play beyond the confines of the playing areas occurs in those plays influenced by Western models, such as those of Okamoto Kido, which have been written within the last fifty or sixty years. (Ernst, 1974, p. 121)

Its power also spills into contemporary documentary film practice.[18] Douglas Gordon and Philippe Parreno's, *Zidane: A 21st Century Portrait* (2006), was filmed in *real time* using 17 synchronized cameras positioned around the perimeter of a football pitch, constantly tracking Zinédine Zidane throughout a match, (until he is given the red card 5 minutes before the end of the match). Tremendous effort has been made to capture the subtlest of detail and nuance within the visuals. If we consider location sound, however we find that out of a team of 18 in the sound department, with numerous credits for post production – Foley artists, sound editors, sound effects editor and a sound designer (Hollywood designer Randy Thom) with help from Skywalker Sound – there is only one boom operator. Why this unspoken unbalance between visual and aural *actuality*? Do the directors feel that location sound recording is not convincing enough to accompany, underscore or supplement the visual account of Zidane's action and the prevailing environmental context in which he is finds himself twice a week?

Reflecting further on this salient question, why we require 'illusionary sound to vivify the production', Barry Truax provides an explanation. On discussing the notion of 'sound romance' (Truax, 2001, p. 28), the feeling of nostalgia attached to a sound linked to 'a time and circumstance that no longer exists' (*ibid.*, p. 29), there is a tendency to idealize those sounds and the context in which we were accustomed to hear them. With this attitude to listening: 'The mind discards irrelevant detail; hence the sound "resonates" in the memory, much as the past become idealized as the "good old days" for many people' (*ibid.*, pp. 29–30).

It is this idealization of sound, Truax asserts, that is exploited in the deployment of *sound effects*. Thus a successful *sound effect* efficiently and effectively refers to an ideal notion of a sound or soundscape rather than an assiduous attempt at *authenticity*. And again this is contingent on the shared literacy of signs:

---

[17] Of course in the right hands the hackneyed sound effect pertains great comedic quality. I refer you to the 2nd episode of the 3rd series of *Father Ted* titled '*Chirpy Burpy Cheap Sheep*'.

[18] Remember John Grierson's often quoted authoritative axiom: 'documentary is the creative treatment of actuality' (Grierson, 1933, p. 8).

any ... sound can represent an object or idea as long as it is 'agreed to' by the community, patterns, and associations in the soundscape, which are built up over the years around specific sounds, and therefore their qualities become associated with their meanings. (*ibid*, p. 164)

Or in the words of Crook: 'When it becomes stereotypical and clichéd it is almost inevitable that the sound [effect] conveys by way of cultural codification a mood, idea or feeling' (Crook, 2001, p. 72).

More fundamental to culture than the notion of the 'sound romance' is linguistics, the operation of which we may extend to the codification of the *sound effect*. In Roland Barthes *Elements of Semiology* (1964), he stresses the inflexibility of the process of signification:

> The association of sound and representation is the outcome of a collective training (for instance the learning of the French tongue); this association – which is the signification – is by no means arbitrary (for no French person is free to modify it), indeed it is, on the contrary, necessary. (Barthes, 1964)

It may not necessarily be 'necessary' for *sound effects* to issue such rigid signification, however it offers the contemporary sound designer a tool kit to convey the full range of linguistic expression: irony, pathos, ambiguity, sublimity, comedy, synecdoche, and so on.

SOUND OBJECT: A RETURN TO THE 'INNOCENT EAR'

So if the current practice of *sound effects* is confined to the strictures of a standardized convention based on supposed (albeit illusionary) cause related to a rigid system of signification, what other options does the sound designer have?

On his trajectory of demystifying the practice of Western painting in *Art & Illusion*, Ernst Gombrich reflects for a moment on the onomatopoeic use of language. He arrives at the notion that due to 'habitual interpretation ... there is no innocent ear'.[19] Gombrich tries out a simple experiment to test out this concept. On considering the name we have attributed to the sound a clock makes in English, 'tick-tock', he tries out an alternative *interpretation* of what perhaps should be more like a 'tick-tick':

> since the units of sound are almost identical, and yet I feel compelled to organize my precepts ... An alternative interpretation may drive out the accepted one and reveal a glimpse of the reality behind it. Having become critical of my hearing 'tick-tock', I can try to hear something else. I can adopt the tentative hypothesis of making the clock say 'tick-tick-tock', and when I succeed in projecting this alternative, I can conclude that the stimuli I group in these different ways must be neutral. (Gombrich, 1993, p. 307)[20]

---

[19] Just as John Berger spelled out, 'The way we see things is affected by what we know or what we believe' (Berger, 1972, p. 8) can we not equally replace 'see' with 'hear'?

[20] In Michel Chion's *Audio Vision* (Chion, 1994, pp. 120–1) he refers to the research of François Delalande and Bernadette Céleste (*L'Enfant; Du a sonore au musical*) that explores the relative innocent ear of the child at play. They surmise that the child's accompanying sounds to a toy

To hear what is in fact present in a sound without 'habitual interpretation' intervening is a matter that led to an extensive methodological study by Pierre Schaeffer and the *Groupe de Recherches Musicales* in Paris in the 1950s and 1960s. In this case the primary motivation was a musical one: to develop a new music theory that dealt with sound on a fixed medium (disc, tape, etc.) freed from the confines of extant practice: a practice that was deferential to an abstract notation systems (ocular), predicated on the lineage of Western Music underpinned by such a system.

In, what Pierre Schaeffer named *musique concrète*, the artist works with the sounds themselves directly, using his/her ears and perceptual processes to shape and assemble the composition: calling for the 'primacy of the ear' (*primauté de l'oreille*) (Schaeffer quoted in Dack, 1999), 'rather than a priori assumptions regarding musical materials and how they might function' (Dack, 2002). Denis Smalley regards such a relationship with the listener and the object being listened to as 'interactive': '[A]n active relationship on the part of the subject in continuously exploring the qualities and structure of the object' (Smalley, 1992, p. 520).

A common misunderstanding is that *musique concrète* is limited to, as the *Oxford English Dictionary* states, 'music produced by combining various recorded natural sounds' (*OED*, 2007). On the contrary it could be any sound ('natural' is not a prerequisite), which has been recorded and fixed onto a medium for playback. In fact at the stage of composition the sound's history (i.e. its initial source), or implied history, is regarded as inconsequential. The distinctive method of *musique concrète* is thus the endeavour to focus on and exploit the intrinsic qualities of sounds – attending to the dynamic combination of frequencies and amplitudes as they change over time[21] and feed that perceptual knowledge into further embellishment, filtration, juxtaposition and or superimposition of sound:

> As a sculptor chisels stone, the acousmatic[22] musician fashions his sound material, shaping it and often completely changing its nature. Like a painter, he juxtaposes his colours, mixes them, modifies them, composes and blends them. Like a photographer, he captures a particular moment, centres his 'picture', chooses his lighting, makes use of double exposure. Like the film-maker, he chooses his timing, creates movement and contrast, edits, brings into play fluidity and clashes, repetition, delay, continuity, breaks. (Dufour and Brando, 2000)

Pierre Schaeffer started this journey in the late 1940s with his *Concert de Bruits* in 1948 comprising of 5 studies. The first study, *Etude aux Chemins de Fer*, featured

---

car, etc. are not 'literal reproduction' (Chion, 1994, p. 121), rather 'to evoke the thing's movement by means of isomorphisms, that is by "a similarity of movement between the sound and the movement it represents"' (Chion, 1994, p. 121), for example, its trajectory. Chion concludes that this approach is maintained in audiovisual practice in animation and cartoons.

[21] I.e. spectromorphology (Smalley, 1986).

[22] Acousmatic music is in a sense the follow-up to *Musique Concrète*, but with less disciplinary dogma. The term *Acousmatics* refers to 'a sect of the disciples of Pythagoras who were said to follow a form of teaching where the Master spoke to them hidden behind a screen' (Chion, 1983, p. 2).

a collage of sounds recorded at a train switching yard at Batignolles, Paris. Despite innovative recording, editing and mixing techniques, the sound of trains as trains are clearly legible in the final work: 'With the trains I was far removed from the domain of music and, in effect, trapped in the domain of drama' (Schaeffer, 1952, p. 21).[23]

Addressing this composerly anxiety he developed three techniques to conceal the source, engendering a return to the 'innocent ear':

1. *The sound object*: 'isolating[24] a sound from its context, manipulating it, and thus creating a new sound phenomenon which could no longer be traced directly to its cause ...' (Schaeffer, quoted in Chion, 1983, p .2), which psychologically we would regard as a discrete unit – a gestalt.
2. *The closed groove* (*sillon fermé*) (*Chion, 1983*, p. 2): by cutting into a groove on a disc rather than it spiralling centripetally, forming a circle it is thus destined to repeat.[25] This technique predates tape, but is a precursor to the ubiquitous technique of looping.
3. *The cut bell* (*cloche coupée*) (*ibid.*): the fragmenting of a sound. For example the attack from a recording of a bell is erased, leaving only the ensuing resonance, and then applying the closed groove technique to this resonance. On carrying out such a procedure the bell sound now resembled more like a flute' (Schaeffer quoted in Chion, 1983, p. 2).[26]

Appropriating the phenomenology of Edmund Husserl (1859–1938), as a result of these '*experiments in interruption*' (*ibid.*) a new mode of listening is encouraged: *reduced listening*. Unlike *causal listening* and *semantic listening,* it requires an unlearning of listening habits. It is only concerned with the relation of listening to the intrinsic qualities of sound. Linked to the notion of reduced listening is Husserl's notion of the *époché* (phenomenological reduction) or 'bracketing'. Through Schaeffer's acousmatic listening[27] situation, 'experiments in interruption' and repeated listening of the *sound object*, thanks to its fixed medium, we steadily get closer to the sound, circumventing the more seductive modes of causal and semantic tendencies.

A primary contribution of Schaeffer and his colleagues' research was the devising of a topology of the *sound object,* resulting in the tome *Traité des objets musicaux* (1966) and related annotated audio examples *Solfège de l'objet sonore* (2000, first published 1967). Chion reduced and rationalized the *Traité* in his *Guide des*

---

23 Translation by J. Dack and C. North (unpublished).
24 'The esthetic procedure of isolating sonic objects is analogous to the sculptor's or the decorator's isolating a marble work against a black velvet draping: This procedure directs attention to it, alone not as one element among many in a complex framework' (Moles, 1968, p. 117).
25 'a fragment of life caught in a trap, torn from its context, placed outside time and normal limits, repeated tirelessly' (Chion and Reibel, 1976 quoted in Dack, 1994).
26 This procedure highlights the role a sound's attack plays in source recognition.
27 I.e. Listening to a sound without seeing its source.

Objets Sonores (1983) and Denis Smalley has helped articulated this trajectory even further with his 'Spectro-morphology and Structuring Processes' (1986).

For the sound designer this approach opens up a greater qualitative experience of sound from both an acoustic and perceptual perspective than the causal (index-ical) and semantic (symbolic) strictures of the *sound effect*, suggesting new config-urations and assemblage. Schaeffer's colleagues at the GRM embraced this approach as the foundation for their compositional practice, resulting in *musique concrète* and acousmatic music masterpieces as Pierre Henry's *Variations pour une porte et un soupir* (1963) (Variations for a Door and a Sigh), Denis Smalley's *Pentes* (1974), Bernard Parmegiani's *De Natura Sonorum* (1975), Jonty Harrison's *Klang* (1982), Trevor Wishart's *Vox V* (1988) and Francis Dhomont's *Novars* (1989).

'FRIGHT EFFECT'

There is an aspect of non-semantic and non-causal listening that can accompany the *sound effect*. François Jost in his paper 'The Voices of Silence' on the precur-sors of sound in cinema, reflects on the status of sound effect as *icon*: '[S]ound produced must resemble the object it represents enough for spectators to identify it' (Jost, 2001, p. 48). However, on occasion this can be: 'less a matter of resem-blance between sounds than it is between the frights effected by the surge of some unexpected noise' (*ibid.*, p. 49).

He cites Handel's opera *Amadigi di Gaula* (1715) of which in the original staging required a: 'sudden, explosive irruption of thunder ... produced by a device made of alternated barrel staves and metal sheets onto a rope and let loose from the top of the flies' (*ibid.*, p. 48). Such an effect skips cognitive faculties, exercising a flight-or-fright response, with the release of hormones including adrenaline and subsequent endorphins into the blood stream and in general resulting in a feeling of hyper-arousal. All this before we translate the bodily experience into a sign.

In Hollywood sound design we have come to expect such stimulation aroused by sound, however this may not be necessarily *audible* sound design. The threshold for human perception of a continuous tone for low frequencies is commonly stated as 20Hz (Howard and Angus, 2001, p. 79), and as a correlate subwoofers tend not to have frequency response lower than 20–25 Hz.[28] In comparison, for a standard clas-sical orchestra the lowest sound that can be generated is the double bass' open E string at 41.245 Hz (Roads, 2002, p. 17). Below 20 Hz is the mysterious territory of infrasonic, where sound can be *felt* and help *colour* qualities of the audible sound, but may not be directly audible. An arts/science project led by Sarah Angliss (Infrasonic, 2008) exploring the influence of infrasonic frequencies (in this case 17Hz) in a music context, presented a concert of contemporary music in the Purcell Room (31 May 2003), with the addition of sporadic diffusion from a specially made 'acoustic cannon' (Infrasonic, 2008) designed by researchers at NPL. The audience's

---

[28] It is interesting to note that the lower limit of the discrete subwoofer channel on a profes-sional Dolby surround sound system is 3 Hz (Dolby, 2008).

responses to this addition included some esoteric reports such as: "'sense of cold-ness', 'anxiety' and 'shivers down the spine', 'calmness' and 'moments of clarity'" (O'Keeffe and Angliss, 2004, p. 132).

SOUND EVENT: CONTEXTUAL LISTENINGS

Returning to *The Judge*, what of this baby and why is/was it crying? We know when it was recorded, but we don't know its name or its parents. Through its audible distress it has unwittingly (that is, without consent) joined the cast of a theatre production, and as such was required to provide convincing crying (by means we can only imagine) of a fictional baby. The baby has undergone a process of appro-priation.[29] Through the recording process the crying earns the status of *sound effect*, hence transferable, anonymous, generic, idealized, archetypical. To the baby's parents this is not necessarily the case, as the acoustic bond between mother and baby tends on the indefectible. To her we may surmise that her child's role in the play is incidental and the background noise of the phonograph inaudible – the cries of her baby remaining intact: 'I see only the referent, the desired object' (Barthes,1988, p. 7). This attitude is concurrent with a bullet-point in Edison's marketing scheme. For as well as preserving the voices of 'our Washingtons, our Lincolns, our Gladstones, etc.', (Edison, 1878, p. 534) the phonograph could be used as a 'family record': 'For the purpose of preserving the sayings, the voices, and *the last words* of the dying member of the family – as of great men – the phonograph will unquestionably outrank the photograph' (*ibid.*, pp. 533–4).

In the field of soundscape studies we find analogous concern for archiving, history and sentiment in regards to time and place.[30] *Soundscape* is an overused term in sound design today. To reclaim is values we need to return to its inception, as coined and elaborated on by R. Murray Schafer and the World Soundscape Project: 'Technically, any portion of the sonic environment regarded as a field of study' (Schafer, 1994, p. 274).

But this is not some dispassionate 'field of study'. The key to understanding the soundscape is through the listener(s). Truax develops this definition: 'An environ-ment of sound with emphasis on the way it is perceived and understood by the indi-vidual, or by a society. It thus depends on the relationship between the individual and any such environment' (Truax, 1999).

The environment and its aural architecture[31] physically mediates sound,

---

[29] 'To photograph is to appropriate the thing photographed' (Sontag, 1984, p. 4).

[30] It is interesting to note that the earliest sound effect disc according to Robert and Celia Dearling's research, proclaimed in *The Guinness Book of Recorded Sound* (Dearling and Dearling, 1984), is *London Street Sounds* by Columbia: 'the result of a microphone being set up in Leicester Square at 2.30pm on Tuesday, 11 September 1928' (Dearling and Dearling, 1984, p. 181).

[31] 'aural architecture refers to the properties of a space that can be experienced by listening. An aural architect, acting as both an artist and a social engineer, is therefore someone who selects specific aural attributes of a space based on what is desirable in a particular cultural frame-work. With skill and knowledge, an aural architect can create a space that induces such feelings

consequently the listener cognitively mediates sound. The human role in the constitution of the soundscape is not only cognitive. We contribute to its very make-up as we carry out our day-to-day life. Soundscape studies (aka acoustic ecology) is the study of these relationships.

It is within this set of relationships that we approach the notion of the *sound event*: 'event' here is taken to mean 'something that occurs in a certain place during a particular interval of time'. (Schafer, 1994, p. 274). Unlike the self-referential perceptual unit of the *sound object*, the *sound event* however encompasses and extends beyond the intrinsic to include all 'social and environmental' (Truax, 1999) aspects of its original 'spatial and temporal' (*ibid.*) context: 'a nonabstractable point of reference, related to a whole of greater magnitude than itself' (Schafer, 1994, p. 274). Moreover, in contrast with the *sound object* that eschews context, the *sound event* is a context-specific phenomenon: 'the environmental sound signal, whether foreground or background in perception, *only* acquires meaning through its context, that is, its complete relationship to the environment' (Truax, 2001, pp. 52–3).

The interpretation of a *sound event* therefore requires in-depth knowledge of that context. The greater the contextual knowledge the more understanding there is of the operation of the *sound event*. Likewise the *sound event* can impart distinct information on the prevailing social and environmental context. '[T]he general acoustic environment of a society can be read as an indicator of social conditions which produce it and may tell us much about the trending and evolution of that society' (Schafer, 1994, p. 7).

The founding tenants of acoustic ecology including an outline of a topology of the *soundscape* and *sound event* are presented in Murray Schafer's *The Soundscape: Our Sonic Environment and the Tuning of the World* (1994)[32] and elaborated further in Barry Truax's *Acoustic Communication* (2001).[33] Discourse and study is promoted today though the World Soundscape Community and its regional satellites such as the UK and Ireland Soundscape Community.

ACOUSTEMOLOGY

A related term to soundscape is *acoustemology*, a concept developed by the ethnomusicologist and anthropologist Steven Feld on studying the Kaluli people of the Bosavi forest, Papua New Guinea.

> [Acoustemology explores] acoustic knowing as a centrepiece of Kaluli experience; how sounding and the sensual, bodily, experiencing of sound is a special kind of knowing, or put differently, how sonic sensibility is basic to experiential truth in the Bosavi forests. Sounds

---

as exhilaration, contemplative tranquillity, heightened arousal, or a harmonious and mystical connection to the cosmos. An aural architect can create a space that encourages or discourages social cohesion among its inhabitants. In describing the aural attributes of a space, an aural architect uses a language, sometimes ambiguous, derived from the values, concepts, symbols, and vocabulary of a particular culture' (Blesser and Salter, 2007, p. 5).

[32] First published in 1977.
[33] First published in 1984.

emerge from and are perceptually centred in place, not to ment'
places. Just as 'life takes place' so does sound; thus mor'
accounts of the Kaluli sound world have become acoustic
place and places make sense. (Feld, 1994, p. 4)

For many of us, our sensibilities to sound, culture, soc
not be as acutely interlinked as those of an indigen.
however, from my own[34] preliminary studies of the inhabitan.
South West of England (2000–2) I have learnt of the deep, often unconsu.
placed on ones prevailing soundscape (Drever, 2007).

Location recording is central to soundscape studies: pedagogic creative listening experiments, interpretative artistic compositions, sound archive, material for study in the laboratory. All these approaches can be heard in *Soundscapes of Canada* (1974): 10 one-hour radio programmes based on the sounds of Canadian acoustic environment (World Soundscape Project, directed by Schafer, 1974).

Composition and acousmatic music have had a close relationship with soundscape composition resulting in a rich and diverse archive of artistic responses to sound, sentiment and place: Luc Ferrari's *Presque Rein Le lever du jour au bord de la mer* (1970), World Soundscape Project's *The Vancouver Soundscape* (1973), Hildegard Westerkamp's *Kits Beach Soundwalk* (1996), Murray Schafer's *Winter Diary* (1997), Steven Feld's *Rainforest Soundwalks* (2001), Drever's *Phonographies of Exeter* (2002), Chris Watson's *Weather report* (2003), and so on.

Ironically, in the film word, the pretty well one-man production team of Philip Gröning, in his documentary film, *Die Große Stille* [*Into Great Silence*] (2005), elicits more sonic detail than the efforts of Gordon and Parreno's multi-pronged production squad. Equipped with one Sony CineAlta 24P HDCAM (the same model used in Sokurov's *Russian Ark*, 2002), the 169 minute fly-on-the-wall style documentary is the result of 6 months living with and filming the everyday activities of the hermit-like community of the Carthusian order of the Grande Chartreuse in the French Alps. There is no Foley or library sfx required here. Rather through the long takes of this still community we begin to savour the particular creaking motion of a well used oak prayer stall; the undulating filtersweep of antiquated electric shavers, sonifying the unique contours of the monks' foreheads as they undergo their monthly trim.

In some soundscape studies local communities have been invited to represent themselves through the editing, treatment and arrangement of recordings they have made of the sounds they hear everyday, for example, the *Sound Portraits* from *The Sounds of Harris & Lewis* (2002), directed by Gregg Wagstaff and Sonic Arts Network's *Sonic Postcards* (2006). Often projects ask for the nomination of sounds to form the basis of the study, for example, Peter Cusack's *Your Favourite London Sounds* (2001).

Despite the preponderance of field recording and editing in soundscape studies, Schafer regards the pervasiveness of electroacoustic technology as partly responsible

---

[34] In collaboration with Touring Exhibition of Sound Environments, the Digital Crowd (University of Plymouth) and Aune Head Arts.

Of greater significance to field recording in soundscape studies methodology however, is the practice of sound walking, as developed by Schafer, Westerkamp, and others. In its most elemental of form: '[A]ny excursion whose main purpose is listening to the environment' (Westerkamp, 2007, p. 49). It can be done alone or organized as a group experience. Before a sound walk we may predict what sounds we will hear, using our past experience, existing knowledge of context, and so on. However in practice sound walks are full of surprise and serendipity. Unlike the controlled lab or isolated sound studio environment, here we are listening *in situ*, where all sounds are site-specific: '[B]ringing us closer to the ultimate goal of aural awareness on a wider scale' (Westerkamp, 2007, p. 52).

A more recent contribution to this emerging field is the concept of the 'sonic effect'. Eruditely weaving together the threads of the Schaeffer and Schafer schools, with an up-to-date knowledge of acoustics, psychology, architecture, aesthetics and sociology, is Augoyard and Torgue's *Sonic Experience: A Guide to Everyday Sounds* (2005).[35] The book is formed of a glossary of what they have coined 'sonic effects'. 'The concept of the sonic effect seemed to describe this interaction between the physical sound environment, the sound milieu of a socio-cultural community, and the "internal soundscape of the individual"' (Augoyard and Torgue, 2005, p. 9). Such research is designed as a tool kit for the analyst and sound designer alike, helping provide a fuller, even holistic understanding of the soundscape.

CONCLUSION

Beyond the subservient and closed system of the *sound effect,* the qualitative self-reference and autonomy of the *sound object* and the contextual concerns of the *sound event* offer a wide ranging and yet closer engagement with auditory materials for the sound designer and as a corollary, for the director, cast, production team, audience and a theatrical work's overall dramaturgy. It must be stressed that these are challenging and time-consuming approaches. It can involve assiduous fieldwork

---

[35] First published as À l'écoute de l'environement. Répertoire des effets sonores by Editions Parenthèses in 1995.

and engagement with communities and environments outside of the theatre, sociological, acoustic and psycho-acoustic study, and prolonged experimentation with materials in the field, studio, stage, and throughout the whole auditorium. Moreover for such approaches to work, they must be considered as a central concern for the devising of a work and verging towards an equal footing with words and music. With faith they will lead us towards Artaud's 'fragile music' and 'crystal swarms'.

Conclusion: The Theatre of Sound II

I said at the beginning that this was not a how-to-do book. How-to-do books often contain a few afterthoughts about auditory culture, dramaturgy and auditory concepts. Given that this book has been all about those things, I'll end with some afterthoughts on 'how to do'.

So, I first offer six suggested conceptual headings for thinking about or discussing theatre sound, which recap and summarize the main themes of this book. They might make useful seminar topics or help someone facing a creative block find an oblique strategy to get the ideas flowing again. Then I end with my own, brief, personal suggestion of 'how to do' theatre sound design.

HOW TO THINK ABOUT THEATRE SOUND DESIGN

Re-Arranged Hearing

The dramaturgy of sound is not only a process of arranging sound, it is also a process of arranging hearing. Try this exercise (or imagine it, perhaps, if you are reading this on a train).

Stand in a quiet room. Breathe deeply and regularly. Listen to your breathing. As you begin to breathe more slowly, listen to the sounds your body makes between breaths. Don't worry if it is so quiet that you are not sure whether you are imagining things.

Now extend the range of your hearing a little further – listen to the room. If you are with other people, listen to their bodies.

Think about what you just did when you extended the radius of your hearing. Where are you extending it from? Where is the centre of your auditory sphere?

Count the number of different sounds you can hear in this room. Now find five more (there are always more, don't worry if you think you might be imagining them, imaginary sounds are valid).

Now widen the sphere of your hearing yet further. Listen to whatever is immediately the other side of the walls. Check on your breathing again, and then check back on the sounds in the room, then go back to the sounds outside the room and find five more – if you can't hear any, try to imagine some that you think might be out there.

Now widen your sphere to its full extent, to its event horizon, to the distant hazy drone of unimaginably vast sound and any faintly discernible details you can pick out (real or imagined). If you are in the city, listen to the skyline of distant traffic, building works and aeroplanes. If you are in the country, listen to the wild blue yonder. How far can you hear? What does the horizon sound like and what do you think lies beyond it?

Now, gradually, move the focus of your hearing back into the room and back into your body – but this time, not letting go of the more distant sounds, until eventually you can hear it all – the whole sphere of sound, centred on your consciousness. Fly around it, move from the most distant aeroplane to nearest saliva-swallow or half-imagined wheeze. As your attention flits from focus-to-focus, think about how often it is taken by the words in your head. Are your thoughts sounds?

Sound is what you hear. But is it only that? What about the sound that you listen to? Is that different from the sound you hear? Isn't sound also something you download, something that you make and sell, something that you feel in the pit of your stomach, something that you notate on a stave in dots and lines? Another exercise: Say the words *theatre* and *sound* in your head. (Did you hear them?)

What comes to mind when you say those words? Loudspeakers? Coconut shells? Thunder-sheets? Microphones? Computers? Wires? Knobs? Faders? Atmospheric soundscapes of montaged noises? Dogs barking? Doorbells? A department? A job? A degree? You could write a list.

Would voice, body, movement, smell, touch, silence be on the list? Would music? Say the words *theatre* and *sound* again (in your head or out loud) but this time, listen to the gap between the words. What's in there? Nothing? Listen again (leave a longer gap if you like).

Now imagine the words *theatre* and *noise* and what comes to mind? Mobile phones perhaps? Sweet wrappers? Police sirens from outside the theatre? The hum of a crowd milling around the foyer and bars? The bumps and thuds of a scene change? You could write another list. Why do you think it would be different from the *theatre* and *sound* list?

… *and relax* … exercise over.

Cultured Hearing

Hearing is arranged spatially by environmental circumstances such as architecture and is calibrated by the dynamic range of sound one is situated in and the scale of sounds one is listening for. It is also arranged in and around thoughts, which are, in some senses, audible and co-inhabit the same, or at least a very proximate, spatiotemporal field. Hearing is also arranged by categories of cultural preconception (and one might say that hearing also arranges the world into cultural categories). It is possible to choose whether to hear something and how to hear it; those choices are culturally informed.

The ways in which contemporary auditory culture categorizes *noise, music* and *sound* separately have been thoroughly described in relation to acoustic ecology and the sonic arts, for example by R. Murray Schafer (1994), Douglas Kahn (1999), Jacques Attali (1985), and Paul Hegarty (2007). I would recommend each of these books as part of any thorough theatre sound bibliography, for between them they constitute a historiography of how people hear art and how art hears the world. Theatre, though, is more than art. It is also a room. We encounter *noise, music* and *sound* in the room as well as in the art.

While they are empirically cognate concepts (each is heard) *noise, music* and *sound* are culturally arranged, usually by adjectives, within a kind of aesthetic taxonomy. For example, noise might be *raw*, sound *prosaic* and music *poetic*. Musical noise, prosaic music or noisy sound are contradictory concepts – either interestingly or problematically so. Noise is barred by convention, prevented, abated, or made deliberately to shock or alarm; it lacks sense. Music, on the other hand, is traditionally a manifestation of form itself; a performance of order and sense. Sound is more functional, is *of* something ... the sound of a dog barking, the sound of the actor's voice; *a* sound is something distinct from the general field of noise and is different from noise; it is a signal to which we tune-in; as opposed to noise, it is wanted.

But music, noise and sound have not always been so separate. It has not always been considered improper to talk or make noise while music is being played or theatre is being performed. The mediaeval English collective word for publically performing musicians was a *noise* of musicians, as in *Henry IV Pt.2*: Act 2; Scene 4: 'see if thou canst find out Sneak's *Noise*. Mistress Tearsheet would fain hear some music.' Environmental urban noise has not always been a nuisance (in some historical instances, quite the contrary).

The contemporary connotations of these words are cultural positions, which also affect the ways in which sound is heard within theatre. For example, early-modern English ears around the time of Shakespeare appreciated a healthy, panoramic balance between noise, sound and music because this demonstrated a 'oneness' between the natural and human spheres. Music was appreciated in relation to noise, not despite it. Late twentieth-century ears, culturally trained to appreciate 'hi-fidelity' and a 'high signal-to-noise ratio', by contrast, prefer drama or music to be performed in silence and find intermingling noise, music and sound confusing (except, perhaps, in a pub or some other place where it might be acceptably 'atmospheric').

People, like sponges, absorb their acoustic environment and conform to it in their behaviours and in the sounds and noises they make. In Part II, John Levack Drever described Stephen Feld's anthropological study of 'acoustemology' – the cultural relationship between societies and their sonic environments. It is a concept manifest throughout historical theatre sound practice. When, in *The Tempest*, Caliban says 'the isle is full of noises, sounds and sweet airs', he is describing an exotically broad and diverse sonic ecology (not a series of separate contradictory categories), but he is also describing himself. The island's strange and wonderful acoustemology partly defines Caliban's exoticism, and is reflected in the frequent aural allusions and odd rhythms of his verse (see Smith, 1999, pp. 333–9). Shakespeare's contemporary audience, whose ears were only just beginning to become 'modernized',[1] would have picked up on this perhaps more instinctively than a modern-day audience. A slight difference in emphasis within the verse would have hinted at a whole other world of sound in a way that a modern audience simply would not hear. Neither would a modern audience 'get' the slight timbral difference between the sounds of different kinds of trumpets used to announce entrances at the top of scenes, which would have very precise codified meanings to early-modern ears and set up a scene just as suggestively as a theme tune.

The very thought of *sound* and *hearing* as separate categories is somewhat culturally predicated. Recent studies of sensual culture[2] (for example, Howes 2005 and Erlmann 2004) challenge the modernist categorization of perception into discrete senses and the attendant categorization of the phenomenal universe into objects grouped according to the senses (sounds, smells and so on). The 'meaning' of a sight, it is proposed, cannot be dissociated from the ambience of its place of reception, which is experienced synaesthetically within the *sensorium* (the mediaeval concept revived as a trope for holistic sensual perception).

Not only does one sense impinge on and affect the others, but perception is affected by cultural histories associated with the senses. As David Howes, one of the leading figures in the field explains:

> To a greater or lesser extent, every domain of sensory experience, from the sight of an artwork to the scent of perfume to the savour of dinner, is a field of cultural elaboration. Hence the necessity of adopting an anthropological approach to the study of the sensorium. (http://www.david-howes.com/DH-research.htm, accessed 6 Jan 2009)

Contemporary perception of sound is affected by a complex and multifarious cultural history which can, very broadly, be summarized in two major narratives.

The first of these is the history of noise, particularly the growing opposition during the modern period between culturally 'wanted' *sound* (music, clear speech and so on) and unwanted *noise* (which some theorists such as Attali (1985) have described as a political story). A postmodern history of noise is perhaps still unfolding around us (and I describe some of this in the Introduction). Noise is important enough to have its own heading (see below).

The second is the *objectification* of sound and the narrowing of its definition from earlier, more holistic concepts of analogically sonic ontology. In this

---

[1] By the empirical rationalism and categorization that would become associated with the European 'Enlightenment'

[2] An emergent field, manifest in the recent *Sensory Formation* series of Readers (Berg).

narrative, vision and the visually-orientated tropes of the Enlightenment are often portrayed as culprits in the demotion of sound as the softer sense of the dominant pair – the 'touch feely' sense, so to speak; or else the sense of spirituality and emotion, but not of rational thought or detached observation.

It is hard sometimes to avoid talking about sound in binary opposition to vision and detached objectivity, perhaps even to logic and reason. In order to theorize and discuss sound it is sometimes necessary, as Bruce R. Smith (1999, p. 26) puts it, 'to counter the tyranny of Cartesian philosophy, with its privileging of visual experience, its ambition to speak with a single authoritative voice'. Sometimes, though, this countering can be taken too far, and a kind of audio/visual competition ensues which I regard as a discursive red-herring. Or else, and more insidiously, a evangelical hijacking of aural concepts for political purposes can take place, which it is worth spending some time summarizing.

Enlightenment processes, it is claimed, falsely rationalized the mind into thinking about sounds as independent objects, and falsely rationalized the body by disaggregating the field of bodily sensation into five sensual categories, only one of which was associated with sound. According to some, such as the new age writer E. J. Berendt, who has had some 'cross-over' influence on academic aural theory through his books *Nada Brahma* (1983) and *The Third Ear* (1988), the En*light*enment was something like visualist colonialism, occupying languages and ways of thinking for political reasons as well as philosophical ones. It *seeks* in*sight* by dividing the holistic continuum into discreet events, objects and ideas; submitting them to detached inspection; categorizing them; measuring them; demanding that they be independently verifiable. In doing so, it corrodes spiritual consciousness (this was Berendt's position). European languages became awash with visualist tropes (if you *see* what I mean? Seeing is believing, and so on) and vision became regarded as the objective, compellingly logical and therefore the primary sense. Berendt, with some witty allusions to psychoacoustic theory, talks of analogical 'ear thinking' versus logical 'eye thinking', with the ear thinker as hero:

> Logic aims at security
> The ana-logician has the courage to embark on risk and adventure.
> Logic is goal-orientated and passes judgement
> Analogy ponders and establishes relationships.
> The logician sees
> The ana-logician listens.
>
> (Berendt, 1988, p. 60).

Berendt (1988, passim), analogically, describes the Enlightenment as a *hypertrophy* of the eye and an atrophy of the ear. Earlier mythologies, philosophies and belief systems that were built on tropes of orality, aurality and embodiment, gave way to abstract ideas and reason (I am still characterizing a broad school of thought here). Starved of its discursive premises and thus of its lifeblood, ear-thinking and the expanded consciousness of being aurally 'in-tune' with the universe, shrivelled into disuse.

An alternative view might be that they became embalmed in occultist hippy sub-culture ... relaxation CDs of whale song, surf or rainstorms; the generic joss stick scented ambience of 'world' music and sounds; expanded consciousness through auditory massage. One must ask who is making the 'ontotheological' portrayal of hearing as a special, spiritual sense in binary opposition to vision, and why. In a list of clichés he calls the 'audiovisual litany', Jonathan Sterne shows how sound is often characterized as *spiritual* because it is spherical, immersive and to do with interiors whereas vision is characterized as *intellectual* because it is directional, offers perspective and is concerned with surfaces.

[Sterne's Audiovisual Litany]
- hearing is spherical, vision is directional;
- hearing immerses its subject, vision offers a perspective;
- sounds come to us, but vision travels to its object;
- hearing is concerned with interiors, vision is concerned with surfaces;
- hearing involves physical contact with the outside world, vision requires distance from it;
- hearing places us inside an event, seeing gives us a perspective on the event;
- hearing tends toward subjectivity, vision tends toward objectivity;
- hearing brings us into the living world, sight moves us toward atrophy and death;
- hearing is about affect, vision is about intellect;
- hearing is a primarily temporal sense, vision is a primarily spatial sense;
- hearing is a sense that immerses us in the world, vision is a sense that removes us from it (Sterne, 2003, p. 15)

Some of this is indeed true. The mathematical models that describe acoustics and auditory perception may *indeed* be less linear than those of vision; the spatial/temporal properties of sound *do* make it difficult to establish a firm distinction between object and environment in a way that linear logic may find it difficult to accommodate;[3] auditory attention *may* be given more through psychoacoustic processing than by a beam-like visual gaze. But it is important to remember that these characteristics have evolved in interdependency with the other senses within a synaesthetic sensorium. We hear a slight noise in the undergrowth behind us, or maybe it's just an illogical 'feeling' that something is wrong, and we turn round to check it out; we visually identify it and categorize it and then we act. Without this process of

---

[3] A good example of this difficulty is Brian O'Shaughnessy's 'The Location of Sound' (1957), 'The peculiar thing about [a sound]' he muses, 'is that it appears to wear its spatial "properties" like a quality. If one pictures space as a vast ocean and a sound as a small sponge, then it is as if the sponge were situated in a vast ocean which it had, at the same time, absorbed' (p. 490).

immersive aurality triggering objective analysis, humankind would long ago have been eaten by tigers, so there is clearly evolutionary advantage in possessing a combination of logical, detached analysis and circumstantial aural 'hunch' or feeling. And yet proponents of the audiovisual litany, according to Sterne, idealize hearing as the open channel to 'pure interiority', while denigrating vision as a wordly sense, for political reasons:

> The audiovisual litany is ideological in the oldest sense of the word: it is derived from religious dogma. It is essentially a restatement of the longstanding spirit/letter distinction in Christian spiritualism. The spirit is living and life-giving – it leads to salvation. The letter is dead and inert – it leads to damnation. Spirit and letter have sensory analogues: hearing leads a soul to spirit; sight leads a soul to the letter. A theory of religious communication that posits sound as life-giving spirit can be traced back to the Gospel of John and the writings of Saint Augustine. These Christian ideas about speech and hearing can in turn be traced back to Plato's discussion of speech and writing in the Phaedrus. (*ibid.*, p. 16)

Sterne also points out that hearing underwent its own cultural process of modernization – that the Enlightenment was also an 'En*son*iment'. It is possible, if not entirely comfortable, to consider sounds as significant objects in isolation from the rest of the aural field, and it was through the development of stethoscopes and ear trumpets that the technology of sound developed towards telegraphy, telephony, sound reproduction and storage. These technologies changed the way we hear, just as the current sonification of objects and user-interfaces will change the way we hear in the future. Technologies cannot be un-invented, and modern hearing cannot be unpicked to retrieve some primally 'natural' state.

Together these narratives of *noise* and *objectification* tell a lot about the modernization of hearing. One might also consider the effect of acoustemological diasporas in postcolonial and migrant cultures, and the history of gendered hearing. But within modern, culturally arranged hearing, non-modern sonic understandings continue faintly to resonate. As Veit Erlmann suggests in the introduction to his edited volume *Hearing Cultures*:

> The modern sonic self is defined by complex dialectical processes insecurely poised between the modern and the 'primitive', between the rational and the affective, the discursive and the embodied (Erlmann, 2004, p. 13).

Erlmann suggests a residual cultural memory in the modern psyche of a time when sound was conceptually different; was more than packets of communication delivered through auditory apparatus; more than the medium of the verbal idea or the musical artwork. In various 'primitive' understandings (some of which Don Ihde describes in *Listening and Voice: a Phenomenology of Sound* (1976) and others which Berendt covers in *The Third Ear* (1988) sound is a philosphical analogy by which existence itself is understood.

Conceptual Hearing

At several times during the course of this book, I have discussed how sound, both within the controlled arrangements of aesthetic theatre and within the personal theatre of daily life can be a theoretical as well as an acoustic environment. The constancy of the universe, according to some belief systems and philosophies, consists in a balance between the elemental chaos of unformed energy and sonic order (for example the harmonically ordered energy of aligned celestial orbs and bodily organs in the notion of *harmonia mundi*). In Chapter 3 we saw how Boethius' version of this philosophy (his musical trinity *mundana/humana/instrumentalis*) would have conditioned the sonic dramaturgies and conventions of Shakespearian theatre.

There is a part of the 'modern sonic self', to whom the composer or theatre sound designer speaks through their designs, that retains a cultural memory of this wider sonic significance. Indeed, for many it is still a live trope. Sound is the visiting voices of the angels, the stories of Babylon and Jericho and so on:

> The beginning of man is in the midst of word. And the center of word is in breath and sound, in listening and speaking. In the ancient mythologies the word for soul was often related to the word for breath. In the biblical myth of the creation, God breathes life into Adam, and that breath is both life and word. (Ihde, 1976, p. 3)

> The primary presence of the God of the West has been as the God of Word, YHWH. 'And God said, let there be ...' 'The creative power of the Hebrew God is word which is spoken forth as power: from word comes the world. And although God may hide himself from the eyes, he reveals himself in word which is also event in spite of the invisibility of his being. Human life, too, as the word-breath which unites the human with others and the gods is a life in sound. (*ibid.*, p. 15)

> In the Tibetan Book of the Dead, the deceased, on his migration through the intermediate state between death and rebirth, hears 'innumerable kinds of musical instruments that fill entire world-systems with music and cause them to vibrate, to quake and tremble, with sounds so mighty as to stun one's brain'. (Berendt, 1988, p. 38)

These analogies speak to people's daily experience of acoustic sound in order to imagine metaphysical environments and experiences. Through sonic tropes (breathing, music and so on) imponderable notions such as *self* and *other*, *inspiration* and *spiritual migration* become metaphorically articulated and hence more reconcilable or tangible to the grasp. While I do not make the kinds of ontotheological claims that Sterne warns against (see above), I think that sound designers or composers do well to be aware that they are working very close to this territory; that sounds of breath and resonance in particular have the ability to recall larger themes.

The Aural Body

In Part II we looked at sound understood according to the modern theory of corporeal subjectivity known as phenomenology (in which a trace of *musica humana* faintly resonates). We saw how sounds originate in points in *space-time*, but inflate at the speed of sound to become part of the immersive acoustic environment; a theatre of sound. When sitting as part of the theatrical congregation called *an audience* in a Theatre with a capital T, one tends to (or is supposed to) focus one's ears on the points of origin of the words or music that form the auditory programme. But one is also aware of one's material surroundings, not by sight, which is (supposedly) directed forward and whose peripheral zones are normally darkened, but by the closely interrelated skin/air senses (hearing, smell, touch). I describe these as aural senses not because of a connection to the ear, but because the etymology of the word aural connects with the Latin word *aura* (breeze or zephyr – that airborne, tactile, mnemonic sense of place). This synaesthetic, general background awareness of ambient environment, of noise, resonant space and *others*, is the atmosphere within which any perception is made, and modifies the meaning of any received communicative signal. It takes the foreground during silence, and is a perceptual experience of the whole body.

The concept of the *aural body* is important to the understanding of theatre sound because it admits that hearing is not *only* a process of the cultured intellect. Just as they are in the psyche, hearing and sound production are interrelated within the body. In its organic, sympathetically resonant response to external, air-based acoustic energy, and in the sound that it produces, the aural body is also a sonic instrument. Its sounds might be deliberately communicative – vocal production, kinetic sound production (for example, clapping) – or it might be involuntary: the personal soundscape, which one continually inhabits, of one's own breathing, wheezing, rumbling, swallowing, sniffing, coughing and so on. Resonance – whether in the ear canal and drum or within the bowel or stomach – is a kinetic process; and processes of corporeal (as opposed to psychoacoustic) hearing are very close to being tactile sensations such as itches or physical pleasure or pain. The sound of a low bass frequency is defined as much by the tingling vibration it causes within the chest and lower body as it is by its auditory appearance. A shrill sound can hurt. Try swallowing some saliva. Where does the sound end and the tactile sensation begin? The subjects of hearing and sound often lead to *koans* (or enigmatic sayings – the one hand clapping, trees in forests and so on). Or else to florid figurative prose, such as the writings of Michel Serres:

> By the ear, of course, I hear: temple, drum, pavilion, but also my entire body and the whole of my skin. We are immersed in sound just as we are immersed in air and light, we are caught up willy-nilly in its hurly-burly. We breathe background noise, the taut and tenuous agitation at the bottom of the world, through all our pores and papillae, we collect within us the noise of organization, a hot flame and

a dance of integers. My acouphenes, a mad murmur, tense and constant in hearing, speak to me of my ashes, perhaps, the ones whence I came, the ones to which I will return. (Serres, 1995, p. 7)

The aural body is the intimate theatre we live in, and all wider theatres are experienced through it. Listening out from the point of sentient awareness that is the constant, blinking cursor point of *me being awake* (located, it seems, somewhere behind my sinuses) I have largely learned to be deaf to my own constant noise, only becoming aware of it in moments when I am alone or silent, but it remains the live context of everything I perceive.

Not All Sound is Real

But when I am alone or silent I am also aware that there is sensation other than acoustic sound within my aural body – the ghosts of sounds and sounds yet to happen. Partly this is *phonomnesis* – imagined or recalled sound: the sounds of these words in my head as you read this sentence. These are within your body as thoughts, but have the potential to be spatial. I can imagine a sound to my left or right; above me or below me. I can remember the sound of my parents downstairs as I lay in bed as a child and these imagined sounds come from the direction *down*. I sometimes ask students to remember sounds such as these, and then ask them to listen to something present in the room while remembering their sound at the same time. This usually proves impossible, as if trying to remember was the same as listening (and while one may hear polyphonically, one cannot listen to two things at the same time).

But the sonic ghosts are not only in my head; they are also in my bodily sensations; they are my corporeal imaginings of aural feelings: the recollection of the internal vibration of standing by the sea or the roadside; the impetus to wince remembered from a shrill sound; the complex emotional arrangement of vibration, flushes, prickling skin and adrenal activity of engaging with music. Augoyard and Torgue (2005, p. 85) describe a phenomenon they call *anamnesis*: the physical recollection – literally the re-*membering* – of sound through the body. This might be triggered empathetically by sensual perception or through imagined or remembered sound. One might remember music in one's head (phonomnesis) and also experience its effect in the body (anamnesis). Anamnesis is produced either by sound or memory; indeed, one might view it as a form of memory or imagination experienced in the aural body.

In a way, sound is all in the mind; a figment of the imagination, or at best an imaginative psychoacoustic guess at what is going on. Just to be difficult, let me say this: 'sound' does not exist, *per se*, as an independently verifiable energetic phenomenon of the universe like wind, or even like light (which aside from illuminating objects in order for us to see them, also produces photosynthesis and can be farmed for energy). Light is measurably 'out there' in the universe as photon particles. Sound is only in our minds. It is nothing but effect. The cliché is true. A tree falling in a forest when nobody is there sends ripples through the air, but only the ear knows them as sound-waves. What we call acoustic energy is one way of looking at the variations in air pressure produced by the vibration of an object. It is an analogue inscription within a medium, a form of weather even, but it is not 'sound' without a body to feel it and a mind to 'think' it as such. One might say this of light, but light transmits through a vacuum whereas sound is carried in a medium, so it has an independence which sound does not. What we experience as acoustic (as opposed to imagined) sound is the neural analogue of a kinetic process created by vibrations in a tiny reservoir of air which is in direct, tactile contact with the flesh, hair and membrane of our ear. When you probe the furthest reaches of your hearing, you are in fact reaching no further than the immediate tactile interface between your inner ear and the small inlet of air that is your outer ear canal. Either that or you are probing the realm of the imagination.

Contained in the ripples in this little auricular harbour of air is a microcosm of all the activity in the vast ocean of energetically charged air beyond. These ripples contain data which are transduced by your flesh, membranes, nervous tissue and bone into thoughts. This is where sounds originate. Hearing infers environmental sound from *within* the ear.

The sound of my fingers typing these words appears to come from the keyboard in front of me, but I know it is happening in my head. There is no 'sound particle'[4] moving between the keyboard and my ears. I am detecting vibration in my auditory canals, creating a mental image of a sound and projecting it onto the keyboard. It is a psychoacoustic trick called localization – there is no sound actually 'on' the keys as there seems to be. I am imagining it. A sound is not an object in the universe like a piece of scenery – what we perceive as *a sound* is a psychoacoustically projected image.

Imaginary hearing and perceived hearing are merely different registers of a larger mechanism of audition. I can imagine the sound of my parents downstairs because imagined sounds and perceived sounds seem to share auditory space. As Don Ihde points out:

> As a field phenomenon, auditory imagination apparently displays the same general features that its perceptual base does, i.e., imagined sounds may be presented as coming from any direction or may surround the subject. Again the space of auditory imagination is *surrounding*. (Ihde, 1973, p. 54)

In most circumstances we do not project the images of imaginary sound into the world outside our heads. There are, however, some circumstances where

---

[4] Apparently things called sound particles and phonons do exist, but only as theoretical tools used for describing wave activity in quantum terms rather than observable phenomena, see Haughton (2002).

a suggestion of projection 'beyond' is experienced. This happens in some cases of synaesthesia or schizophrenia, or when we are tired, spooked, trying very hard to hear something which we think might be there, or when we vividly remember something. Neurologists now know, through modern scanning technologies, that the same combination of areas of the brain lights up when a schizophrenic or a synaesthetic hears a sound that nobody else does as they do when that sound is made in the room. The subject really is hearing the imagined sound. Theatre conventions such as ghost voices, voiceovers, or the portrayal of someone's inner mental state through external sound (for example, in Irving/Leopold Lewis's melodrama *The Bells*) demonstrate that theatre audiences recognize that phonomnesis and anamnesis can manifest as auditory hallucination.

In the mediaeval tradition of sonic 'conjury', strange sonic happenings, apparitions, screaming earth and talking objects (which we encountered in Chapter 4) were openly heard by all as portentous magic. As the modern age dawned, supernatural phenomena gained a new ambiguity.

Theatre Noise

The alternative history of theatre sound is the history of theatre noise. From the classical certainty that tempestuous noise indicated cosmic disharmony to the intense silence of a modern theatre auditorium, where a mobile phone ring or an ill-timed cough causes deep annoyance, it is against the noises which are not sound that theatre sound is heard.

> Noise is negative: it is unwanted, other, not something ordered. It is negatively defined – by what it is not (not acceptable sound, not music, not valid, not a message or a meaning) – but it is also a negativity. In other words, it does not exist independently, as it exists only in relation to what it is not. In turn it helps structure and define its opposite (the world of meaning, law, regulation, goodness, beauty, and so on). Noise is something like a process. (Hegarty, 2007, p. 5)

A necessary process: noise might be unwanted, but it is from, despite, on top of, because of *noise*, that sound can have meaning, make sense, or show intelligent design.

> Background noise is the ground of our perception, absolutely uninterrupted; it is our perennial sustenance, the element of the software of all our logic. It is the residue and the cesspool of our messages. No life without heat, no matter, neither; no warmth without air, no logos without noise, either. Noise is the basic element of the software of all our logic, or it is to the logos what matter used to be to form. Noise is the background of information, the material of that form. (Serres, 1995, p. 7)

We do not listen to it (for to do so would be to make it the signal), but noise is always there in our hearing. Within our contemporary culture, it has tended to be viewed as a bad thing: something to pay to avoid, something to abate, limit or prevent. To the audiophile or hi-fi enthusiast it is an anathema. You may find it surprising, therefore, that a sound designer might write in defence of noise. I do so, because I believe the role of the sound design in theatre is sometimes to be noisy – to distract, to create a dialectic between the alternative reality being presented 'over there' on the stage, and the personal reality being experienced 'over here' in row J.

Theatre sound provides a spatial continuity between the audient's psyche and the world of empirical phenomena – it unites thought, memory and perception in one spatial field. Immersion in a designed soundscape engages both the body and the mind in a theatrically effective way which can be sublime. As I hope the extracts in this book have shown, sound does more in the theatre than merely underscore emotional vectors in a melodramatic way. Before there were sound designers, there were *noisemakers*, and in some respects I prefer that epithet, because part of the potency of theatre sound is in its capacity to irk or annoy; sometimes almost imperceptibly to undermine; to create doubt in the audience's mind about what is intended; to recall other corporeal feelings and make them resonate in the consciousness; to give aural glimpses of another narrative which somehow seems pertinent or indeed a parallel world.

The convention of silence dominates auditoria tyrannically, but is an unattainable ideal. Theatres, guiltily, are creaky, leaky, humming places of stifled sound. The philosopher Alphonso Lingis in *The Community of Those Who have Nothing in Common* (1994) claims that noise has a necessary part to play within the ideal forum of communication. Noiselessness, he points out, far from being ideal, would in fact, be bad for you.

> In the absence of auditory, visual, and tactual background signals, one no longer senses the boundaries between outside and inside, past and present, perception and images, and one soon hallucinates. If the reception of a determinate signal is impossible beyond a certain level of background noise, the intention to emit a determinate signal becomes unrealizable without a certain level of ambient drone to escalate, punctuate, and redirect. Recorded white noise – forest murmurs, the rumble of the city – was added to space capsules; the recordings are sold to terrestrials living in sound-proofed apartments. (Lingis, 1994, p. 93)

Lingis contends that sonic noise is essential in communications – both in the background and also in the internal imperfections of our messages to each other. While noise is often assumed, by definition, to be insignificant, it is inevitable and omnipresent, and our psychoacoustic and imaginatively discursive processes have come to rely on its ambiguities and interference as part of the negotiation of meaning. In short, 'we' (as a plural collective) need it. Communities, who may well have very little else in common, form around the need to overcome noise in order to transact communications. Lingis goes even further than this, to suggest that the noise we make in our cities, as we go about our daily business, is not necessarily the environmental 'pollution' that those who would politically idealize silence might claim it to be; it is, rather, a cultural performance:

> All these stammerings, exclamations, slurrings, murmurs, rumblings, cooings, and laughter, all this noise we make when we are together makes it possible to view us as struggling, together, to jam the unequivocal voice of the outsider: the facilitator of communication, the prosopopeia of maximal elimination of noise, so as to hear the distant rumble of the world and its demons in the midst of the ideal city of human communication. (*ibid.*, p.105)

Communities make, allow and value noise, like a masking scent, to block out the noise of *other* and the *beyond*; but also as the necessary evil which must be overcome within the daily travail in order to achieve ideal discourse. When an audience listens to the words of an actor, it is a community of people defined by a shared interest in hearing those words, and in overcoming the distraction of being themselves. But it is in the dialectic between the 'pure' reception of the signal (the staged performance) and the noisy circumstance of audience that the full meaning of going to the theatre is completed. Sound design, very often (and especially with the advent of surround sound) is often more concerned with creating noisy circumstance than with enhancing pure reception.

HOW TO DO THEATRE SOUND DESIGN

Know How Your Kit Works

But remember that each human being walks into the theatre in an unsurpassable piece of sound technology – the human body. No loudspeaker can surpass it for vocal quality; no microphone or processing algorithm for sound-field imaging or dynamic range; no computer for storage capacity, speed of data retrieval or random memory access.

Do Your Text Analysis

But remember that your text is not just the words and ideas on the page, nor the conceits of the devising process. Neither should your approach to textual analysis be confined to these things. Get to the theatre or the rehearsal room early and sit there in silence. Sit and breathe as a member of the audience would: still, and self-aware. Let the room envelope you, listen to its character and the tricks it plays, listen to its noises and the noises that leak in from outside. Listen to your breathing in the space – this is a good way to get a sense of aural scale. Then, before anyone else arrives, get to know its resonance. Use your voice. Find its resonant frequencies and its echoes and reverberations; stamp on its floors and clap your hands; knock its walls and run up and down its aisles and corridors. Find out what sounds come in

when you open its doors. As people arrive, as activities happen, as people start to rehearse on the stage, let their sounds surround you and vie for your attention with the noises that were there before.

Watch The Rehearsals

Listen to the sounds of the actors moving around as well as the sound of the words and the resonance of their voices; but also listen to the sounds in your head – the imagined sounds, the sounds that you are reminded of. If a random tune pops into your head, do not ignore it just because it seems to have no logical reason to be there. Take note of the moments when your mind begins to wander. Listen to your boredom, your personal responses and any mischievous thoughts. Do this as well as the things it tells you to do in the other textbooks or do it instead of them.

Be an Artist

You are not just there to serve the director and the play. Some of the textbooks will tell you that is your job, but that is nonsense. Every theatre production is a new work of art; your ideas, solutions and negotiations are dramaturgy, and your creativity as a designer can come from anywhere that works for you. Don't be afraid to bring your own ideas to bear on the text, no matter how personal or irrational they seem.

Immerse Yourself in the Wider Theatre of Sound and Sonic Possibility

Here I am where I began in the Introduction to this book, writing on my PDA. I have headphones in my ears and music is playing, but the artificial sound-effect which the device makes to describe the keystrokes that make up these words clicks audibly in counterpoint with the music. (In case you're interested, these words were written to Jimmy Webb's *Carpet Man* performed by the easy-listening group Fifth Dimension. Would you ever have guessed?) The tube stops and I can hear that the driver is announcing something. I get out at Swiss Cottage and walk through the street market opposite the Hampstead Theatre, still easy-listening, but also remembering that I stood here in silence at 12 noon on 14 July 2005, when all of London, it seemed, observed a two minute silence one week after the terrorist attack on its public transport system.

On that day, a strange thrall descended on such local scenes of remembrance, to which the urban permadrone, distant sounds of building works and individual locomotive events, formed a distant perimeter. On pavements outside workplaces, in shopping centres and in tube stations, people paused their journeys, set down their bags, and adopted familiar poses of silent memorial. The two minutes passed, but here, in this pedestrian concourse, people did not move. The two minutes became five, ten even, before people gently went away.

Within the period of the silence, the soundscape seemed to arrange itself around a personal fleshbound moment. It was not a silent moment, but a stilled one, without laughs, coughs, conversations, ipods, ringtones and the other noises we make and surround ourselves with in the course of the usual daily journey. Instead, because this was a serious moment, we stood to address the noise beyond these local soundscapes. Each passing car; each distant horn; each stray stifled vocal sound and footfall from the oblivious tourist passing by; each line of phase-modulating aeroplane noise, passing over the scene in the aural equivalence of a vapour trail; each of these events seemed to be in some kind of golden proportion to the general background drone of London. And each spoke with poignancy to the occasion; to the remembrance of the passer-by victims of immersive warfare; to the continuing life of a city built of noise; to that particular moment in my particular day when my hearing was re-arranged and recalibrated by a larger thought.

I mention that soniferous silence, because I think of it whenever I think about what theatre sound might be able to do. I imagine an entire piece of theatre comprising nothing more than the same sublime, anxious thrill of pause, in which nothing is said, but in which the mundane becomes monumentally strange-yet-fond; in which audience becomes performance; in which the body tingles with memory and sound; in which noise and stray thoughts are allowed to be exquisite rather than guilty interruptions and in which all technology becomes redundant.

Bibliography

A Miniature Library of Philosophy, http://www.marxists.org/reference/subject/philosophy/works/fr/barthes.htm (accessed 12 Jan 2009).

Ackroyd, P. (2000) *London: The Biography* (London: Chatto and Windus).

Alström, T. (2004) 'The Voice in the Mask', *TDR: The Drama Review*, 48, 2 (T 182), 133–5.

Altman, R. (1992) *Sound Theory/Sound Practice* (New York, London: Routledge).

Appia, A. (1962) *Music and the Art of Theatre*, trans. R. W. Corrigan, and M. Douglas Dirks (Florida: University of Miami Press).

Aristotle (1898) 'Poetics', trans. S. H. Butcher, *Aristotle's Theory of Poetry and Fine Art with a Critical Text and Translation of The Poetics*, 2nd edn (London: Macmillan).

Aristotle (1931) *Metaphysica*, in W. D. Ross (ed.), *The Works of Aristotle Translated into English* (London: Oxford University Press).

Arnott, P. D. (1989) *Public and Performance in the Greek Theatre* (New York: Routledge).

Arns, R. G. and Crawford, B. E. (1995) 'Resonant Cavities in the History of Architectural Acoustics', *Technology and Culture*, 36, 1 (January), 104–35.

Artaud, A. (1974) *Collected Works of Antonin Artaud: Volume 4*, trans. V. Corti (London: Calder & Boyars).

Attali, J (1985) *Noise, the Political Economy of Music*, trans. B. Massumi (Minneapolis: University of Minnesota Press).

Augoyard, J. and Torgue, H. (2005) *Sonic Experience: A Guide to Everyday Sounds*, trans. A. McCartney and D. Paquette (Montreal, Kingston: McGill-Queen's University Press).

Auslander, P. (1999) *Liveness: Performance in a Mediatized Culture* (London: Routledge).

Barker, A. (1982) 'The Innovations of Lysander the Kitharist', *The Classical Quarterly*, new series, 32, 2, 266–9.

Barker, G. (1995) *Granville Barker's Prefaces to Shakespeare: Romeo and Juliet* (Portsmouth, NH: Heinemann).

Barron, M. (1993) *Auditorium Acoustics and Architectural Design* (New York: E. & F. N. Spon).

Barry, Peter (1995) *Beginning Theory: An Introduction to Literary and Cultural Theory*, 3rd edn (Manchester, UK: Manchester University Press).

Barthes, R. (1964) *Elements of Semiology* (New York: Hill and Wang).

Barthes, R. (1968) *Elements of Semiology*, trans. A. Lavers and C. Smith (New York: Hill and Wang).

Barthes, R. (1977) *Image, Music, Text* (New York: Hill and Wang).

Barthes, R. (1988) *Camera Lucida* (London: Fontana).

Bate, J. (1654) *The Composing of all Manner of Fier-Works for Triumph and Recreacion* (London: R. Bishop).

Baudrillard, J. (1994) *Simulacra and Simulation*, trans. S. F. Glaser (Ann Arbor: University of Michigan Press).

Beacham, R. C. (1993) *Adolphe Appia: Texts on Theatre* (London: Routledge).

Beckett, S. (1959) *Waiting for Godot* (London: Faber and Faber).

Bell, K. (1997) 'The Art of Theater Sound', http://www.svconline.com/mag/avinstall_art_theater_sound/index.html (accessed 12 March 2008).

Bentley, E. (ed.) (1978) *The Theory of the Modern Stage*, rev edn (1983) (Middlesex: Penguin).

Bentley, R. (1971) Dyce, A. (ed.) *Works of Richard Bentley (1836–38)*, vols 1–2 (New York: Georg Olms).

Berendt, J. E. (1983) *Nada Brahma: a música e o universe da consciência* (São Paulo: Ed. Cultrix).

Berendt, J. E. (1988) *The Third Ear* (Vermont: Destiny Books).

Berendt, J. E. (1991) *The World is Sound: Nada Brahma* (Vermont: Destiny Books).

Berger, J. (1972) *Ways of Seeing* (London: Penguin).

Billington, M. (2004) 'The Horror, the Horror', *The Guardian*, 22 December.

Blauert, J. (1997) *Spatial Hearing: The Psychophysics of Human Sound Localization* (Cambridge, MA: MIT Press).

Blesser, B. and Salter, L. R. (2007) *Spaces Speak, Are You Listening?: Experiencing Aural Architecture* (Cambridge, MA: The MIT Press).

Blin, R., Artaud, A., Kirby, V. N., Nes, N. E., and Robbins, A. (1972) 'Antonin Artaud in "Les Cenci"', *TDR: The Drama Review*, 16, 2, Directing Issue, (June), 91–145.

Böhme, G. (1995) *Atmosphäre. Essays zur Neuen Ästhetik* (Frankfurt: am Main: Suhrkamp).

Böhme, G. (2000) trans. N. Ruebsaat, 'Acoustic Atmospheres: A Contribution to the Study of Ecological Aesthetics', *Soundscape: The Journal of Acoustic Ecology*, 1, 1, 14–18.

Böhme, G. (2003) 'The Space of Bodily Presence', in M. Hård, A. Lösch and D. Verdicchio (eds), *Transforming Spaces. The Topological Turn in Technology Studies*, http://www.ifs.tudarmstadt.de/gradkoll/Publikationen/transformingspaces.html (accessed 25 October 2007).

Boulez, P. (1971) *Boulez on Music Today* (London: Faber and Faber).

Bracewell, J. L. (1993) *Sound Design in the Theatre* (Englewood Cliffs, NJ: Prentice Hall).

British Library Archival Sound Recordings, http://sounds.bl.uk/ (accessed 12 August 2008).

Brown, J. A. C. (1963) *Techniques of Persuasion* (Harmondsworth: Penguin Books).

Brown, R. (2005) 'The Theatre Soundscape and the End of Noise', in *Performance Research*, 10, 4, 'On Technê'.

Burris-Meyer, H. and Mallory, V. (and Goodfriend, L.) (1959) *Sound in the Theatre* (Mineola, NY: Radio Magazines, Inc.).

Busia, K. A. (1954) 'The Ashanti of the Gold Coast', in D. Forde (ed.), *African Worlds* (London: Oxford University Press).

Butterworth, P. (2005) *Magic and the Early English Stage* (Cambridge: Cambridge University Press).

Cage, J. (1978) *Silence*, New edn (London: Marion Boyars Publishers).

Calaprice, A. (2005). *The New Quotable Einstein* (Princeton, NJ: Princeton University Press).

Capra, F. (2000) *The Tao of Physics: An Exploration of the Parallels Between Modern Physics and Eastern Mysticism* (Berkeley, CA: Shambhala).

Carpenter, E. and McLuhan, M. (eds) (1960) *Explorations in Communication* (Boston: Beacon Press).

Chan, Mary (1980) *Music in the Theatre of Ben Jonson* (Oxford: Clarendon Press).

Chion, M. (1983) *Guide des Objets Sonores: Pierre Schaeffer et la Recherché Musicale*, trans. J. Dack and C. North (Paris: Institut National de l'Audiovisuel & Editions Buchet/Chastel).

Chion, M. (1993) 'The State of Musique Concrète', in F. B. Mâche (ed.), *Music, Society and Imagination in Cotemporary France*, vol. 8, pt 1 (Switzerland: Harwood Academic Publishers), 51–5.

Chion, M. (1994) *Audio-Vision – Sound on Screen*, trans. C. Gorbman (New York: Columbia).

Chion, M. (1999) 'Silence in the Loudspeakers, or – Why, with Dolby Sound in Films, it is the Film which is Listening to Us', trans. S. Muecke, *Framework: The Journal of Cinema and Media*, 40, April, 106–10.

Cibber, C. (1889) *An Apology for the Life of Mr. Colley Cibber, Volume I*, http://etext.lib.virginia.edu/toc/modeng/public/Cib1Apo.html (accessed 21 March 2007).

Clapp, S. (1998) 'Theatre', *The Observer*, 15 March.

Clapp, S. (2004) 'Noises On and Off', *The Observer*, 26 December.

Collison, D. (1982) *Stage Sound*, 2nd edn (London: Cassell).

Connor, S. (2004) *Windbags and Skinsongs*, http://www.bbk.ac.uk/english/skc/windbags (accessed 9 October 2007).

Corbain, A. (1998) *Village Bells – The Culture of the Senses in the Nineteenth-Century French Countryside* (New York: Columbia University Press).

Crary, J. (1990) *Techniques of the Observer: On Vision and Modernity in the Nineteenth Century* (Cambridge, MA, and London: MIT Press).

Crook, T. (1999) *Radio Drama: Theory and Practice* (New York and London: Routledge).

Cusack, P. (2001) *Your Favourite London Sounds*, London Musicians' Collective (RESFLS1CD).

d'Hertefelt, M. (1965) 'The Rwanda of Rwanda', in J. L. Gibbs (ed.), *Peoples of Africa* (New York: Holt, Rinehart & Winston).

Dack, J. (1994) 'Pierre Schaeffer and the Significance of Radiophonic Art', *Contemporary Music Review*, 10, 2, 3–11.

Dack, J. (1999) 'Systematising the Unsystematic', first published in *Diffusion*, 7, Sonic Arts Network, http://lansdown.mdx.ac.uk/lceaSite/about/staff/JohnDack/JohnDack.html (accessed 12 August 2008).

Dack, J. (2002) 'Histories and Ideologies of Synthesis', http://www.sonic.mdx.ac.uk/research/dackhis.html (accessed 28 December 2007).

Davies, J. B. (1978). *The Psychology of Music*. Stanford, CA: Stanford University Press.

de Nebesky-Wojkowitz, R. (1956) *Oracles and Demons of Tibet* (London: Oxford University Press).

Dearling, R. and Dearling, C. (1984) *The Guinness Book of Recorded Sound* (Enfield, Guinness Books).

Dejong, G. (1989) 'The Role of Explanation in Analogy; Or, The Curse of an Alluring Name', in S. Vosniadou and A. Ortony (eds), *Similarity and Analogical Reasoning* (Cambridge: Cambridge University Press), 346–65.

Dekker, T. (1953–61) *The Dramatic Works*, edited by Fredson Bowers, 4 vols (Cambridge: Cambridge University Press).

Deleuze, G. (1989) *Cinema 2: The Time-Image*, trans, H. Tomlinson and R. Galeta (London: Continuum).

Devereux, P. (2001) *Stone Age Soundtracks: The Acoustic Archaeology of Ancient Sites* (London: Vega).

Devereux, P. and Jahn, R. G. (1996) 'Preliminary Investigation and Cognitive Considerations of the Acoustical Resonances of Selected Archaeological Sites', *Antiquity*, 70, 665–6.

Dhomont, F. (2001) *Novars, Cycle du son, empreintes*, DIGITALes (IMED 0158).

Dolby (2008) http://www.dolby.com/consumer/technology/dolby_digital.html (accessed 12 August 2008).

Douglas, M. (1954) 'The Lele of Kasai', in D. Forde (ed.), *African Worlds* (London: Oxford University Press).

Douglas, M. (1966) *Purity and Danger* (London: Routledge & Kegan Paul).

Drever, J. L. (2003) *Phonographies of Exeter*, Sound-Marked (SM03-01CD).

Drever, J. L. (2007) 'Topophonophilia: A Study of the Relationship Between the Sounds of Dartmoor and its Inhabitants', in A. Carlyle (ed.), *Autumn Leaves: Sound and Environment in Creative Practice* (Paris: Double Entendre), 98–100.

Dufour, D. and Brando, T. (2000) 'The Acousmatic Genre', http://www.myspace.com/acousmaticart (accessed 12 August 2008).

Durkheim, E. (1961) *The Elementary Forms of the Religious Life*, trans. J. W. Swain (New York: Collier).

Ebrahimian, B. A. (2004) *The Cinematic Theater* (Lanham, MD: Scarecrow Press).

Edison, T. A. (1878) 'The Phonograph and its Future', *The North American Review*, 126, 262, 527–37, http://moa.cit.cornell.edu/cgi-bin/moa/sgml/moa-idx?notisid=ABQ7578-0126-62 (accessed 12 August 2008).

Egan, R. B. (1988) 'Two Complementary Epigrams of Meleager (A.P. vii 195 and 196)', *Journal of Hellenic Studies*, cviii, 24–32.

Eliade, M. (1964) *Shamanism: Archaic Techniques of Ecstasy*, trans. W. T. Trask, rev. edn (London: Routledge & Kegan Paul).

Elzenheimer, R. (1999) 'Silence – The Development of a New Musical Category', *Performance Research*, 4, 3, 25–33.

Erlmann, V. (ed.) (2004) *Hearing Cultures: Essays on Sound, Listening and Modernity* (Oxford and New York: Berg).

Ernst, E. (1974) *Kabuki Theatre* (Hawaii: Honolulu University of Hawaii Press).

Feld, S. (1994) 'From Schizophonia to Schismogenesis: On the Discourses and Commodification Practices of "World Music" and "World Beat"', in S. Feld and C. Keil (eds), *Music Grooves* (Chicago: The University of Chicago Press) 257–89.

Feld, S. (2001) *Rainforest Soundwalks: Ambiences of Bosavi, Papua New Guinea*. Earth Ear (ee1062).

Feld, S. (2003) 'A Rainforest Acoustemology', in M. Bull and L. Back, (eds), *The Auditory Culture Reader* (Oxford, New York: Berg).

Ferrari, L. (1995) *Presque Rein*. INA (ina c 2008).

Finelli, P. (1989) *Sound for the Stage* (New York: Drama Book Publishers).

Folkerth, W. (2002) *The Sound of Shakespeare* (London and New York: Routledge).

Foucault, M. (1972) *The Birth of the Clinic: An Archaeology of Medical Perception*, trans. A. M. Sheridan Smith (New York: Pantheon).

Frazer, J. (1922) *The Golden Bough* (London: Macmillan).

Freedman, M. (1967) *Rites and Duties, or: Chinese Marriage* (London: Bell).

Fuchs, E. (1985) 'Presence and the Revenge of Writing: Re-Thinking Theatre after Derrida', *Performing Arts Journal*, 9, 2/3, 10th Anniversary Issue: The American Theatre Condition, 163–73.

Galpin, F. W. (1965) *Old English Instruments of Music*, 4th edn rev. with supplementary notes by Thurston Dart (London: Methuen).

Godman, R. (2005) 'The Enigma of Vitruvian Resonating Vases and the Relevance of the Concept for Today', Conference paper at 'Harvest Moon Symposium', Concordia University, Montreal, Canada September, http://cec.concordia.ca/econtact/Harvest_Moon/files/Vitruvius_Godman.pdf (accessed 21 December 2008).

Gombrich, E. H. (1993) *Art & Illusion: A Study in the Psychology of Pictorial Representation* (London: Phaidon).

Gordon, D. and Parreno, P. (2006) *Zidane: A 21st Century Portrait*. Artificial Eye (ART332).

Green, M. (1958) *Stage Noises and Effects* (London: H. Jenkins).

Grierson, J. (1933) 'The Documentary Producer', *Cinema Quarterly*, 2, 1, 7–9.

Gröning, P. (2005) *Die Große Stille* [*Into Great Silence*] (Warner Bros., 8671995).

Gurr, A. (1980) *The Shakespearean Stage 1574–1642* (Cambridge, UK and New York: Cambridge University Press).

Gutman, R. W. (1968) *Richard Wagner: The Man, His Mind, and His Music* (New York: Harcourt Brace and World, Inc).

Hall, D. (1991) 'Reviving a Forgotten Pyrotechnical Art Form: Pyrotechnics and Twentieth-Century Performance Art', *Leonardo*, 24, 5, 531–4.

Handel, S. (1989) *Listening: An Introduction to the Perception of Auditory Events* (Cambridge, MA: MIT Press).

Hardcastle, E. (1823) *Wine and Walnuts: Or After Dinner Chit-Chat* (London: Longman, printed for Hurst, Rees, Orme and Brown).

Harrison, J. (1996) *Klang*, NMC (D035).

Harwood, R. (1992) *Reflected Glory* (London: Faber and Faber).

Hattaway, Michael (1982) *Elizabethan Popular Theatre: Plays in Performance* (London: Routledge and Kegan Paul).

Haughton, P. M. (2002) *Acoustics for Audiologists* (Oxford: Academic Press).

Hawking, S. (1998). *A Brief History of Time* (New York: Bantam Books).

Hegarty, P. (2007). *Noise/Music: A History* (New York: Continuum).

Helmholtz, H. (1954) *On the Sensations of Tone* (New York: Dover Publications).

Henry, P. (1987) *Variations pour une porte et un soupir*, Harmonia Mundi (HMC 905200).

Henslowe, P. (1907) *Henslowe Papers*, edited by W. W. Greg (London: A. H. Bullen).

Henslowe, P. (1961) *Henslowe's Diary*, edited by R. A. Foakes and R. T. Rickert (Cambridge: Cambridge University Press).

Hollier, D. (1997) 'The Death of Paper, Part Two: Artaud's Sound System', in *October*, Vol. 80, Spring (Cambridge Mass.: MIT Press).

Holman, T. (2001) 'Future History', *Surround Professional*, March–April, 58+.

Holman, T. (2007) *Surround Sound: Up and Running*, 2nd edn (Burlington: Focal Press).

Howard, D. M. and Angus, J. (2001) *Acoustics and Psychoacoustics*, 2nd edn (Oxford: Focal Press).

Howes, D. (2005) *Empire of the Senses: The Sensual Culture Reader* (Oxford and New York: Berg).

Hull, J. M. (1990) *Touching the Rock: An Experience of Blindness* (London: Arrow Books Ltd).

Ihde, D. (1973) *Sense and Significance* (New York: Humanities Press).

Ihde, D. (1976) *Listening and Voice: A Phenomenology of Sound* (Athens, OH: University Press).

Infrasonic (2008) http://www.spacedog.biz/Infrasonic/infrasonicindex.htm (accessed 12 August 2008).

Irving, L. (1951) *Henry Irving: The Actor and his World* (London: Faber and Faber).

Isaacs, J. (1933) *Production and Stage-Management at the Blackfriars Theatre* (London, Oxford University Press).

Iselin, P. (1995) 'Music and Difference: Elizabethan Stage Music and its Reception', in J.-M. Maguin and M. Willems (eds), *French Essays on Shakespeare and his Contemporaries* (Newark: University of Delaware Press).

Jahn, R. G., Devereux, P. and Ibison, M. (1996) 'Acoustical Resonances of Assorted Ancient Structures', *Journal of the Acoustical Society of America*, 99, 2, 649–58.

Johnson, B. (2005) 'Hamlet: Voice, Music, Sound', *Popular Music*, 24, 2, 257–68.

Jost, F. (2001) 'The Voices of Silence', in R. Abel and R. Altman (eds), *The Sounds of Early Cinema* (Bloomington, IN: Indiana University Press), 48–65.

Kahn, D. (1992) 'Histories of Sound Once Removed', in D. Kahn and G. Whitehead (eds), *Wireless Imagination: Sound, Radio and the Avant-Garde* (Cambridge, MA and London: MIT Press).

Kahn, D. (1999) *Noise Water Meat: A History of Sound in the Arts* (Cambridge MA and London: MIT Press).

Kaye, D. and Lebrecht, J. (1992) *Sound and Music for Theatre* (New York: Back Stage Books).

Kershaw, B, (2007) *Theatre Ecology: Environments and Performance Events* (Cambridge, Cambridge University Press).

King, R. (2001) *The Works of Richard Edwards: Politics, Poetry and Performance in Sixteenth Century England* (Manchester: Manchester University Press).

Kitto, H. D. F. (1951) *The Greeks* (London: Penguin).

Koller, A. M. (1984) *The Theater Duke: Georg II of Saxe-Meiningen and the German Stage* (Stanford, CA: Stanford University Press).

Krige, J. D. and Krige, E. J. (1954) 'The Lovedu of the Transvaal', in D. Forde (ed.), *African Worlds* (London: Oxford University Press).

Kuhn, H. P. (2000) *Licht und Klang* (Heidelberg: Kehrer Verlag).

Kurosawa, Akira, (1983) *Something Like an Autobiography*, trans. A. E. Bock (New York: Vintage Books Edition).

Laermans, R. (1999) 'Performative Silences', *Performance Research*, 4, 3, 1–6.

Landels, J. G. (1967) 'Assisted Resonance in Ancient Theatres', *Greece and Rome*, 2nd series, 14, 1, 80–94.

Landis, C. and Bolles, M. (1950) *Textbook of Abnormal Psychology* (New York: Macmillan).

Lawrence, W. J. (1935) *Those Nut-Cracking Elizabethans: Studies of the Early Theatre and Drama* (London: The Argonaut Press).

Leach, E. R. (1961) *Rethinking Anthropology* (London: Athlone Press).

Lefkowitz, M. (2007) 'Antimasque', *Grove Music Online* L. Macy (ed.), http://www.grovemusic.com (accessed 21 March 2007).

Leggatt, A. (1992) *Jacobean Public Theatre* (London: Routledge).

Levi, D. M. (ed.) (1993) *Modernity and the Hegemony of Vision* (Berkeley and Los Angeles: University of California Press).

Lévi-Strauss, C. (1964) *Le cru et le cult* (Paris: Plon).

Lévi-Strauss, C. (1966) *Du miel aux cendres* (Paris: Plon).

Lindley, D. (2006) *Shakespeare and Music* (London: Thomson Learning/Arden Shakespeare).

Lingis, A. (1994) *The Community of Those Who Have Nothing in Common* (Bloomington, IN: Indiana University Press).

Linz, R. (1996) 'Towards the Design of a Real-Time Interactive Performance Sound System', *Leonardo Music Journal*, 6, 99–107.

Loehlin, J. (2006) *Chekhov: The Cherry Orchard* (Cambridge: Cambridge University Press).

Long, J. H. (1961–71) *Shakespeare's Use of Music*, 3 volumes (Gainesville: University of Florida Press).

Loraux, N. (2002) *The Mourning Voice: An Essay on Greek Tragedy*, trans. E. T. Rawlings (Ithaca: Cornell University Press).

Maeterlinck, M. (1890) *The Intruder*, http://www.theatrehistory.com/plays/intruder.html (accessed 20 October 2008).

Maeterlinck, M. (1897) *The Treasure of the Humble*, trans. A. Sutro (London: George Allen).

Manning, P. (1993) *Electronic and Computer Music* (Oxford: Clarendon Press).

Martin, J. (1993) *Downcast Eyes: The Denigration of Vision in Twentieth-Century French Thought* (Berkeley and Los Angeles: University of California Press).

Mauro, D. G. (2006) 'The Rhythmic Brain', *The Fifth International Conference of the Cognitive Sciences* (Vancouver, BC).

McLuhan, M. (1962) *The Gutenberg Galaxy: The Making of Typographic Man* (Toronto: University of Toronto Press).

Moles, A. (1968). *Information Theory and Esthetic Perception*, trans. J. E. Cohen (Urbana: University of Illinois Press).

Moore, B. C. J. (2003). *An Introduction to the Psychology of Hearing*, 5th edn (San Diego: Academic Press).

Mott, R. L. (1990) *Sound Effects: Radio, TV, and Film* (London: Focal Press).

Mumford, L. (1934) *Technics and Civilisation* (New York: Harcourt Brace and Co.).

Munrow, D. (1976) *Instruments of the Middle Ages and Renaissance* (London: Oxford University Press).

Nagler, A. M. (1959) *A Source Book in Theatrical History* (New York: Dover Publications).

Napier, F. (1936) *Noises Off – A Handbook of Sound Effects* (London: F. Muller Ltd).

Nattiez, J. J. (1990) *Music & Discourse: Toward a Semiology of Music*, trans. C. Abbate (Princeton: Princeton University Press).

Naylor, E. W. (1931) *Shakespeare and Music*, 2nd edn (London: Dent).

Needham, R. (1967) 'Percussion and Transition', *Man*, 2, 606–14.

Neher, A. (1962) 'A Physiological Explanation of Unusual Behaviour in Ceremonies Involving Drums', *Human Biology*, 34, 151–60.

Norman, K. (2004) *Sounding Art: Eight Literacy Excursions through Electronic Music* (Aldershot, UK: Ashgate).

O'Shaughnessy, B. (1957) 'The Location of Sound', *Mind*, new series, 66, 264 (October), 471–90.

Oberg, K. (1940) 'The Kingdom of Ankole in Uganda', in M. Fortes and E. E. Evans-Pritchard (eds), *African Political Systems* (London: Oxford University Press).

O'Keefe, C. and Angliss, S. (2004) 'The Subjective Effects of Infrasound in a Live Concert Setting', CIM04: Conference on Interdisciplinary Musicology (Graz, Germany: Graz University Press), 132–3.

Ong, W. J. (1991) 'The Shifting Sensorium', in D. Howes (ed.), *The Varieties of Sensory Experience* (Toronto: University of Toronto Press), 47–60.

Ong, W. J. (1982) *Orality and Literacy: The Technologization of the Word* (New York: Routledge).

Oxford English Dictionary (2008) http://www.oed.com (accessed 12 August 2008).

Paget, Sir R. A. S. (1924) 'The Musical Nature of Speech and Song', in *Proceedings of the Musical Association*, 50th Session (1923–4), 67–83.

Parmegiani, B. (1991) *De Natura Sonorum*, INA (ina c 3001).

Parret, H. (1995) 'Synesthetic Effects', in T. A. Sebeok and J. Umiker-Seboeok (eds), *Advances in Visual Semiotics* (Berlin: Mouton de Gruyter).

Peirce, C. S. (1955) *Philosophical Writings of Peirce*, J. Buchler (ed.) (New York: Dover Publications).

Plimpton, G. (1984) *Fireworks: A History of Celebration* (Garden City, NY: Doubleday).

Proschan, K. (1981) 'Puppet Voices and Interlocutors: Language in Folk Puppetry', *The Journal of American Folklore*, 94, 374, "Folk Drama" (Oct–Dec), 527–55.

Rebellato, D. (1999) *1956 And All That: The Making of Modern British Theatre* (London: Routledge).

Reynolds, V. (1965) *Budongo: A Forest and its Chimpanzees* (London: Methuen).

Reynolds, V. and Reynolds, F. (1965) 'Chimpanzees of the Budongo Forest', in I. DeVore (ed.), *Primate Behavior* (New York: Holt, Rinehart & Winston).

Richardson, E. G. (1936) 'The Science of Voice-Production', *The Musical Times*, 77, 1121, (July), 599–602.

Ridgeway, W. (1915) *The Dramas and Dramatic Dances of Non-European Race* (Cambridge: Cambridge University Press).

Roads, C. (2002) *Microsound* (Cambridge Mass.: MIT Press).

Schaeffer, P. (1966) *Traité des Objets Musicaux* (Paris: Editions du Seuil).

Schaeffer, P. (2000) L'Œuvre *musicale l'intégrale*. EMF & INA (ina c 1006-07-08).

Schaeffer, P. and Reibel, G. (2000) *Solfège de l'objet sonore* (réédition), Ina (ina c 2010-11-12).

Schafer, R. M. (1994) *The Soundscape: Our Sonic Environment and the Tuning of the World* (Vermont: Destiny Books).

Schafer, R. M. (1997) *Winter Diary*, in *Angewandte Musik [B] Musik Für Radio: Das Studio Akustische Kunst Des WDR*, RCA Red Seal (74321 73522 2).

Scheer, E. (ed.) (2004) *Antonin Artaud: A Critical Reader* (London and New York: Routledge).

Schopenhauer, A. (1911) *Samliche Werk: Erster Band, Die Welt als Wille und Vorstellung*, P. Deussen (ed.) (Munich: Piper).

Schutz, A. (1964) *Collected Papers*, 2 (The Hague: Nijhoff).

Secrets Of The Dead: Sounds From The Stone Age, UK Television, Channel 4, 12 November 2001, 2100–2200 hrs.

Sellars, P. (1992) 'Introduction', in D. Kaye and J. Lebrecht, *Sound and Music for Theatre* (New York: Back Stage Books).

Serres, M. (1995) *Genesis*, trans. G. James and J. Nielson (Ann Arbor: University of Michigan Press).

Shepherd, S. and Wallis, M. (2004) *Drama, Theatre, Performance* (London and New York: Routledge).

Shingler, M. and Wieringa, C. (1998) *On Air: Methods and Meanings of Radio* (London: Arnold).

Singer I. and Mels, E. (2008). *Chronegk, Ludwig*, http://www.jewishencyclopedia.com/view.jsp?artid=492&letter=C (accessed 12 August 2008).

Smalley, D. (1986) 'Spectro-Morphology and Structuring Processes', in S. Emmerson (ed.), *The Language of Electroacoustic Music* (London: Macmillan), 61–93.

Smalley, D. (1992) 'The Listening Imagination: Listening in the Electroacoustic Era', in J. Paynter *et al.* (eds), *Companion to Contemporary Musical Thought: Volume 1* (London: Routledge), 514–54.

Smalley, D. (2000) *Pentes*, Empreintes Digitales (IMED0054).

Smith, B. R. (1999) *The Acoustic World of Early Modern England – Attending to the O-Factor* (London: University of Chicago Press).

Sokurov, A. (2002) Russian Ark. Artificial Eye (256 DVD).

Sonic Arts Network (2006) *Sonic Postcards*, http://www.sonicpostcards.org/ (accessed 12 August 2007).

Sonnenschein, D. (2001) *Sound Design: The Expressive Power of Music, Voice, and Sound Effects in Cinema* (California: Michael Wiese Productions).

Sontag, S. (1984) *On Photography* (Harmondsworth, UK: Penguin Books).

Sound Ideas (2008) http://www.sound-ideas.com (accessed 12 August 2008).

Soundscapes of Canada (1974) World Soundscape Project, directed by R. M. Schafer.

Stanislavski, C. (1968) *Stanislavski's Legacy: A Collection of Comments on a Variety of Aspects of an Actors' Art and Life*, ed. and trans. E. R. Hapgood (New York : Theatre Arts Books).

States, B. (1985) *Great Reckonings in Little Rooms* (Berkley and Los Angeles: University of California Press).

Stedman, J. W. (1976) 'Enter a Phonograph', in *Theatre Notebook: A Journal of the History and Technique of the British Theatre*, XXX, 1.

Sterne, J. P. (1978) *Nietzsche* (Fontana Modern Masters) (London: Fontana/Collins).

Sterne, J. P. (2003) *The Audible Past* (Durham and London: Duke University Press).

Sturtevant, W. C. (1968) 'Categories, Percussion and Physiology', *Man*, new series, 3, 133–4.

Tarkovsky, A. (1998) *Sculpting in Time: Reflections on the Cinema* (Austin: University of Texas Press).

Tarkovsky, A. (2002a) *Solaris*. Artificial Eye (ART211).

Tarkovsky, A. (2002b) *Stalker*, Artificial Eye (ART215).

Thaut, Michael H. (2005) *Rhythm, Music and the Brain*, (New York: Routledge).

Thomas, R. K. (2001) 'The Function of the Soundscape', *Theatre Design and Technology Journal*, 37, 1, 18–29.

Thomas, R. K. and Bell, K. (1995) 'Sound in the Performing Arts: The Dramatic Auditory Space', *Theatre Design and Technology Journal*, 31, 1, 16–26.

Thompson, E. (2002) *The Soundscape of Modernity: Architectural Acoustics and the Culture of Listening in America, 1900–1933* (Cambridge, MA and London: MIT Press).

Toop, D. (2004) *Haunted Weather: Music, Silence and Memory* (London: Serpents Tail).

Truax, B. (1999) *Handbook for Acoustic Ecology*, 2nd edn (Vancouver: Cambridge Street Publishing) (CD-Rom).

Truax, B. (2001) *Acoustic Communication*, 2nd edn (Westport, CT: Ablex).

Turnbull, C. M. (1965) 'The Mbuti Pygmies of the Congo', in J. L. Gibbs (ed.), *Peoples of Africa* (New York: Holt, Rinehart & Winston).

Unruh, Delbert, with Marilyn Rennagel and Jeff Davis (2006) *The Designs of Tharon Musser* (Syracuse NY: Broadway Press).

Van Gennep, A. (1960) *The Rites of Passage*, trans. M. B. Vizedom and G. L. Caffee (London: Routledge & Kegan Paul).

Van Leeuwen, T. (1999) *Speech, Music, Sound* (London: Palgrave Macmillan).

Vernon, J., Marton, T. and Peterson, B. (1961) 'Sensory Deprivation and Hallucination', *Science*, 133, 1808–12.

Vitruvius (1914) *Ten Books on Architecture*, trans. M. H. Morgan (Cambridge MA: Harvard University Press).

Waaser, C (1976) *The Theatre Student: Sound and Music for the Theatre* (New York: Richard Rosen Press).

Wagner, G. (1954) 'The Abaluyia of Kavirondo', in D. Forde (ed.), *African Worlds* (London: Oxford University Press).

Wagstaff, G. (2002) *The Sounds of Harris & Lewis*, Touring Exhibition of Sound Environments.

Walne, G. (1981) *Sound for the Theatre* (London: A&C Black).

Walter, G. (1961) *The Living Brain* (Harmondsworth: Penguin Books).

Wardle, I (1978) *The Theatres of George Devine* (London: Cape).

Watson, C. (2003) *Weather Report*. Touch (TO: 47).

Webster's Seventh New Collegiate Dictionary (1963) (Springfield, MA: G&C Merriam Company).

Welsch, W. (1993) 'Auf den Weg zu einer Kultur des Hörens?', *Paragrana*, 2, 1–2, 87–104.

Westerkamp, H. (1996) *Kits Beach Soundwalk*, Transformations, Empreintes DIGITALes (IMED 9631).

Westerkamp, H. (2007) 'Soundwalking', in A. Carlyle (ed.), *Autumn Leaves: Sound and Environment in Creative Practice* (Paris: Double Entendre), 49–54.

Wickham, G. (1992) *A History of Theatre*, 2nd edn (London: Phaidon).

Williams, G (2003) *British Theatre in the Great War: A Revaluation* (London: Continuum).

Wishart, T. (1990) *Vox V*, Virgin Classics (VC7 91108-2).

Wishart, T. (1996) *On Sonic Art*, rev. edn (London: Routledge).

Witmore, C. L. (2006) 'Vision, Media, Noise and the Percolation of Time: Symmetrical Approaches to the Mediation of the Material World', *Journal of Material Culture*, 11, 3, 267–92.

World Forum for Acoustic Ecology, http://interact.uoregon.edu/MediaLit/WFAE/home (accessed 12 August 2008).

World Soundscape Project (1997) *The Vancouver Soundscape 1973/Soundscape Vancouver 1996*. Cambridge Street Records (CSR-2CD 9701).

Wright, L. B. (1927) 'Juggling Tricks and Conjury on the English Stage before 1642', *Modern Philology*, 24, 3, 269–84.

Wrightson, K. (2000) 'An Introduction to Acoustic Ecology', *Soundscape: The Journal of Acoustic Ecology*, 1, 1, 10–13.

Yalman, N. (1964) 'Sinhalese Healing Rites', *The Journal of Asian Studies*, 23, 115–50.

Yewdall, David (2007) *The Practical Art of Motion Picture Sound* (Oxford: Focal Press).

Index

Note: an 'n' after a page number refers to a note on that page.